TOP MANAGEMENT

Paul E. HOLDEN
Professor of Industrial Management, Emeritus

Carlton A. PEDERSON
Professor of Business Management

Gayton E. GERMANE
1907 Foundation Professor of Logistics

TOP
MANAGEMENT

A research study of the
management policies and practices
of fifteen leading
industrial corporations

Conducted under the auspices of the
Graduate School of Business
Stanford University

McGraw-Hill Book Company

New York
San Francisco
St. Louis
Toronto
London
Sydney

TOP MANAGEMENT

Printed in the United States of America.

Library of Congress catalog card number: 68-8551

1 2 3 4 5 6 7 8 9 0 PEPE 7 2 1 0 6 9 8

2 9 5 4 5

FOREWORD

The top management of American business is well known throughout the world for its dynamism, its competitiveness, and its increasing professionalization. Since 1941 when the Stanford University Press published *Top Management Organization and Control* by Holden, Fish, and Smith, there have been many challenges to American management's capacity to respond to technological change, to the needs of world markets, as well as domestic demand, and to the necessity for improving productivity to offset increased costs.

In general, the record has been excellent. So much so that we have heard the cry of "le défi américain" from Europe describing American superiority in technology and managerial skills as threatening to European industrial independence. Though the "technology gap" is significant, it is not decisive. Outstanding scientific achievement and managerial competence are found on both sides of the Atlantic. Nonetheless American management, with certain natural advantages, has exploited with energy and imagination the research output since World War II and has applied it efficiently and profitably to the economic improvement and growth, not only of the United States but also of foreign markets.

What are the characteristics of American corporate management which have brought this about? What changes in American corporate practice, in organization, in attitudes, in the past 30 years have been significant in this achievement? What innovations and adaptations can be expected in the future?

This study attempts to answer some of these questions. It provides the reader with insights into how successful companies cope with the managerial problems constantly confronting top management when complexity, change, new competition, and the expanding dimensions of the market are the order of the day. It describes the best current managerial practice in fifteen successful U.S. industrial companies and discusses in a lucid and interesting style how they cope with today's problems (as contrasted with 30 years ago) in the areas requiring executive leadership and action.

The authors are well qualified for their task.

Professor Paul E. Holden, now emeritus professor at the Graduate School of Business and author of the first study in 1939-1941, has the advantage of hindsight and is in a unique position to compare and evaluate corporate policy and practice today with that of 30 years ago. Professor Holden has taught and consulted in the field of business policy and organization since 1926.

Professor Carlton A. Pederson, who is the recipient of the Mead Johnson Professorship award, has been at Stanford since 1946. He has concentrated his teaching and research in the field of business policy and organization and spent the past six months engaged in this work at the European Institute of Business Administration in France, in 1968, studying European corporate practice.

Professor Gayton E. Germane, who is the 1907 Foundation Professor of Transportation and Logistics at the Stanford Graduate School of Business, is an authority in the logistics field and has been on the Stanford faculty since 1952. During this period he spent a year as Director of Transportation Policy, Department of Defense, in Washington, D.C., and three years as Director of Transportation Planning and Research, Traffic Division, for the U.S. Steel Corporation in Pittsburgh. He is currently Assistant to the Moderator of the Transportation Association of America.

Top-level managers, not only in business but also in other organizations, will find this book useful and helpful. What is "best practice" for one company may not be as successful or effective in another, but this book enables the reader to compare his own technique, methodology, and philosophy with those of fifteen successful and well-managed business organizations throughout the country, and this in itself will make an important contribution to the effectiveness of management. Hopefully, too, the reader will find this volume to be predictive of trends which will be anticipated in developing corporate strategies and plans of the future.

Ernest C. Arbuckle

Chairman of the Board, Wells Fargo Bank

*Formerly Dean, Graduate School
of Business, Stanford University*

PREFACE

Something over twenty-five years ago, under the imprimatur of the Graduate School of Business at Stanford University, a book was published with the title of *Top Management Organization and Control*. It presented the findings of an extensive field study of the then current top management practices of thirty-one large industrial companies in the United States. The authors were Professor Paul E. Holden of the Graduate School of Business, and two research assistants, Lounsberry

S. Fish and Hubert L. Smith, both at that time members of the Department on Organization of the Standard Oil Company of California.

The project was an early, if not a pioneering, venture to explore the manner in which major manufacturing corporations were handling their common activities and problems. An immense amount of first-hand information was gathered, analyzed, and finally assembled into a document which for many years enjoyed gratifying readership, both in the business community and in business education, abroad as well as in the United States. The book was translated into Japanese, French, German, and Spanish.

During the quarter century since that study was made, many significant changes have occurred in the external as well as the internal environment of American industry. Despite the vast literature that has evolved and the countless meetings that have been held in the meantime, all dealing with the management process, the authors believed that another study patterned somewhat on the first one was an appropriate undertaking.

As an initial step, three basic objectives were established:

1. To determine the current top management policies and practices with respect to a selected number of major top management involvement areas.
2. To identify and evaluate the major changes in top management policies and practices between the current findings and those reported in the earlier study. This explains the frequent references made to the first study throughout the various chapters that follow.
3. To interpret the implications of the current policies and practices and the changes in terms of the probable trends and direction of future policies and practices in the field of top management organization, direction, and control.

The next step was the selection of the particular areas of top management involvement on which to concentrate the field investigation. The following areas were chosen:

1. Overall control
2. Management of the corporate income
3. Long-range planning

  4. Organization structure
  5. Centralization versus decentralization
  6. Committees
  7. Composition, functions, and use of boards of directors
  8. Research and development
  9. Product-line direction and control
 10. Mergers and acquisitions
 11. International operations
 12. Management information systems
 13. External relations
 14. Employee relations
 15. Development of executive personnel

The third step had to do with the nature and extent of the field work suitable to the project. Again, it was decided in the interest of comparability to restrict the coverage to a diversified group of large manufacturing companies rather than include financial, distribution, transportation, or other types of enterprise. However, it was decided that a smaller number of companies would adequately provide the variety and volume of information desired.

Fifteen companies participated. During recent years, their annual contribution to the G.N.P. has been approximately 8%.

The authors wish to express their profound appreciation to these fifteen participating companies who, in the course of the field work, extended every possible courtesy, and to the 268 executives in those companies who gave so freely of their time and cooperated so helpfully in making available the information around which this book is developed. We are indebted to several of our colleagues on the faculty of the Stanford Graduate School of Business for suggestitions made and technical evaluation of certain data gathered. Particularly, we want to extend our sincere thanks to Ernest C. Arbuckle, Dean of the school at the time of this study, for his wholehearted encouragement and support of this undertaking from beginning to end. Grateful acknowledgement is made to the Graduate School of Business, the Stanford Research Institute, The Merrill Foundation, The Alfred P. Sloan Foundation, The John A. McCarthy Foundation, and to Mr. Ralph K. Davies for providing the funds that made possible the conduct of this study.

It is the genuine hope of the authors that the material presented in this document will have met, at least to some degree, the original objectives established at the outset and will be found useful to top corporate executives in comparing and evaluating their management practices with those of other successful companies.

P.E.H.
C.A.P.
G.E.G.

CONTENTS

Foreword   *v*

Preface   *ix*

1 SYNOPSIS   **1**

OVERALL CONTROL   **2**

MANAGEMENT OF THE CORPORATE INCOME   **3**

LONG-RANGE PLANNING   **3**

ORGANIZATION STRUCTURE   **4**

RESEARCH AND DEVELOPMENT   **7**

PRODUCT LINE DIRECTION AND CONTROL   **9**

MERGERS AND ACQUISITIONS   **10**

xiii

INTERNATIONAL OPERATIONS	11
MANAGEMENT INFORMATION SYSTEMS	13
EXTERNAL AND EMPLOYEE RELATIONS	14
SELECTION AND DEVELOPMENT OF EXECUTIVE PERSONNEL	16
ROAD TO THE TOP	19

2 OVERALL CONTROL AND MANAGEMENT OF THE CORPORATE INCOME   **22**

OBJECTIVES	23
BUDGETARY CONTROL	23
PROFIT AND LOSS CONTROL	24
RETURN ON INVESTMENT	25
POLICIES	27
OTHER OVERALL CONTROLS	32
MANAGEMENT OF THE CORPORATE INCOME	34

3 LONG-RANGE PLANNING   **37**

CURRENT OBSERVATIONS	38
The five-year projection	39
The comprehensiveness of the plans	41
The extent of top management involvement	42
Participation by line executives	44
The role of the central planning staff	45
EXAMPLES OF LONG-RANGE PLANNING PROCEDURES	48
Company A	48
Company B	50
Company C	52
A LOOK AHEAD	53

4 ORGANIZATION STRUCTURE   **57**

ARRANGING THE STRUCTURE	58
SPAN OF CONTROL	60
MULTIPLE EXECUTIVE VICE PRESIDENTS	61
VICE PRESIDENT FOR ADMINISTRATION	62
OTHER DEPARTMENTAL GROUPINGS	63
MANAGEMENT INFORMATION SYSTEMS	64
PRODUCT MANAGERS	64
ORGANIZATION PLANNING DEPARTMENTS	67
CENTRALIZATION VERSUS DECENTRALIZATION	68
INTERNATIONAL OPERATIONS	71

Contents

COMMITTEES 71
BOARDS OF DIRECTORS 73

5 MANAGEMENT OF RESEARCH AND DEVELOPMENT 77

ESTABLISHING OBJECTIVES AND A RESEARCH PHILOSOPHY 78
ORGANIZING, DIRECTING, AND CONTROLLING THE RESEARCH
    AND DEVELOPMENT EFFORT 85
A LOOK AHEAD 91
EXAMPLES OF RESEARCH AND DEVELOPMENT POLICIES AND PRACTICES 94
    Company A 94
    Company B 97
    Company C 98

6 PRODUCT LINE DIRECTION AND CONTROL 101

PLANNING THE PRODUCT LINE 103
    Balance and emphasis 103
    Pricing and timing 104
    Use of management information systems 105
DIRECTING AND CONTROLLING THE PRODUCT LINE 107
    Use of product, project, and program managers 108
    Control over inventories and spare parts 110
    Product authorization 111
    Product safety 111
TYPICAL QUESTIONS ASKED BY TOP MANAGEMENT 112
    Planning 112
    Organization 112
    Direction and control 113
A LOOK AHEAD 114
EXAMPLES OF PRODUCT LINE PROGRAMS 119
    Corporation A 119
    Corporation B 120
    Corporation C 122
APPENDIX: THE MARKET PROVINCE CONCEPT 123
    General 123
    Policy 124
    Responsibility 124
    Procedure for establishing provinces 124
    Objectives 125
    Working relationships 125
    Systems selling 126
    Evaluating performance 127
    Charters 127

7   MERGERS AND ACQUISITIONS   128

TOP MANAGEMENT INVOLVEMENT   129
A LOOK AHEAD   132
APPENDIX: CHECKLIST USED BY ONE COMPANY TO DEVELOP
    INFORMATION FOR EVALUATING AN ACQUISITION POSSIBILITY   133
    Personnel   133
    Financial   133
    Marketing   135
    Engineering   135
    Patents   135
    Asking price   135
    Manufacturing   136

8   INTERNATIONAL OPERATIONS   137

FACTORS INFLUENCING INTERNATIONAL OPERATIONS   138
    Cost   138
    Government policy   139
    Market characteristics   142
    Changing conditions   144
MANAGEMENT FUNCTIONS ABROAD   145
    Top management direction   146
    Marketing   147
    Manufacturing   148
    Research and development   149
    Finance and control   150
    Long-range planning   153
    Personnel management   154
APPRAISING PATTERNS OF ORGANIZATION   158
    Foreign agents and representatives   159
    International division   160
    Foreign subsidiaries   161
    World marketing by product divisions   163
    Inquiries by management   164

9   MANAGEMENT INFORMATION SYSTEMS   166

PROBLEMS IN DEVELOPMENT   167
    Fact and fancy   167
    The reasons why   168
APPLICATIONS OF MANAGEMENT INFORMATION SYSTEMS   170
PROVIDING THE SERVICE   172
    Data center development   172
    Scope of services   174
    Customer freedom   174

IMPACT ON THE ENTERPRISE 175
   Centralization versus decentralization 175
   Impact on middle management 176
   Role of top management 178
IMPLICATIONS OF TECHNOLOGY 180
   Computer capacity and cost 180
   Computer speed and flexibility 180
   Auxiliary equipment 181
   Communications facilities 182
   Software 182
   Mathematical developments 183
A LOOK AHEAD 183
SUGGESTED QUESTIONS FOR MANAGEMENT 189

10 EXTERNAL AND EMPLOYEE RELATIONS 191

SHIFT IN EMPHASIS 192
ORGANIZATION POSITION AND ACTIVITIES 192
COMMUNITY AFFAIRS 196
STATE AND NATIONAL AFFAIRS 197
CORPORATE INFORMATION 198
MANAGEMENT-LABOR RELATIONS 199
APPENDIX: OUTLINE OF DECENTRALIZED LABOR CONTRACT
   NEGOTIATION METHODS USED BY A PARTICIPATING COMPANY 200
APPENDIX: AGENDA FOR A MONTHLY MEETING OF A CORPORATE
   RELATIONS COMMITTEE WITH SOME NOTES BY THE CHAIRMAN 201

11 SELECTION AND DEVELOPMENT OF EXECUTIVE PERSONNEL 203

REQUIREMENTS FOR SUCCESS IN TOP MANAGEMENT 205
   Comments by executives 205
   The generalist versus the specialist 207
PLANNING AND ORGANIZING FOR EFFECTIVE SELECTION, EVALUATION,
   AND DEVELOPMENT 207
   Use of committees 208
   Administration without the use of a committee 209
   Recent changes and future trends 211
SELECTION AND EARLY IDENTIFICATION OF POTENTIAL EXECUTIVE
   PERSONNEL 212
   Recruitment of college graduates 212
   Obtaining experienced executives from outside 213
   Early identification of executive potential 213

APPRAISAL AND EVALUATION   217
  Formal programs   217
  Nature and scope of top management's involvement   217
  Counseling as part of the appraisal process   218
  Most significant changes in appraisal and evaluation   219
DEVELOPMENT OF FULL POTENTIAL   219
  Internal development   220
  External developments   223
KEY QUESTIONS BEING ASKED BY TOP MANAGEMENT   224
EXAMPLES OF SUCCESSFUL EXECUTIVE SELECTION AND DEVELOPMENT
  PROGRAMS   225
  Corporation A   225
  Corporation B   229
  Corporation C   230

12 ROAD TO THE TOP   233

PERSONAL AND EDUCATIONAL BACKGROUNDS   236
  Age   236
  Years with company   236
  Education   236
  Personal characteristics   239
EXPERIENCE BACKGROUNDS   239
  Line and staff experience   240
  Analysis by functions   240
  Multidivisional experience   244
VARIATIONS IN CAREER PATTERNS   245
THE GENERALIST-SPECIALIST DICHOTOMY   245
A LOOK AHEAD   246
APPENDIX: TABULATED DATA ON TOP MANAGEMENT   249
  Age distribution   249
  Years with company   250
  Academic degrees   251
  Major fields of study   253
  First jobs   254
  Primary fields or functions   254
  *Functions from which top management was promoted into general
    management*   255
  Functions prior to promotion into present positions   255

INDEX   257

TOP MANAGEMENT

SYNOPSIS

1

It may well be said that this book is of top management, by top management, and for top management. The authors' role has been planning and organizing the project, gathering information at firsthand through the interview process, analyzing and interpreting the material, and presenting the findings.

To permit a quick overview of the material contained in the chapters that follow, this opening chapter is intended to highlight the significant conclusions pertaining to each of the top management involvement

1

areas studied in depth. The reader may then follow the dictates of his own interest as to which topics he will examine in more extended fashion and in what sequence.

OVERALL CONTROL

The essence of good administrative practice is delegation of responsibility and authority to the fullest practicable degree, that is, to place decision making at the lowest level at which needed facts are available. However, delegation never relieves a manager from ultimate responsibility. The chief executive officer is inescapably accountable for corporate performance. This position of extreme vulnerability calls for appropriate protective measures which take the form of adequate and timely controls.

A number of control devices were found in the participating companies, although not all were in universal use. The starting point in many companies is the establishment of corporate objectives. If these meet certain criteria, top management has taken a fundamental step in providing the basis for other controls. Perhaps the second most effective instrument of control is a set of corporate policies that implement the attainment of predetermined objectives. Again, several criteria must be met if policies are to serve the purposes for which they are intended.

The budget in its various applications is unquestionably the most widely used control mechanism. The initial review and approval of the budget by top management is the first control step. Then the periodic comparison of actual expenditure with budget provides a continuing measure of results in terms of planned performance. This recurring evaluation, when accompanied by an explanation of variances, equips top management with an invaluable and opportune means of control.

Companies organized on a product or geographic divisional basis frequently use several other types of control, with profit and loss and return on investment being the more common. A few chief executives hold to the opinion that the most effective control under this plan of organization is gained through visits with operating managers at divisional headquarters. There can be little argument that this confrontation can provide an examination of many vital aspects of divisional performance and prospects in an expeditious manner.

Other control devices are briefly described in Chapter 2. Some documents used in this connection and sample statements of policy are also presented.

MANAGEMENT OF THE CORPORATE INCOME

Disposition of income is an annual determination in any well-managed enterprise. Stated in simple terms, it is the allocation of those funds remaining after obligatory expenditures have been covered. Basically, this area of discretionary action is concerned with two responsibilities: the declaration of dividends and the underwriting of corporate growth and protection.

The first of these responsibilities, for well-established and profitable companies, involves very little deliberation upon most occasions. The second, however, entails many decisions and calls for the exercise of business judgment of the highest degree. Thus it is that the management of the corporate income becomes the sole prerogative of a company's top executives, with the board of directors having the final authority.

LONG-RANGE PLANNING

Forward planning is accepted practice today in well-managed industrial enterprises. The men in top management have a keen awareness of their corporate obligation to plan for the future and to do so with an unmistakable seriousness of purpose. There are, of course, significant differences among companies in their depth of experience with the process, the degree of sophistication developed, and the means of implementation applied. There is little difference, however, in the involvement of the chief executive officers who devote from 25 to 70 percent of their time to long-range planning. This involvement occurs, customarily, in the initial steps and at the final-approval stage, but in some cases there is participation at each significant point in the development of the overall plan.

Other members of line management carry a heavy responsibility for advance planning in their respective areas of accountability. An increasing emphasis will be given to the line executives' role; to qualify for an important position an individual will have had to demonstrate a capacity to plan ahead.

Although the involvement of line management from bottom to top in the planning process is general practice, the participation of the board of directors follows no common pattern. Occasionally, the board will be called upon to contribute to the establishment of corporate objectives as an initial step and to approve the final plan. More often, the board is simply advised by the chief executive officer of the salient features of the plan. In these instances, the board does not relinquish its authority to control capital expenditures, as this is achieved through its final approval of the capital budget.

Despite the major role assumed by line management in long-range planning, a central agency continues to be involved in the process. The headquarters group may be one or two individuals, a committee, or a fully constituted staff department. There is also marked dissimilarity in the extent of participation of the central agencies. Duties may range from developing the format for submitting plans and providing assistance and advice to serving in the capacity of monitoring, auditing, reviewing, and finally consolidating divisional plans into an overall corporate plan.

In contrast to early corporate planning, the current practice is to develop comprehensive projections involving product line, sales, facilities, research and development, manpower, organization structure and, of course, finances. Particularly noteworthy is the present-day arrangement for a heavy marketing input to provide the basis for deriving the divisional plans as well as the overall program.

Although a five-year planning cycle is the prevailing pattern, some notable exceptions are found. Some companies with multiple product lines plan only for three years ahead for consumer products, but project eight years or more for products destined for heavy industry or other applications necessitating long lead times for facilities and development. Other exceptions to the five-year cycle relate to certain elements of the overall plan such as managerial manpower development, research, diversification through acquisition — all longer-time projections. Companies that have had successful experience in long-range planning and that are cognizant of the need to extend the cycle for certain elements are either moving rapidly to a ten-year program or are giving serious consideration to that eventuality.

Chapter 3 discusses long-range planning in detail. The actual procedures followed by three companies well advanced in planning techniques are set forth.

ORGANIZATION STRUCTURE

Over the years countless words, written and spoken, have been devoted to the subject of organization. This is, of course, a measure of its importance, and no document relating to top management could properly omit a discussion of it. In the course of this particular undertaking, the topic was explored at some depth with major executives in the participating companies. Certain practices, developments, and trends were observed with sufficient frequency to be representative.

Relative stability of organization structure appears to be a general characteristic, but this does not imply that changes are not made as occasion warrants. The point is that change for its own sake is strictly avoided, if for no other reason than the disruptive effect of a major rearrangement of structure. If a basic reorganization is to be made, the decision lies with the chief executive officer, as he is in the best position to observe the need and to do something positive about it.

Decentralization through the medium of product or geographic divisionalization of large industrial enterprises has been the custom for many years, is still the general pattern and, if the opinion of many top executives has validity, will continue to be the accepted plan for years to come. The innate advantages are so pronounced, and corporate experience is so convincing, that this judgment is impressively supported. However, it must be reported that over a substantial time span there has occurred some lessening of the autonomy exercised by divisional management. This reflects simply the influence of evolving situations, largely environmental, and does not indicate any doubt as to the soundness of the basic concept of the decentralization of operations.

The attitudes toward committees are as diverse and disputatious today as ever. Some top executives are unequivocally opposed to this organizational device, while others are equally convinced that committees fulfill a need not met as well in any other manner. It can be stated that, in general, fewer standing committees are to be found — even in the companies where committees are highly regarded — than was the case some years previously. The alternative practice is the use of ad hoc task forces. Those committees that have regular and continuing status are, for the most part, high-level and serve primarily in an advisory capacity to the chief executive officer or the chief operating officer.

At one time, the position of executive vice president connoted just one thing: the incumbent was next in line to the chief executive and, to all intents and purposes, was destined to be his successor. Today, a quite common corporate practice is to have several executive vice presidents, any one of whom may accede to the top position. This optional situation is not the fundamental reason for this organizational development, but merely a by-product. The real purpose for having multiple executive vice presidents (the position of group vice president may be regarded as comparable) is to reduce the load carried by the chief executive officer and the chief operating officer — in short, to narrow the span of control for these two top administrative posts.

The executive vice president or group vice president, as mentioned, ordinarily functions in a line capacity. In a few instances, however, the same titles are attached to positions with jurisdiction over a number of central staff departments. Another designation for this assignment, and one found more frequently, is administrative vice president. Although there is no standard composition of the grouping of staff departments assigned to an administrative vice president, certain ones appear frequently; for example, employee relations, public relations, secretary, treasurer, and legal. In addition to shortening the span of control for chief executives, this organizational arrangement is designed to serve other useful purposes.

New and noteworthy developments appear on the organizational scene only occasionally. One such relatively recent occurrence is the position of product manager. Somewhat similar to, but not identical with, this position are others designated as project managers and program managers.

The product manager is generally visualized as the planner, coordinator and, particularly, the promoter of a single product or a closely related group of products. He is neither line nor staff, yet in most instances he is responsible for the profitability of his line.

The project manager has a product and market orientation, but is concerned with an entirely new venture rather than an existing line of products. His assignment occurs when research and development come up with a process or product that gives real promise. The customary practice is to organize a task force of research, development, manufacturing, and marketing people under a project manager to carry the undertaking to successful commercialization or to demonstrated impracticability.

The program manager is usually found in a company involved in a substantial defense effort. When a contract is consummated, he is appointed and becomes the principal contact with the procuring agency. His responsibility, without line authority, is for the completion of his program on time, within budget, and in full compliance with requirements.

Organization planning departments, as a high-level staff agency, appear to have had their day, albeit a useful one. There are a number of reasons for this turn of events. Where they do exist, they have other functions to perform, including providing consultative services to operational units of the enterprise, particularly foreign.

Perhaps it is not surprising to find that the composition and role of the board of directors has undergone very little change over the years. Today, the size, proportion of outside members, committees, and duties of the board are about the same as they were a quarter century ago. Now, as then, the board of directors is vested with the trusteeship function, and all that that term implies.

A few developments with respect to boards of directors can be noted, and would appear to be trends that will continue into the future. First, board compensation fees are higher, and the practice of an annual retainer for outside members is growing in acceptance. Second, the establishment of a retirement age for directors, outside as well as inside, is found with increasing frequency. Third, the scheduling of fewer full board meetings per year seems to be gaining favor, as is the practice of holding one or more such meetings at important geographic locations of company operations. Fourth, there is some evidence that the ratio of outside members to inside members will increase, particularly in those companies where the latter category has been in subtial majority.

RESEARCH AND DEVELOPMENT

During the past fifteen years there has been an approximately fourfold increase in research and development expenditure in the United States, and the rate of growth of research activities is likely to increase rather than decrease. Top management is very much involved in the planning, direction, and control of the research and development efforts.

Typical subjects of concern to top management include: patterns and methods of corporate growth, either by acquisition or by internal product development; the corporate image as viewed by the scientific community and by the customer; the competitive position of the product lines; the balance between fundamental research and applied research and development; the utilization of outside research capabilities of universities, research institutes, and the government; and the maintenance of an appropriate balance between the management or profit point of view and the scientific point of view.

The use of specific research objectives and goals varies among the companies studied. Likewise, the expenditures for research and development, as a percentage of sales, range from a low of 1 percent to a high of 10 percent. In recent years market opportunities and product line needs have been widely used as guides for applied research expenditures. "Keeping the pipeline filled" or "pumping money into the technology bank" represent an extension of the same general approach to basic or long-range research. In addition, most of the companies follow a practice of making annual allocations of research funds between the central research organization and the operating divisions. Allocations normally are also made by product lines in relation to the expressed needs of operating divisions, by customers needs, and by types of research, such as basic or applied.

Fourteen of the fifteen companies studied have central corporate research organizations. The vice presidents or directors of research all report to the president and/or chief executive officer, to a committee of the board of directors, or to an executive or senior vice president. Corporate research and development committees usually include representatives of both the central research organization and the operating divisions. During recent years top management has been particularly concerned in getting increased multifunctional inputs at earlier stages in the research and development process. In some instances this is accomplished by assigning top-level marketing and engineering executives to membership on the research and development committees. In other cases project teams with multifunctional membership are utilized to achieve this purpose.

New tools, techniques, and organization structures are being used in several companies to shorten the time between the development and the commercialization of new products and to ensure that good new product ideas do not die in the research laboratories. Improved quantitative and behavioral science tools and techniques are being used in simulation or consumer studies to provide top management with more complete information for decision making on new products. The creation of "new venture" or "new product transition" departments and the establishment of multiple routes by which products are advanced to the marketplace are increasing the effectiveness of the new product development program in a number of companies.

Top management anticipates a number of changes in the future administration of the research and development activities. Some of these changes include:

1. A continuing, and perhaps increased, emphasis upon applied research geared to the specific needs of the operating departments and to the desires in the marketplace.

2. Improved coordination and communication between the corporate research organization and the research personnel at universities, private research institutes, and governmental organizations.
3. More effective use of quantitative and behavioral skills in forecasting customer demands for new products.
4. Greater use of "new venture" departments, special task forces or committees with multifunctional membership, and the project form of organization to expedite the development of new products.
5. A closing of the gap between management's profit point of view and the researcher's scientific point of view. This is likely to result from more effective controls over research expenditures, from better communication between central research and the line operating departments, from an increase in multifunctional inputs at various stages of development, and from the use of a greater number of "look-see" evaluation points in the research and development process.

Descriptions of successful research and development programs of three of the participating companies are included in Chapter 5, "Research and Development."

PRODUCT LINE DIRECTION AND CONTROL

Top management considers product line direction and control to be one of its major responsibilities. The president and his team of top executives constantly utilize both leadership and pressure to improve product line competitive positions and to make distinctive contributions within the industry or particular area of operations.

Effective product line direction and control requires that top management has exceptional skill in coordination. Frequent conflicts occur among engineering, research and development, production, marketing, and finance personnel. It is the responsibility of top management to anticipate and prevent these conflicts, to solve those that arise, and to develop a spirit of teamwork among all segments of the organization. This responsibility for the overall coordination and control of the product line cannot be delegated to subordinates.

Top management anticipates a number of changes in the future problems involving the establishment of the most effective division of the product line among operating divisions; maintenance of an appropriate balance in terms of an engineering orientation of the product line versus a marketing orientation; the extent to which certain phases of product line control should be decentralized; where the responsibility for pricing should rest; reduction of time from conceptualization of a new idea to the sale of the product; use of project management; use of improved information systems for product design and inventory control; elimination of unprofitable items from the product line; and evaluation of new product or product modification proposals in terms of return on investment and discounted cash flow.

In Chapter 6, "Product Line Direction and Control," the nature of top management's involvement is described, and an extensive list of questions being asked by top management is included. The product line programs of three companies are described. Two of these companies have centralized programs, and the third has a highly decentralized plan.

Future changes in product line direction and control are likely to include:

1. An increased rate of product change caused by more severe international competition, greater research efforts, and more effective cost control and information systems.
2. An increased emphasis on marketing inputs at several stages in the development of new products.
3. Improved and more extensive use of new quantitative techniques to reduce inventories and to eliminate unprofitable items from the lines. Increased control of inventories on a vertically integrated basis from raw materials to finished goods in the dealer's stock, particularly in the field of spare parts.
4. Greater and more enlightened participation by line management through its involvement in long-range and short-term planning and through its increased emphasis upon the "management by objectives" concept.
5. An increase in the use of product value analysis programs and product competitive cost comparison programs.

MERGERS AND ACQUISITIONS

One method of expanding or diversifying a product line, for many companies and for many years, has been through mergers or acquisitions. Today the climate for this type of corporate action is, to say the least, uncertain. For large companies, particularly if they are dominant in their respective industries, the enlargement of present product lines, or the addition of a closely related product line by means of mergers or acquisitions is not in the realm of reality. The situation, however, is somewhat different in the area of product line diversification and in the foreign field.

Regardless of the degree of corporate activity or the extent to which the procedure has been formalized, there are six steps in the merger or acquisition process: identification, initiation, evaluation, negotiation, consummation, and integration. As expected, there is no uniform pattern as to who does what and when in this process. A key role is universally played by the chief executive officer, but the nature and extent of his involvement varies from company to company. Other high-level management people, committees, staff departments, and the board of directors have a part in putting together a merger or acquisition as found among the participating companies.

In Chapter 7, "Mergers and Acquisitions," specific examples are presented showing how a few companies with years of experience have developed guidelines and other helpful aids to implement various steps in carrying out a merger or acquisition.

INTERNATIONAL OPERATIONS

Growth prospects for United States business abroad are spectacular, in most cases outstripping the probable expansion in the domestic market. All the companies participating in this study are giving careful attention to overseas plans and operations.

Government influence on international operations is effective in many areas, from tariffs and exchange controls to personnel policy. More, rather than less, government involvement seems likely in the future. Market characteristics, such as product preferences and requirements, distribution patterns, and the need for interchangeability, are also important factors in international operations. These factors are often distinctly different from those in the United States. Both government policy and market problems are complicated by continuing changes as one group or another takes control of government, economies develop, and customer tastes evolve. As a result, a current and intimate knowledge of each major market is necessary for most effective international operations.

This need has led to the increased emphasis on the international aspects of various management functions and to the handling of some parts of these activities abroad. Thus, marketing, production, research and development, finance and control, long-range planning, and personnel management are of greater importance overseas than before in the operations of many of the companies studied. This emphasis is likely to continue as foreign markets grow in importance.

As these changes have taken place, there has been an interesting pattern of organization developments in many companies. Generally, the old system of foreign agents and representatives is being abandoned in favor of arrangements providing more effective control and development. The international division is a feature of the organization structure of most of the companies visited. This organization may provide direction only for product lines not having a volume adequate to support separate representation overseas, or it may be a means of coordinating all international operations of the firm. Because of its flexibility, it appears that the international division will be a part of the foreign operations of many United States companies in the future.

The foreign subsidiary is another device that has gained favor as international operations have expanded. Two problems of importance require careful management attention now and in the future. One problem is the demand of various foreign nationals, often supported by their governments, for a share in the ownership of the overseas subsidiary. Some United States companies have resisted this. Others have accepted or encouraged minority stock ownership for foreigners in overseas subsidiaries, and a few of the companies studied have accepted a minority stock position for themselves. An interesting development in this last case is the experimentation with operating contracts as a means of assuring effective management control of a foreign subsidiary, and possibly increasing the United States company's return on investment, while it holds a minority stock position in the foreign subsidiary. This arrangement is expected to offer both profit and public relations advantages abroad. The second problem concerning overseas subsidiaries is that some of them were organized as national companies. Now expansion of business and new technology make multinational operations appropriate. To deal with this, regional international holding and operating companies are being established by some firms to provide the regional coordination required among their foreign subsidiaries without disturbing national feelings. This pattern also is likely to continue as other markets develop in size.

Many firms hope to move from foreign agents, through the international division stage, to a concept of world marketing by product line divisions of the company. It will require time to develop the necessary skills and to build a staff of executives with international experience at the product division headquarters. In addition, foreign markets must become sufficiently large to support separate product line operations. In some cases, the interrelationships among the products of the company, or the distinctive patterns of the overseas markets and organizations, will make this an undesirable objective for the United States business firm. The pattern of organization best suited to each firm will depend on the present and prospective characteristics of its international markets, manufacturing requirements, and other factors. Each pattern will have to be developed in detail. There is no such thing as a "best organization" for international operations for all companies, or for any one company at all times and in all places.

MANAGEMENT INFORMATION SYSTEMS

The development of management information systems has progressed rapidly in recent years. Without exception, the companies participating in this study plan to extend further the use of computers and mathematical techniques in the handling of their affairs. It seems clear that the emphasis in these new applications will be on operating controls and on improved methods for testing and analyzing decision alternatives at various management levels.

The major problem observed concerning management information systems was shared to some degree by all the companies contacted. This common problem is the gap in communications between the line manager and the computer or operations research specialist. Typically, the specialists were technique-oriented rather than problem-oriented. They frequently were not aware that they lacked an adequate understanding of the nature or ramifications of the management problems on which they sought to provide assistance. This, coupled with an intellectual arrogance in some cases, substantially reduced their effectiveness. On the other hand, many senior executives did not have an adequate understanding of computer or operations research concepts. This limited their ability to utilize the skills of their management information system specialists. In the short run, the most effective solution to this manager-specialist communications problem appears to involve a task-force approach. In many cases, experienced managers with some knowledge of these new techniques, plus a number of management information system specialists, can work together to provide improved problem analysis and recommendations for their firm.

As an additional benefit, they may educate one another further in the process.

The implications of technology in the management information systems field indicated that there would be faster, more versatile machines with larger capacity available in the future, and that mathematical techniques would be more powerful and more generally applied than in the past. The combination of economical, long-distance data transmission and the low cost per unit of work on the giant computers of the future was expected to lead to a centralization of data processing capacity in many firms. It was suggested that, in some cases, the data processing capability would be provided by a public utility type of enterprise, serving many different customers to achieve the maximum economies of scale.

In spite of these technical possibilities there was a striking similarity in views concerning the impact of management information systems on the enterprise, whether the speaker was a chief executive officer, the manager of data processing, or the head of the operations research group. All agreed that the computer and the new mathematical techniques had not, and would not, increase the centralization in management. In fact, there was substantial evidence that the effect had been to make decentralization more practical and profitable. This evidence was contrary to some of the literature published in the past few years. Another reversal of the forecasts of various authors was the finding that computers and mathematical techniques would not decrease the authority or significantly affect the numbers of executives in middle management. This, of course, is consistent with the continuing trend to decentralized operations as organizations grow in size.

EXTERNAL AND EMPLOYEE RELATIONS

The striking increase in emphasis on external and employee relations was highlighted by one firm which has increased sevenfold its budget and staff for public relations during the past decade. Although this was the greatest change observed among the fifteen participating companies, all the firms reflected more emphasis on external and employee relations during the past ten years. This change appears to be a result of increasing government involvement in business affairs, greater use of national collective bargaining, larger and more diversified stockholder groups, a broader interpretation of the social responsibility of business, and a shift in management emphasis from meeting problems as they arise to anticipating problems and change in the external and employee relations areas.

The importance with which these functions are viewed is indicated by the fact that the senior executives in charge of external and/or employee relations usually report directly to the president or chief executive officer and always have direct access to him when required. In addition, other line executives are spending more time than before on these functions. Many of the companies visited maintain a Washington office, and some have regional offices with external relations functions. The number of these offices probably will increase somewhat in the next decade.

Another development of importance has been the greater attention given to problems of the future in considering external or employee relations. In almost every participating company, collective bargaining strategy, executive reference materials, and public information on the company situation are prepared well in advance of the start of actual negotiations. In some cases, public tours and plant visits are encouraged several months before contract termination, to improve public knowledge about working conditions.

Looking still further ahead, many external relations groups are now trying to anticipate major issues and problems for their companies. In one large firm, a separate long-range planning section has been established in the public relations department. A somewhat different approach was taken by another company which set up a corporate relations committee, including five executives of vice-presidential rank or above, to look ahead and recommend policy on external affairs.

Perhaps as a result of looking ahead, a broader and more mature viewpoint on external and employee relations appears to have developed in management over the preceding decade. Executives from almost all the participating companies indicated that their organizations are now more favorable than in the past toward employee activity in community affairs and political campaigns. A number of firms have sponsored courses of instruction on political action, have invited rival candidates to speak at company plants or offices, and have encouraged employees to accept appointive positions or to run for elective offices. The underlying reason appears to be a desire for community service, blended with a belief that if government officials understand business problems government action is likely to be more intelligent. These excursions into community and political affairs have resulted in serious problems for some of the firms visited. However, none of them plans to be less active in these areas, and many of them expect to be more active in the future.

This more mature viewpoint seems to have affected both management and union negotiators in many cases. There appears to be a feeling of respect for one another and a degree of mutual trust not present ten years ago. In some cases, it was pointed out that union officials (both national and local) understood and discussed management problems so well that they found it difficult to retain the support of their union members. The increased understanding on the part of management is indicated by the fact that several of the companies have successfully resisted union organizing efforts since World War II. Looking at the several examples, the key to their effective resistance appears to have been that they provided good wages, good working conditions, and fair treatment, so that there was no basis for an effective union organizing campaign. With better understanding on both sides and a willingness to work together, the employee relations area may see more constructive action in the future than we have commonly encountered there in the past.

SELECTION AND DEVELOPMENT OF EXECUTIVE PERSONNEL

The chairman of the board, the president, and other top-level executives in all the participating companies are significantly involved in the selection and development of executives. Typical comments by presidents were: "It's my number one job." "I spend more time on this than on any other activity." "The basis of our success is people. I am constantly searching for men with outstanding managerial capability."

There was recognition by the chief executive officer in all fifteen companies that there is an extremely short supply of men with the executive capacities required to meet the future challenges of increased competition and of technological, social, and political change. In every company visited there was evidence that increased emphasis is being given to the early identification of young men with general management capability and to the development of the full potential of executives and managers at all levels.

In the opinion of the top executives interviewed, there is no clear-cut stereotype for success in top management. Changing conditions require different executive capabilities. There was general agreement among the top executives, however, that the individuals with the greatest promise for success in top management usually possess most of the following qualities:

1. Drive
2. Initiative and enthusiasm
3. Flexibility
4. Objectivity
5. Decisiveness
6. Imagination
7. Emotional stability
8. Mental alertness and analytical skill
9. Breadth of knowledge and understanding
10. Good judgment
11. Effective human relations and communication skills
12. Willingness to take risks
13. Loyalty and dedication to purpose
14. Toughness (ability to stand up under pressure and to take action even though the action is unpopular)
15. Unselfishness

Most of the qualities listed above are nonquantifiable and therefore hard to measure. It is difficult to determine whether an individual possesses these qualities until he has had the opportunity to perform on the job. Consequently, top executives place major emphasis upon performance as the basis for promotion. They are also firm believers in the concept, "You learn to manage by managing."

On the subject of the generalist versus the specialist, the top executives interviewed were unanimous in the opinion that success in general management requires broad experience and understanding rather than narrow specialization. They were also in agreement that line experience is almost mandatory for success in a general management position.

There was wide variation among the companies visited in the degree to which their executive evaluation and development programs are formalized. Most of the companies utilize formal organization charts which include backup lists or replacement schedules. Several companies have three- or four-year specific development programs for each executive. One of the most comprehensive programs includes personal history, promotability, replacement, and individual development records for 10,000 management and professional personnel. Several companies, however, have discarded highly formalized programs in favor of simpler programs that focus attention upon a relatively small number of "key men" or "comers."

In most of the companies visited the chairman of the board and the president are personally involved in the evaluation and promotion of several hundred executives. The nature and scope of this involvement are described in Chapter 11.

Four of the fifteen participating companies use top-level committees to evaluate and promote executives. In one company the committee reviews annually the records of approximately 1,500 executives and approves 225 appointments. In all instances where committees are used, the top line executives of the company are members of the committee.

Top management expressed considerable interest in the need to develop improved programs for the early identification of individuals who possess general management capability. At present this identification is generally accomplished through day-to-day observations of executive performance. A few companies have plans whereby the president and a select number of board members and/or executives visit the operating divisions periodically for the specific purpose of evaluating executive personnel. Other companies rely exclusively on "key men" lists to identify young men with unusual potential. Only one of the participating companies is doing significant research in the area of early identification of executive talent.

During the past few years a number of changes have taken place in the methods used to develop executives. These changes include:

1. Greater emphasis upon the use of individually tailored development programs geared to the specific needs of each executive.
2. Increased use of university and other outside development programs to provide breadth and understanding in general management and to update management in special fields of study.
3. More attention to the development of middle and upper levels of management through special seminars, committee and task-force assignments, and project assignments.
4. An increase in the use of job rotation to provide multifunctional and multidivisional experience at various levels of management.

Chapter 11 includes a list of key questions being asked by top management concerning the selection, evaluation, and development of executive personnel. It also includes a detailed description of the executive selection, evaluation, and development program of one company and descriptions of certain phases of the programs of two other companies.

ROAD TO THE TOP

This chapter includes a detailed analysis of the personal characteristics, the educational achievements, and the experience backgrounds of 310 top executives in the fifteen participating companies. The group was selected after interviewing over 260 individuals and after reviewing the personal history records of over 450 executives. The 310 executives chosen truly represent top management in that they spend all or most of their time in performing the following functions:

1. Determining company objectives
2. Developing long-range plans
3. Establishing policies to implement long-range planning
4. Developing and modifying the organization structure
5. Selecting and providing a continuous flow of qualified key personnel
6. Setting short-term goals
7. Appraising overall results and applying corrective measures
8. Managing the corporate income

The analysis includes breakdowns by age, years with the company, types and number of academic degrees, major fields of study while in school, and functional areas of work experience. Experience is analyzed according to first jobs with the company, functions in which the majority of time was spent, and functions from which executives moved into general management positions. Career experience patterns are examined as related to multifunctional and interdivisional experience. The authors also project likely changes in the method and nature of developing future members of top management.

The major findings and observations in this chapter include the following:

1. There was a high degree of maturity and seniority among the top executives. The median age was 57 and the median number of years with the company was 30. About 3 percent of top management has been with the company less than ten years.
2. All the participating companies rely primarily on promotion from within.

3. Top management is a highly educated group. The 310 executives studied have earned 388 degrees, 32 percent earned two or more degrees, and 8 percent have Ph.D. degrees.

4. Over 50 percent of the top executives' academic fields of specialization were in the technical areas of engineering and the physical sciences. The second most frequent area of specialization was a combination of business administration, accounting, and economics.

5. After employment, the first jobs to which the top executives were assigned fell into the following areas:
   a. Engineering and production (44 percent)
   b. Accounting and finance (21 percent)
   c. Sales and marketing (14 percent)
   d. Physical sciences (13 percent)
   e. All others (8 percent)

6. In terms of the functions in which the top executives spent the greatest number of years during their careers, the combined functions of production and engineering represented the largest segment (48 percent), followed by sales and marketing (17 percent), research and development (7 percent), and all others (9 percent).

7. The last functional jobs of the top executives prior to their present assignments in general management were distributed among the functions as follows: production (45 percent), sales and marketing (27 percent), accounting and finance (12 percent), engineering (11 percent), research and development (2 percent), and all others (2 percent).

8. Multifunctional experience of the top executives was not as widespread as might be expected: 44 percent had experience in only one function, 40 percent in two functions, 11 percent in three functions, 4 percent in four functions, and the remainder had experience in more than four functions or came directly into general management from another company. Multifunctional experience was more prevalent among the executives of companies that operated on a decentralized and profit-responsibility basis. There was considerable movement of executives back and forth between such functions as production and engineering, engineering and research, and sales and production. On the other hand, there was very little movement in and out of the accounting

and science functions. The greatest concentration of single functional experience was in the fields of law and accounting.

9. Although there was considerable variation in the career patterns of the top executives, the most common promotion path on the road to the top was through line operating positions rather than through staff positions. There was no evidence that the channels of mobility into top management had changed during the past two decades, and it was the unanimous opinion of both line and staff executives interviewed that the future top executives would be individuals with both breadth and depth experience in operations.

10. In the years ahead, there are likely to be a number of improvements made in the process of developing future top executives. Some of these will include: increased emphasis upon the early identification of executive potential, more sophisticated executive development programs geared to the individual needs of executives, increased use of committee, task-force, and job-rotation assignments.

OVERALL CONTROL
AND MANAGEMENT OF
THE CORPORATE INCOME

2

Regardless of the extent of decentralization and the degree of autonomy granted divisional managers, the ultimate responsibility for corporate performance and end results resides with the chief executive officer. The buck can be passed no further. Hence, it is prudent practice and basic administrative procedure to institute effective and timely controls. This area of top management involvement was explored during the course of this study, as it was many years ago in a prior study to which frequent reference is made.

Several of the same fundamental control devices were in use then as now, although found less often in the first study. During the intervening years, additional control instruments have been developed and have gained increasing acceptance. In the paragraphs that follow, brief discussions will be devoted to the more frequently used means of overall control.

OBJECTIVES

Underlying the direction and control of an enterprise are the corporate objectives as conceived and established by top management. Objectives, to be purposeful, must be: unmistakably clear as to purpose and intent, reasonably and practicably attainable, and capable of measurement in finite terms. In addition, objectives should cover all significant areas of corporate performance and not just a single goal such as a specific volume of business or a given amount of profits. Wise top management well knows that if there is but a single objective, it may be achieved at the expense of other desirable attainments or induce short-term action to the detriment of long-range corporate interest. Thus, objectives should have a check-and-balance characteristic.

Once corporate objectives have been established, top management has taken the primary step toward providing the basis for controls that will permit appropriate delegation of responsibility and authority. Top management is thus freed from much decision making and other administrative detail and can devote major attention to forward planning and to the performance of the company as a whole.

BUDGETARY CONTROL

If the practices of the participating companies may be regarded as typical, the budget in its various applications is by far the most widely used control mechanism. In contrast to the situation 25 years ago, when only half the participating companies were employing budgetary control in some manner, the present survey finds universal application among the companies.

It is obvious that during the intervening period the budget has proved fully effective as a control device and has provided top management with a most useful tool for evaluating corporate and divisional performance on a detailed as well as an overall basis. Moreover, from rather primitive beginnings much expertise in the preparation and interpretation of budget data has been acquired by management people at all levels.

Budget preparation, review, and approval is an annual event for the participating companies. Division or other operating segments start the process early enough to permit appropriate examination and final consolidation. The initial review and approval of the budget serves as the first control step. The periodic comparison of actual expenditure with budget throughout the fiscal year provides the continuing control. For most companies this comparison occurs monthly, although one company that is highly sensitive to market conditions carries out this step on a weekly basis. In all cases, vital features of the periodic comparison are the highlighting of variances, the causes thereof, and determining what action is to be taken. This reporting is customarily in narrative form and to a standard format which readily permits of subsequent reference as to what action was promised, what actually occurred, and with what results.

One of the cooperating companies prefers the term "targets" to "budgets" on the grounds that the latter carries the implication that a budget item has been authorized to be expended. However, as a planning and control device, the budget in its various applications, such as operating, cash, capital expenditures, project, is so widely and thoroughly used that there is little evidence that it will be abandoned in the foreseeable future. To be sure, top management uses and will continue to use many other methods of control, some of which will be discussed in subsequent paragraphs.

PROFIT AND LOSS CONTROL

Since most of the companies in this study have structured their operations on a divisional basis, either product or geographic, it is natural that profit and loss performance is another commonly used control. It should be noted that the determination to divisionalize was induced by the very practical recognition that the traditional functional basis of organization was incapable of meeting performance objectives under conditions of an ever-extending and diverse line of product, an ever-expanding market area, an ever-accelerating advance of technology, and an ever-increasing degree of complexity in doing business. The total enterprise had to be broken up into more manageable segments, and the highly effective profit and loss control resulted.

The format for deriving the profit or loss figure for a division closely follows that for the company as a whole; it has changed very little over the years and is the same for most of the cooperating companies. One company, however, has recently introduced a new form, shown on the following page. This monthly report for each division not only shows the profit and loss situation, but provides top management with a number of other ratios. Because of fundamental differences in the product lines, markets, capital requirements, and other characteristics of the divisions, this control document is used to compare a given division's achievements from one period to another and not to match the performance of one division with another.

RETURN ON INVESTMENT

Another top management control device in frequent use is return on investment. As might be expected, the value attached to this measure of operating performance varies among the participating companies. As representative of the distinctly plus position, one company states its philosophy thus: "We believe that a manufacturing enterprise can best measure and judge the effectiveness of its efforts in terms of return on investment." In this instance, the same strong endorsement applies to operating segments of the business as well as to the company as a whole. This point of view is underscored by the further statement that "the manager of a division can improve his return on investment ratio by reducing costs or better utilizing existing investment, both of which are within his control." Differences also exist in the derivation of the factors that enter into the calculations.

The principal dissimilarity pertains to (1) the derivation of the investment figure, and (2) the use of before- or after-tax figure for earnings. For the fixed-assets portion of the investment figure, some companies use the net amount after depreciation. Others use the gross investment on the grounds expressed by one company:

> Since plant facilities are maintained in high productive order during their working life, the depreciation reserve is designed primarily to provide for obsolescence. Therefore, it would be inappropriate to consider that operating management was responsible for earning a return on only the net investment. If depreciable assets were stated at net depreciated values, earnings in each succeeding period would be related to an ever-decreasing investment. Even with stable earnings, return on investment would con-

MONTH			INCOME STATEMENT	YEAR TO DATE		
Last year 000's	Budget 000's	This year		Last year 000's	Budget 000's	This year
			Outside sales			
			Internal sales			
			SALES & OPERATING REVENUE			
			Cost of outside sales			
			Cost of internal sales			
			Variance from standard			
			Cost of sales			
			GROSS PROFIT			
			Selling & advertising			
			Administrative			
			Research & development			
			Profit from operations			
			Other income (deduct)			
			PROFIT BEFORE TAX			
			Federal income tax			
			Less 5% of capital employed			
			EARNINGS CONTRIBUTION			
			% GROSS MARGIN			
			Outside sales			
			Internal sales			
			% OF SALES & OPERATING REV. Gross profit			
			Selling & advertising			
			Administrative			
			Research & development			
			Profit before tax			
			Capital employed turnover			
			Return on capital empl. after tax			
			Payroll			
XXXX	XXXX	XXXX	Number of employees			

Above the table: _____ DIVISION   Period ending: _____

tinually rise so that comparative ratios would fail to reveal the extent or trend of management performance.

In determining current assets, some companies deduct current liabilities, others do not. Some include cash as assigned, others exclude the item. In like fashion, practice differs concerning the earnings figure used in the ratio. One school of thought takes the position that operating management should be measured on operative earnings, that is, before income tax. The contrary viewpoint is held by other companies who use the net or after-tax figure; they reason that the net earnings represent a more realistic situation and that operating management should not lose sight of the impact of taxes. Such differences merely reflect unlike top management concepts and are actually meaningless so long as a company is consistent in the particular practice it pursues.

POLICIES

Corporate policies, when thoughtfully conceived and properly promulgated, constitute one of the most effective instruments of overall control. In the earlier study of top management practices, policies were defined as the guiding principles established by a company to govern actions, usually under repetitive conditions. The report resulting from that study went on to say that the distinguishing feature of policies is that they provide the basis for governing future actions and, accordingly, must be made known to those who are responsible for handling such actions.

If corporate policies are to serve their intended purpose, they should meet such criteria as: (1) be capable of uniform and ready interpretation, (2) have a high degree of permanency, (3) be amenable to periodic review and necessary revision, (4) be comprehensive in coverage, and (5) permit being checked for compliance.

It goes without saying that for policies to satisfy these stipulations they should be in written form; however, this is not the general practice. One reason given is that a set of written policies has a restrictive influence on decision-making executives. They are, it is claimed, denied a rightful exercise of individual initiative and judgment. Depending upon the intent and the language used, policies can impose unnecessary and undesirable restraints. But if top management conceives of basic and general policies as those principles that guide executive action so the conduct of the business is consistently directed toward predetermined objectives, policies need not and will not hamstring legitimate management action and performance.

As illustrative of this type of policy formulation, the following examples are taken from the manual of one of the participating companies:

COORDINATION OF BUSINESS INVESTIGATIONS

Business investigations relative to potential acquisitions of equity interests, either capital stock or operating assets, shall be coordinated through the vice chairman's office. The group managers shall be responsible for implementing this policy by ensuring that the vice chairman receives copies of all internal and external correspondence and reports relative to such investigations. This policy applies to the corporation, its subsidiaries, 50%-owned companies, and affiliates.

The vice chairman shall, to the extent he deems necessary, distribute such correspondence and reports to corporate staff departments for review and analysis relative to:

(a) Corporate diversification policy
(b) Department of Justice implications
(c) Federal, state, and foreign income taxes
(d) SEC and stock exchange requirements
(e) Accounting and legal questions
(f) Extent and adequacy of investigation
(g) Fringe benefit liabilities and possible precedents to current practices
(h) Financing requirements

The above requirements are not intended to imply that the group managers or their delegates should not work directly with the corporate staff on business investigation matters, but only that when doing so, they continue to send appropriate material directly to the vice chairman.

Acquisitions require the approval of the executive committee. Following such approval, any commitments, proposals, or letters of intent to be transmitted outside the company must be reviewed by the vice chairman or, in his absence, by another member of the operating committee.

CONTRIBUTIONS

Coordination responsibilities. The director of personnel administration has responsibility for coordinating grants and donations to educational institutions, and his counsel should be sought whenever there is a possibility that more than one of our divisions will be solicited.

The treasurer has responsibility for coordinating contributions outside of the educational field. He should be contacted regarding possible use of foundation funds for any new approved contributions in excess of $5,000.

In areas where a local solicitation may be made to more than one division, the divisions should get together to coordinate their giving and properly allocate their expense. Corporate assistance can be obtained from the treasurer when desired.

Approval levels.   Routine renewals of annual contributions such as United Fund, Community Chest, and so forth, may be made by the appropriate group manager without further approval if the circumstances and conditions remain approximately the same and there were no unusual factors involved in either the current or prior year. All new contributions and increases in established annual contribution programs may be approved as follows:

(a) Executive committee—over $10,000

(b) Any operating committee member—may approve up to $10,000 inclusive

(c) Group managers—may approve up to $5,000

Reporting requirements.   Within 20 days after the end of each calendar quarter, each group, including corporate, is to submit a report to the executive committee listing all contributions over $5,000 approved during the quarter. The report is to be sent to the treasurer, who will compile information on the total corporation. The treasurer will apprise the director of personnel administration of all contributions involving educational institutions.

LABOR CONTRACT CHANGES

Responsibility.   Local management has the primary responsibility for maintaining good labor relations at minimum cost and for negotiating new or revised contracts. Because of the fact that a precedent established at any location can have significant impact at other locations, it is essential that the director of personnel administration be kept fully informed on all negotiations.

Approval levels.   Labor contracts involving less than 500 employees and relatively routine in nature may be approved by any member of the operating committee on the recommendation of the appropriate group manager and the director of personnel administration. Where the rate increase is significantly above other area settlements or there is any likelihood of establishing an undesirable precedent of any nature (unusually high rate of increase, long duration, fringe benefits, and so forth), approval of the operating committee (or executive committee, depending on the importance of the issue) should be obtained.

All labor contracts involving more than 500 employees require approval of the executive committee.

BANK RELATIONS AND CASH MANAGEMENT

The vice chairman is responsible for all bank relations, both domestic and foreign, including determination of bank balance levels and use of bank credit and service facilities.

The vice chairman has assigned to the treasurer certain responsibilities in administering bank relations and cash usage. The following procedures should be observed:

(a) The treasurer is responsible for contacts involving balances, credit, and special service facilities with major banks. Contact with these banks regarding credit or services (other than routine matters in connection with operation of a divisional account) should be cleared with the treasurer, and he should be provided copies of correspondence with these banks.

(b) No new bank relationship (domestic or foreign) should be started without advance approval of the treasurer.

(c) All borrowings and credit facilities from banks or other financial institutions should be approved in advance by the treasurer or vice chairman.

(d) It is corporate policy to maintain divisional bank balances at a level which will compensate the bank for costs incurred by the bank in maintaining the division's accounts plus a reasonable profit. The treasurer is responsible for seeing that this policy is observed. Balances requested by divisions in excess of those necessary to pay a bank for its services in handling an account may only be kept with the approval of the vice chairman or treasurer, and such divisions may be charged a special interest fee at the direction of the treasurer for such excess balances.

(e) Domestic and foreign subsidiaries should report all investments of excess cash to the treasurer.

This standard applies to subsidiaries (domestic and foreign) as well as to divisions of the parent company.

BUSINESS INFORMATION SYSTEMS

Responsibilities. Group and division managers have primary responsibility for the development and implementation of those business information systems, both manual and mechanized, which affect only their own operations. Development of corporate-wide information systems shall be coordinated by the controller. The controller shall establish standard procedures for preparing the written documentation defining formalized business information systems, and for auditing the results of installed systems.

Approvals. Operating management shall formally approve all significant changes in business information systems affecting only their operations. Changes affecting corporate-wide systems require approval of the controller.

Reporting. In order to minimize duplication of business information systems development effort, the controller shall be kept apprised of all significant formalized information systems being developed or planned, and he shall distribute a listing quarterly to all business systems' activities for their use in contacting operations involved with similar problems. Annually, each group, or the divisions within a group, shall prepare a report summarizing the costs of activities which are developing and implementing business systems, the profit contribution realized from systems improvements, and the future plan of business systems development. The controller shall compile these reports for the group managers and operating committee.

DATA PROCESSING AND COMMUNICATION SYSTEMS

General. Data processing shall be operated in the manner which will contribute most to the corporation's profits, taking into account the service level, as well as the costs of personnel, machines, and data transmission. Manual procedures, outside service bureaus, corporation data centers, and locally operated equipment shall all be considered in selecting data processing capacity. Company-controlled data processing equipment shall be operated in accordance with internal control standards established by the controller. The controller is responsible for the management of the interplant wire communications network.

Approvals. In order to ensure the maximum practical compatibility and efficiency in data processing, all additions or changes in mechanical and electronic data processing equipment shall be approved by the controller.

Reporting. Annually, the controller shall prepare a report for the vice chairman summarizing the operating and rental costs of installed data processing equipment, the percentage utilization of this equipment, and the plans for expanding capacity in the next twelve months.

This same company has established policies covering such other topics as:

Capital expenditures
Compensation
   Bonuses
   Stock options
Lawsuits
License agreements
Major sales contracts
General price changes on high-volume items
Purchasing
Appointment of officers
Sales to Iron Curtain countries
Outside consultants
Extension of credit
Cash management
Insurance
Accounting and auditing
Public relations
Advertising
Company aircraft
Capital structure changes

Another company's policy coverage would naturally have different topics, but the foregoing is representative of the specific areas of activity that one top management group decided to control by policy declarations.

OTHER OVERALL CONTROLS

In addition to the more commonly used methods of control discussed in the preceding paragraphs, many other devices are being applied by one or more of the companies in this study. Some have been instituted in recent years, some are of long standing, but all reflect the current philosophy of the top management group of the particular company involved.

Control over pricing in several companies resides at a very high level—either the chief executive officer or, more often, the executive committee. In the words of one president, "There is more money to be made in pricing than in almost any other area of business. It is one of the most overlooked factors in business and often is delegated to too low a level in the organization." There can be little argument that the authority to set prices is not only a powerful means of control over all the operating segments of the company, but is also a prime contributing factor to the overall profit and loss performance of the total enterprise.

Top management review of salaries and promotions with power of veto or approval constitutes another important overall control. The lower the organizational level exercising this control, the more pervasive it becomes. As is pointed out in a subsequent chapter, the chief executive officer, together with members of his top management team, regards this retained authority as indispensable to their ultimate responsibility for corporate results and their obligation to safeguard the future performance of the company.

Another control device found useful by some of the participating companies is what may be termed a "periodic management audit." This is quite apart from the so-called "integrity audit," and is often conducted by a different group. In essence, it is a check on conformance to established procedures and compliance with corporate policies. If it has seemed essential to develop accounting, purchasing, personnel, and other procedures, it is only natural to apply some method to ensure adherence by the operating divisions of a company. Likewise, if policies are to serve their fundamental purpose, steps need to be taken to make sure that there is continuing observance.

Several chief executives expressed the view that probably the most effective overall control was accomplished through visits to the operating people at divisional headquarters. This face-to-face discussion enables the company head, usually with several of his top management team, to evaluate current performance, profit expectancy, anticipated problems, action to be taken, the management personnel situation, and many other matters not always readily translated into monetary figures. In one case, these visitations occur quarterly and are usually of two days duration, with the day starting at 7:30 A.M. and running well into the evening. Under such a program, rugged though it may be for all parties concerned, more ground can be covered, more questions answered, more problems analyzed, and more corrective measures taken than a large sheaf of reports would achieve, and in less elapsed time.

One further control device frequently used is the assembly of many significant financial and other figures on one page to permit top management a quick overview of company and division performance. Usually this document is prepared on a monthly basis. One typical example is shown on the next page.

MANAGEMENT OF THE CORPORATE INCOME

The responsibility and authority for managing a company's income rests finally and exclusively with top management. Actually their responsibility is simply the allocation of that portion of the corporate income available for discretionary action, that is, what is left from gross income after obligatory expenditures such as payrolls, materials and services, taxes, interest, debt retirement, and so forth. It is, incidentally, an area in which the board of directors is perforce vitally involved. Moreover, it demands business judgment of the highest order.

The exercise of this particular responsibility must give full and objective consideration to corporate objectives, policies, stockholder interest, as well as legitimate and often urgent requests from operating executives. As one chief executive put it, "The periodic allocation of residual funds serves two fundamental purposes: the declaration of dividends and the underwriting of future corporate growth." Both purposes obviously are in the interest of stockholders—current as well as long range.

For most long-established and successful companies, the dividend determination is virtually *pro forma,* as over the years a pattern of dividend payout as a percentage of net earnings has frequently been followed. The disposition of the remaining funds, however, is anything but a routine exercise. What new capital investments should be authorized? What reserves should be set aside and for what contingencies? How much additional support should be given to the research effort? Should an enlarged advertising program be endorsed and to what extent? Where and in what amount should foreign operations be expanded? These questions are typical of the many competing claims for financial recognition.

KEY FIGURES
(Thousands of dollars)

Month: Year to:

| Last year | This year | | Income data | Last year | This year | |
	Budget	Actual			Budget	Actual
			Net orders–Commercial			
			Net orders–Defense			
			Backlog–Commercial			
			Backlog–Defense			
			Sales and operating revenue			
			Percent gross profit			
			Selling, administration, and R&D			
			Percent of sales			
			Profit before tax			
			Percent of sales			
			Earnings contribution			
			Division A			
			B			
			C			
			D			
			Etc.			
			Total			
			Capital employed turnover			
			Return on capital employed			
			Net income			
			Percent return on stockholders' equity			
			Number of shares			
			Earnings per share			
			Payroll			
			Number of employees			

| Increase (decrease) from | | Balance sheet data | Last year | This year | |
January 1	Last month			Budget	Actual
		Cash and securities			
		Receivables			
		Inventories			
		Working capital			
		Fixed assets, net			
		Fixed asset additions			
		Depreciation			
		Capital employed–Month			
		Capital employed–YTD average			
		Long-term debt			
		Stockholders' equity			
		Number of stockholders			

35

In any company with a forward-looking, aggressive management, the total dollars requested would exceed the funds available. Hence priorities must be established, and within a given category such as capital expenditures subpriorities need to be determined. Much supporting data will, of course, be developed, and recommendations will ordinarily be submitted by top executives, often through the agency of the finance committee or the executive committee. Nevertheless, the board of directors is customarily the final tribunal and will make the principal decisions relating to management of the corporate income.

LONG-RANGE
PLANNING

3

Mention has been made of a prior study focusing upon the role of top management in corporate operation. The following quotation is from that study:

> There is nothing about an organization more important than its future. Owners, management, employees, and society in general are, or should be, more concerned about where a company is going than where it has been. In any institution the responsibility for visualizing, initiating, and

achieving future objectives rests with its top management. The more specifically the future course of a company is conceived and defined, the more likely is its realization. One of the greatest needs observed during the course of this study is for more adequate planning and clarification of future objectives, both near-term and long-range.

During the more than twenty-five years that have elapsed since that earlier examination of top management philosophies and practices, nothing has occurred that would suggest modification of the above statement except the need described in the last sentence. Currently it is unmistakably evident that the executives who, in any enterprise, determine the destiny of their particular company are fully conscious of the inescapable obligation to plan for the future.

Many influences have brought about this significant change over the past quarter century. Management literature has been replete with reasons for, exhortations concerning, and illustrations of successful practices in the field of forward planning. Numerous organizations such as the Stanford Research Institute have devoted much time and talent to advancing the theory and practice of corporate planning. Then too, the constantly expanding size, complexity, and geographic spread of industrial enterprises have been convincing factors in bringing about a recognition of the imperative need for looking ahead and programming for the future.

Thus, awareness is found among virtually all top management people. To be sure, the years of experience with long-range planning, the degree of formal and systematic approach to the problem, the sophistication of methods, and the means of implementation vary widely, and this is true even among the select companies that participated in this second study.

CURRENT OBSERVATIONS

To the extent that broad generalities can be reported, the following are noteworthy and will be elaborated more fully in subsequent discussion:

1. The five-year projection
2. The comprehensiveness of the plans
3. The extent of top management involvement
4. Participation by line executives
5. The role of the central planning staff

The foregoing features will contrast current practices with the situation twenty-five years ago. This chapter will conclude with some observations regarding the future of corporate long-range planning — a look down the road for a decade or more.

The five-year projection. Whether by design, accident, follow-the-leader, or whatever reason, the period of forward budgeting or planning is more often than not five years. Some striking exceptions to this period were found among the cooperating companies, and these will be commented upon. Normal practice, however, has been a five-year planning cycle. To many managers today it may seem incredible that no longer back than in the early 1940s, many outstanding industrial companies of the country were not projecting operations with precision or comprehensiveness even for the ensuing fiscal year. True budgetary control was known to all, but certainly not practiced by all.

The big leap forward to five-year planning did not occur overnight, nor did it receive sincere acceptance by many companies until relatively recently. Even most of those concerns that used the annual budget with real effectiveness proceeded cautiously and slowly to an extension to five-year plans. Customarily, the practice was first to experiment with a two- or three-year projection; in short, to learn to crawl before undertaking the advanced step of walking. In contrast, the experience of some organizations that ventured the five-year planning in one jump found the exercise a dismal failure and experienced a setback to the effort for an unfortunately long period of time.

A few of the companies cooperating in this current study were forthright in stating that they have been engaged in true long-range planning for only a few years. Others said that they have been seriously involved in the practice for twenty or more years. In no instance, however, was there any expression of doubt as to the justification of long-range planning as a necessary corporate undertaking. As stated by one chief executive, "Virtually 100 percent of the credit for our company's success can be attributed to long-range planning." Another top officer remarked, "Without long-range planning our business would verge on chaos."

Mention was made of striking exceptions to the more frequently found five-year planning periods. These exceptions relate particularly to different product lines and to specific elements of the total plan. Even though a company fundamentally is operating under a five-year plan for overall corporate purposes, it may develop separate plans of varying periods ahead for one or more of the indicated exceptions.

Several companies with multiple product lines plan only three years ahead for those products that are consumer-oriented but go to eight- or ten-year projections for products whose markets are heavy industry, utilities, or advanced military applications. This variable planning reflects the vagaries of consumer markets on the one hand and, on the other, the long-range planning needed for facilities to produce those products requiring expensive equipment, extensive research, development, engineering, and long production lead time.

How do these companies with different product line time projections develop a single corporate plan, for example, a five-year projection? Detailed practice varies, but basically the process is this: (1) In the shorter-term planning, say three years, rough projections are made for an additional two years with the general understanding that there is an extra degree of "blue sky" in the estimates for the fourth and fifth years, and managers of divisions whose products and markets are not readily adaptable to five-year predictions are evaluated on the basis of the validity of their three-year forecasts; (2) for the eight- to ten-year product planning, the shorter five-year picture is often in clearer focus than the longer one so that incorporation in or reconciliation with the overall five-year plan presents no serious difficulty.

Exceptions to the five-year corporate plans are found in not a few companies with respect to certain elements in the total planning process. These are all on the side of the longer planning cycles and generally relate to financial matters (including investments), facilities, raw materials, manpower (particularly managerial), research (contrasted with development), and diversification by the acquisition or merger route. In each instance, the wisdom of projecting needs well into the future and developing plans to meet those needs is quite understandable.

The requirements for facilities to accommodate planned growth — whether by entirely new plants and equipment or by expansion of existing facilities — necessitate for many companies a projection period considerably longer than for the overall corporate plan — twenty years in some cases. If new locations are to be selected, new land acquired, new buildings designed and constructed, and production equipment specified, purchased and installed, it is rather obvious that deliberate rather than hasty action is prudent practice. Then, too, the development of managerial personnel to fulfill the demands brought about by growth, changed organization structure, new ventures, geographical expansion, or other future corporate action is not an overnight process, nor is it a matter to be left for "nature to take its course." Likewise, the critical nature of assured raw-material supplies prompts certain companies to plan for this element much further ahead than is customarily done for other elements of the overall plan.

One company, because of its heavy orientation to the consumer market, gears its basic plan to a three-year cycle, whereas it projects raw-materials planning six to eight years ahead and projects its new product development and facilities for ten years. Natural-resource-based companies have traditionally planned their raw-material supplies much further ahead (40 years to permanently). These situations are peculiar, and in the more typical manufacturing companies such far-out planning is not only unnecessary but impracticable. Again, the fact that certain elements of the corporate program necessitate long planning cycles does not preclude sound overall planning on a relatively short basis.

The comprehensiveness of the plans. Early adventures in long-range planning not only were what would be regarded today as near-term, but were generally confined to capital expenditures and other financial considerations. The present practice of corporations is to provide a heavy marketing input as the foundation for advanced projections. The future marketing outlook is derived from various sources: field sales and service personnel, regional offices, divisional headquarters, central marketing research, and corporate economic research. Virtually without exception the companies participating in this study now build up the total sales figure from considerable detailed information on individual products, appropriate product groups, significant domestic regional areas, broad consuming markets, and foreign markets (usually by countries or established trading areas).

From such basic data, the planning for new facilities' size, nature, location, and capital requirements (both fixed and working) can be done with greater assurance. Similarly, the kinds and extent of supporting services, including research and development, can be gauged and programmed with greater validity. The companion areas of manpower needs and appropriate organization structure can be planned with increased reliability. Thus, present-day forward planning by leading industrial corporations represents a vastly different undertaking, in both sophistication and comprehensiveness, than it was a decade or more ago.

The extent of top management involvement.   The evidence is unequivocally clear that top management is deeply concerned with long-range planning in its respective corporations. This has perhaps been true to some degree ever since the practice has been followed by manufacturing companies. However, the extent and timing of top management planning is unquestionably greater and at more steps today than ever before. In two instances a drastic change in the organization structure was prompted, at least in part, by a determination to enable top management to spend more time in long-range planning. The following quote from the chief executive officer of one of the participating companies is typical of this present-day attitude concerning top management involvement: "Long-range planning is the basis of my job; the entire administrative organization has the primary responsibility for planning where the business is going five to ten years ahead." In similar vein, when asked how much time was devoted to long-range planning, top executives responded characteristically with estimates of 25 percent on the low side to 70 percent on the high side.

Closely related to the time allocated to long-range planning is the personal involvement of the chief executive officer and other members of the top management group at various stages of the annual planning process. Among the cooperating companies, the more common practice is to be heavily involved at the beginning and at the end. The beginning step is ordinarily comprised of two activities: the establishment of overall corporate objectives and the general approval of guidelines related to economic and other environmental prognostications. The concluding step is review and ultimate approval of divisional and corporate long-range programs.

Exceptions to the foregoing are not infrequent wherein top management, particularly the chief executive officer, enters into long-range planning at occasional stages or at each stage in the process. The latter situation is found less frequently, but in one company the president reviews and approves the long-range plan at each of five successive steps: (1) product line programs as developed jointly by marketing and engineering, (2) sales volume estimated and plant capacity available as calculated by the economics group, (3) plant requirements program translated into capital expenditures as determined by manufacturing, (4) divisional operating plans, including manpower needs, as recommended by top divisional executives, and (5) divisional plans consolidated into a set of corporate profit and loss statements for each of the five years ahead.

Referring again to the more common practice of heavy topside involvement at the beginning and end of the long-range planning cycle, the validity of the final program is immeasurably affected by the determinations arrived at in the initial step; viz. corporate objectives and predictions concerning environmental influences. Both, of course, provide the necessary guidelines for executives charged with the responsibility of planning for their respective segments of the business. Objectives underlie the basic corporate strategy and generally set forth specific intent as to the types of business in which the enterprise should be engaged, the market penetration to be achieved, the percentage of annual growth to be attained, the profit improvement per share of common stock equity to be accomplished, the return on investment to be met, discounted cash flow return to be effected, certain balance-sheet ratios to be realized.

Corporate objectives should, and ordinarily do, have a relatively high degree of stability or permanence. However, conditions change, and a periodic review of objectives is a fixed practice with most companies operating under an overall corporate strategy. The outlook regarding economic and other environmental conditions requires an annual examination, and this is part of the built-in planning process. In some companies top divisional executives who may be in disagreement with the forecasts that emanate from a central economics group make divisional plans according to their own judgment. Such divergence usually requires explanation or leads to attempts at reconciliation.

Regardless of any intervening participation in the long-range planning cycle, the end step of review and approval by top management is universal. Even though the seriousness with which this step is carried out is general, the actual manner of performing the concluding action is quite varied. In some instances the chief executive officer, together with a few of the senior top management people (not infrequently the executive committee), conducts the review and makes the final decisions. In other cases the principal corporate executives meet as a group with each divisional manager and go over the divisional plans in considerable detail. This may consume the better portion of an entire month on the part of the reviewing and approving group.

A variant of this practice, followed by several companies, is to bring together the top group and all divisional managers at an annual conference, of several days duration, held at some place remote from headquarters. One company invites to its annual conference twenty or thirty young "comers" as observers for the purpose of gaining executive development values not only from the discussions but also from the associations thus made possible. Proponents of the annual conference find certain advantages to the practice: (1) the conservation of time of the top executives charged with the review and final approval, (2) the benefits derived by having each divisional manager informed on the plans of other divisions and of the total corporate program, (3) the educational value to a division manager new to his job or less able as a planner, and (4) the incidental advantages of developing closer relationships among key operating executives throughout the entire organization, which is often widely separated geographically.

The participation of the board of directors in long-range planning differs markedly among the companies included in this study. At the first step, the board customarily becomes a party to setting objectives and establishing corporate strategy but rarely becomes involved in the formulation of environmental predictions. Board action with respect to corporate objectives more often than not is approval of management proposals rather than direct contribution to such determinations. At the closing step of the planning cycle, board approval is called for in some instances; in other cases the chief executive officer simply reports to the board upon the broad aspects of the forward plans as approved by the appropriate management group.

Participation by line executives. In the words of one chief executive officer, "We want our operating people to be living long-range planning all the time. We expect our line managers to be both planners and doers—to play in the band and lead the band at the same time." Another chief executive stated, "Long-range planning without extensive line participation does not work. Line executives who have the responsibility to implement the plans must also have a chance to do some of the dreaming. A 'planner's plan' has not worked, whereas a 'management's plan' has been effective."

The foregoing statements are fully expressive of the viewpoints held by top management groups in the corporations studied. It is quite a different attitude toward long-range planning than it was when most of these companies first engaged in the activity. The prevailing concept then was to assign long-range planning to a headquarters staff agency. This highly centralized direction of the function failed for the most part to gain acceptance by line people and hence did not enlist their vitally needed support. As one corporate president put it, "The staff planner, no matter at what level he is, becomes a very lonely person."

The general practice today is to start long-range planning at the grass roots and to involve line management from the bottom to the top. Depending upon the organization structure of a company, a number of management levels make significant inputs to the plans as they evolve, and many individuals — both line and staff — take part in the process. The success and practicability of long-range planning is, in the opinion of corporate top management, directly related to the interest and active participation of the chief executive and his line officers.

The role of the central planning staff.   Despite the new attitudes, complete abandonment of a central agency involved in long-range planning has by no means occurred. In one form or another, a headquarters group having a role in the planning process was found in every one of the cooperating companies. The agency consisted of one or two individuals in a few instances, a committee in other cases, and of "full blown" staff departments in still others. Similar variability was observed in the portfolios of the different agencies.

Certain duties and responsibilities, representing perhaps a minimum of involvement, were common to all the organizational schemes. These were: (1) the development of a format for submitting plans so that reasonable comparability could be obtained among many reporting segments of the enterprise, (2) issuance of general instructions on preparation of reports, definitions, schedules for submitting reports, (3) periodic contact with divisions or other reporting segments to ensure that the planning was being accomplished and on schedule, and (4) availability for assistance and advice as desired by line groups.

Advancing up the scale of involvement by these central agencies, other responsibilities were found, such as: (1) forward predictions concerning the economic climate and other environmental factors of significance to company operations, (2) monitoring divisional plans at various stages of development to assure compliance with corporate objectives and other guidelines, (3) a review and audit of final divisional plans before submission to top management for its examination and approval, and (4) consolidation of all divisional plans into an overall corporate plan for decision and action by top management.

The central planning staffs in two companies are of sufficient magnitude and functional composition to warrant special comment. In one company, the director of corporate planning has these six groups comprising his department: product planning and development, industrial marketing planning, consumer marketing planning, distribution planning, management information, and communications research. Collectively these several groups contribute to the company's long-range planning effort in the following ways:

1. Obtain, analyze, and communicate information on economic and business conditions.
2. Forecast economic and business trends over the near term and five years ahead.
3. Define the size and nature of the company's current markets.
4. Obtain and analyze data on industries in which the company participates.
5. Forecast the future market volume in units and dollar value.
6. Develop recommendations for product planning, pricing, and promotion.
7. Analyze distribution trends and report upon the social and economic changes causing these trends.
8. Conduct research into the broad areas of opportunity for feasible participation by the company in products or markets not currently handled by existing divisions.
9. Study the various methods of entry into these new markets and expanding into these new product lines.
10. Develop, prepare, and distribute basic information to line management on long-range plans.

In the other company, the role of the headquarters group in the planning effort could be no better presented than by the executive who heads this group. He is quoted verbatim:

Planning is a decentralized operation in keeping with the organization structure of the company. Each division of the corporation annually prepares both a long-range (five-year) and short-range plan which is submitted to its group manager and subsequently consolidated for the corporation as a whole. The thrust of our major effort is to increase the planning competence of the divisions and groups and the soundness of their individual and collective plans.

The staff, under my direction, acts as the corporation's long-range planning committee. This staff comprises the vice presidents for engineering, manufacturing, marketing, research, and the director of management systems. This group has the responsibility for establishing the basic format for division and group planning each year. At the beginning of each calendar year, we review the experience of the previous year and develop, based on that experience and on newer things which we want to introduce into the process, the procedure and format to be followed in the year's planning activities. The procedure and format, after approval by the president's council, are submitted to the divisions and groups, who begin their planning process about the first of July.

These same people then participate in the review of division and group plans as they are submitted to corporate management. More importantly, however, in their role as staff functional officers, they and their staff specialists work hand in glove with the divisions in the development of their plans and programs. These activities constitute the participation by our people in the group and division planning processes.

In addition to developing and facilitating the planning process of the individual units of the company, our staff directs its attention during the year to strategic planning for the corporation as a whole. This involves the establishment of the corporate purpose, the broad strategies that the corporation should follow in building for the future and conducting studies of business opportunities that do not logically fall within the sphere of one of the groups or divisions. The marketing services department also is responsible for preparing short-range and long-range economic forecasts which are transmitted to the divisions and groups as the basis for their planning and control of operations.

The result of this activity at the corporate level is not a formalized corporate plan in the sense frequently conceived by writers in this field. We feel that long-range planning is essentially a matter of determining what the mission of the organization is, being attuned to probable changes in the environment in which the organization will operate in the future, and the development of specific projects that will take advantage of the opportunities created by the changing environment. This approach has resulted in a number of new ventures for the corporation into some very promising new business areas, but cannot be summarized in a formal planning document.

EXAMPLES OF LONG-RANGE PLANNING PROCEDURES

Among the participating companies were several that had carried out long-range planning on a systemized basis for many years and had achieved a satisfying measure of success with the activity. Although certain elements of their procedures are quite similar, the differences are sufficiently marked to warrant brief descriptions of the individual practices.

The companies themselves have certain characteristics in common but are in completely different industries. All three companies are large, have multiple product lines, are engaged in extensive operations (both domestic and foreign), are organized on a divisional basis with a high degree of autonomy enjoyed by divisional management, and have a heavy technological orientation. Further identification is precluded by the authors' commitment to preserve complete anonymity in presenting the results of this study.

Company A. Long-range planning starts with the individual divisions. In September of each year, the division manager, together with his line and staff people, starts the five-year planning effort. Presentations to the group executive are to be made by mid-December. Experience has shown that some division managers are always high in their estimates of volume and profits, whereas other managers are traditionally low. The group executive factors the estimates down or up as the case may be, and the adjusted figures are used to build the corporate plan. For subsequent follow-up and evaluation, however, the division's performance is checked against the manager's goals, and not the factored estimates.

During the month of January each divisional manager meets with his group vice president and the three top corporate executives. This is the occasion for final review, evaluation and approval of the ensuing five-year plan, and an examination of the division's performance for the past fiscal year as compared with the estimates made five years earlier. The consolidation and summation of the divisional figures provide the corporate plan and equip top management with information on gross sales, total profits, capital outlays, research and development expenses, and other vital information by which to do the financial planning and check expectancies against corporate objectives.

The condensed statement above describes the basic pattern for the company's long-range planning. Further detail concerning the information expected of the division manager is expressed in this quoted admonition: "It is the responsibility of the division manager to ensure that the proposed programs for each of the division plans and product lines represents a balanced plan consistent with his best judgment and one which he supports as realistically obtainable." The division manager is expected to adhere to a company-wide format in preparing his presentation to his group executive and subsequently to the three top officers. The presentation is divided into three parts: the divisional summary, the plant summary, and the product line summary.

The divisional summary will show for each plant in the division and for the division as a whole:

Gross income in dollars
Profits before taxes
   In dollars
   In percent of gross income

} For past fiscal year and estimates for each of the next five years

In this summary, the division manager is invited to comment on the overall plans of his division with such specifics as: comparison of the division's projected volume and profits with the division's objectives; acquisition possibilities being considered which could alter projections; favorable factors that could result in larger volume and profits; unfavorable factors that could adversely affect projections.

The plant summary will show for each plant the following data for each product line:

Gross income, domestic and foreign
Profit over inventory cost
   In dollars
   In percent
Selling and advertising expense
Administrative expense
Research and development expense
Profit from operations before taxes

} For past fiscal year and estimates for each of the next five years

Three other documents to be compiled plant by plant are: (1) capital expenditures for each project, including description, estimated total cost, planned expenditures for each year, expected time schedule (analysis completed, AFE submitted, ordered, to be received, installed); (2) recruitment plan for each position to be filled, including number required, duties involved, education required, experience needed, and other stipulations; and (3) market and competitive standing for each major product line, including total market in dollars and division's share in percent for past fiscal year and next five years.

The product line summary starts with the individual plant and shows for each major product line the dollar and profit contribution of present items and new items to be added in each of the ensuing five years. A time schedule is projected for each new item from completion of development to availability for market, with research and development costs estimated.

Company B. With upward of sixty businesses, distinct profit centers, the problem of implementing long-range planning in Company B is of genuine magnitude. As is generally the case, forward planning starts with the operating divisions, and over the years much assistance has been rendered the divisions by central staff groups. An extensive manual has been developed for guidance to line management based on the belief that "good planning procedures help good managers make better plans."

The company has been engaged in long-range planning for many years; during this period it has modified the basic process from time to time. In the early stages the principal responsibility resided in a central planning staff with a minimum of input from the operating people. This proved unworkable, and currently the focus of responsibility is with the line executives; however, the central planning group continues to make appropriate contributions to the process.

The period of forward projection was once on a seven-year basis but was later reduced to five years. Now the practice is to set a five-year target, retaining that target for at least three years, at which point a new five-year target is set. The purpose of this idea is gradually to sharpen the accuracy of the targets and to strengthen the validity of evaluating divisional performances against profit projections and other divisional objectives.

Fundamental to all planning in this company is a set of corporate objectives developed by top management. Within the framework of these guidelines each division, in turn, establishes its own objectives. The sum total of the objectives constitutes the corporate strategy, which is intended to have a rather high degree of permanency but is nevertheless subject to periodic review and adjustment. Another aid to divisional planning is the forecast by a central planning group as to the future economic, technological, and marketing climate in which the company and its many segments may expect to do business.

Prior mention was made of an extensive manual to ensure comparability of data submitted by divisions and uniformity in the format of presentation. The manual is in two parts, one relating to the profit plan for the next fiscal year, the other to the target year. Both parts contain the various forms to be executed together with full instructions for their completion and a time schedule for preparation and submittal. A controlling factor in the timing as well as the format is the requirement of transmitting the data by teletype to the computer center. The following outline pertains only to the target-year projections:

Market
    Domestic — current product line (in dollars)
    Foreign — current product line (in dollars)
Sales plan
    Domestic — current product line (in dollars)
    Foreign — current product line (in dollars)
    Additions to product line (in dollars)
    Total sales plan (in dollars)
Market penetration — current line
    Domestic percent
    Foreign percent
Operations plan
    Sales billed
    Direct product costs
        Percent of sales billed
    Nondivision costs
    Income taxes
    Income after taxes
        Percent of sales billed
    Corporate investment
    Investment turnover
    Percent of return on investment
Manpower planning — current and target year
    Management
    Salaried — nonmanagement (by functions)
    Hourly (by major skill categories)

With respect to the foregoing tabular data, the division manager is called upon to respond to such questions as:

What changes will likely take place in your business environment by the target year?

What will be the impact on your sales plan as a result of these changes? What basic marketing strategy do you intend to follow for your current line, new product, foreign markets?

What will be the impact on operations as a result of these changes? What are your division's strengths for capitalizing on these changes? What weaknesses in your division require action?

What major facilities or other asset investments do you require to meet these changes?

Company C. The forward planning activity of Company C is the most ambitious and sophisticated of any found among the participating companies. It consists of the following documents prepared annually:

1. A three-year short-term plan developed in full detail.
2. A ten-year long-term plan with somewhat less detail but with major emphasis on capital investment and manpower planning. (This element of the total planning effort could be regarded as the strategic planning phase.)
3. A twenty-year financial model which, in effect, is a condensed balance sheet and income statement by major product groups.

In addition to the above, an effort is just getting underway to make an environmental study looking ahead 25 years. This undertaking would be worldwide in its coverage, and it is anticipated that it would be updated periodically rather than annually. The study at the outset is being conducted by a group of academicians under the general guidance of a corporate executive.

An elaboration of the contents of the several planning documents will be confined to the ten-year plan. The divisions are required to submit first a summary consisting of the following information:

Operating revenue in dollars	
Market position in percentage	
Number of employees	
Total assets in dollars	Data to be presented
Net profit in dollars	for past fiscal year,
Return on total assets in percentage	three years ahead, and
Cash generation from operation in dollars	ten years ahead
Additions to plant in dollars	
Discounted cash flow return in percentage	

Supplementing the above tabular information, the divisions are expected to submit statements on: long-range divisional objectives relating to operations and financial aspects, significant opportunities and problems arising out of environmental factors, justification of the planned capital investment program, contemplated changes in operating practices, and the expected contributions these action plans will make to divisional performance.

In addition to the several reviews through which the divisional long-range plans pass on their way to the top executive group is an unusual step—an early examination by the legal department. This checkpoint is introduced to avoid expenditure of time and effort on developing plans if they are legally impracticable.

A LOOK AHEAD

During the course of this study, specific inquiry was made as to what top executives foresaw as likely or intended changes in the long-range planning of their companies. Several developments or innovations received frequent mention. These will be discussed briefly in the concluding paragraphs of this chapter. It will be observed that prior discussion has alluded to a few such features or actually cited them as being current practices by one or another company. The significance, however, is that the contemplated changes are not isolated instances but typify definite future trends.

One certain and universal expectancy is the predominant role that line management will have in the long-range planning effort. In more recent years this practice has had increasing application in those companies well advanced in their forward planning endeavors, and henceforth operating executives will assume the principal responsibility for charting the future course of their respective organizations. A prerequisite for attainment and retention of an important line position will unquestionably be a demonstrated capacity to plan ahead—to possess the imagination, uninhibited thinking, analytical ability, and sense of timing to visualize corporate and divisional activities well beyond current horizons.

An appreciable number of the participating companies state that the long-range planning process will be extended to central staff departments to much the same degree as is presently being applied to the line organizations. Those staff or service departments having the larger budgets and whose activities produce a greater impact will be the first to undertake a full effort at projecting their plans and programs as far into the future as possible. In companies where they are not already included in long-range planning, primary candidates are research and development, engineering, finance and accounting, employee relations, purchasing and traffic, and management information systems.

The candidacy of the employee relations department stems from the increasing recognition of the need for manpower planning and its underlying requirements of recruiting, training and development, evaluation, and programmed assignments. Secondary candidates will probably be public relations, market research, advertising, legal, and the central planning group itself (including economic research). In the view of those executives whose companies intend to apply long-range planning to selected staff departments, no serious problems are contemplated.

Another apparent trend is to go to a ten-year planning cycle. Although by no means a unanimous determination among the cooperating group, positive and thoughtful consideration is being given to this future development. It is found, naturally enough, in those companies that have had an appreciable and satisfactory experience with a shorter planning period—usually five years. This intention is brought about by the awareness that certain elements in the total planning process need to be projected a decade ahead, and that in due course the overall programming of corporate operations could feasibly and desirably be geared to the same time period. There is no disposition upon the part of these companies to minimize the problems inherent in shifting to the longer cycle. The market and environmental research tools will need considerable sharpening, but even more difficult will be the conditioning of line executives to this transition. In the minds of the authors there is little doubt that ten-year long-range planning will be an established practice in an increasing number of industrial enterprises. After all, projecting operations for half that period was a bold venture not many years ago.

There will unquestionably be greater acceptance of the philosophy of management by objectives. For some companies this is current practice; for others it is audibly endorsed but not followed. Even among those companies who sincerely believe they operate under a well-structured statement of purpose, some disillusion is to be found. Too often the objectives are set forth in broad, high-sounding, almost platitudinous language. In contrast, a few of the participating companies

have delineated their objectives in clear, specific terms readily understood and correctly interpreted by those to be guided. Some go a step
further and require their divisional executives to develop a set of
objectives covering the areas of activity for which this echelon of
management has responsibility. If the destiny of a company is in the
hands of its top management, and if the overriding obligation of these
executives is to ensure a sound, profitable future for the enterprise,
what better guidance to that end can there be than the formulation of
a comprehensive set of intelligible, lucid objectives?

Another likely trend is greater sophistication in the planning
process. Much evidence supports this conjecture. Experience is perhaps the most convincing factor, but also important is the realization
by line management of the tangible benefits that accrue from a formal
program of forward planning. As long as operating executives regarded long-range planning as simply an annual exercise, the end
results were of dubious value and little encouragement was afforded
efforts to systemize and improve the process. When and to the extent
that top management made its position clear, the planning effort could
be measured in new and enlarged dimensions.

One persuasive step was the advent of the annual review by top
management of the projected plans of operating executives and the
critical examination of current performance in terms of prior projections. Somewhere in this evolutionary period, some of the companies
found it expedient to clarify the thinking of the line people concerning
the degree of accuracy expected.

One company put the proposition to its divisional management this
way: "The purpose of long-range planning is not to show how pre-
cisely we can predict the future, but rather to uncover the things we
must do today in order to have a future." Actually, this statement is
an effective paraphrase of an older bit of advice given in the pioneer
days of budgeting: "Men do not shoot because targets exist, but they
set up targets in order that shooting may be more effective." Once the
initial skepticism is removed, the continued refinement of the planning
process is a natural consequence. This is demonstrated by the actions
of many participating companies—development of manuals, enlargement of the marketing inputs, and scholarly research into environmental factors.

Little has been said in this discussion about the computer and the
mathematical techniques customarily related to it. The reason is that
operations research, simulation, probability models, and other similar

developments have found very few applications in the long-range planning practices of the companies involved in this study. It is not that there is a lack of awareness of the technology; but how, when, and where it may be put to practical use are for the most part still undetermined. However, experimentation is underway in several concerns. A typical illustration is the development of models designed to give answers to "what if" questions, such as: What would be the effect if any one of a variety of circumstances occurred, such as price reductions, market invasion, significant political or other environmental changes? It is thus a rather safe prediction that in the years ahead long-range planning will be an area where quantitative techniques and computer capabilities will be found appropriate and helpful.

As a closing observation, there is no question but that long-range planning as a vital corporate activity is here to stay. In many companies one-fourth to one-third of the income dollar is spent with a view to the future — research and development, management training, new facilities, advertising, ventures into new areas, and acquisitions. If such expenditures are to be purposeful and prudent, it is axiomatic that intelligent planning be applied. It is, to be sure, a sobering responsibility for men in top management to exercise judgments, initiate actions, and make decisions when the end results may not be known during their corporate tenure. Put another way, the real measure of a top management team often cannot be fully appraised until after its services have ended.

ORGANIZATION
STRUCTURE

4

During the past quarter century, probably no area of top management involvement has evoked more discussion, written or oral, than that of corporate organization structure. Students of the subject, both practical and theoretical, have expounded at untold length by the printed page and from the platform at countless meetings. What have been the results? The findings of this study lead unquestionably to the conclusion that structuring a company's organization is still a very practical matter, and the theorists as yet have made no appreciable impact.

Furthermore, the design of the basic structure continues to be a responsibility of the chief executive. Finally, organization planning is generally geared to corporate long-range planning, so that attainment of future objectives is not prevented by failure to have the appropriate organization structure in readiness.

The authors were privileged, in most of the companies included in this study, to examine organization charts over a long span of years. The subject of organization was discussed with appropriate top executives in each company. Out of these analyses and discussions certain developments, trends, and practices were observed, and these will be set forth in the following paragraphs.

ARRANGING THE STRUCTURE

The frequency with which basic or major structural changes are made follows no pattern whatsoever. A few of the companies are operating today under the same general organization plan that was adopted many years previously. Others have instituted fundamental modifications from time to time. Still others give the impression of maintaining their organization structure in virtually a constant state of flux. Finally, in an isolated instance, a complete reversal of organizational concept was recently carried out. Why this widely different situation in a group of large, successful, industrial enterprises? There are valid reasons for each grouping, and in no instance is there an unawareness of the vital importance of a company's organization structure nor an absence of perpetual surveillance.

In the first group are those companies that have adhered steadfastly to their early plans, doing so because there has been no justification for changing them. Through innate wisdom and incredible foresight, a prior generation of top executives devised patterns of organization that have stood the test of time. Not only have these organization structures accommodated growth, diversification, global expansion, and the inexorable advance of complexity of operation, but they have established philosophies adopted successfully by other top managements.

An attitude of complacency or "do not argue or tinker with success" is not evident in these cases. To the contrary, the several chief executives would, in the authors' judgment, be the first to restructure their companies' organizations if the existing plans gave indication of inadequacy or ineffectiveness. This latter statement presupposes, and rightly so, that a corporation's chief executive officer not only occupies the best vantage point from which to observe organizational weakness, but also is in the critical position and of the frame of mind to do something about it.

The second group—those who institute fundamental changes upon occasion—comprises the largest number of companies participating in this study. In fact, a substantial majority of all industrial enterprises would fall into this category. More often than not, the occasion for change has been the necessity to shift from a functional to a product or regional division basis.

As was pointed out in the earlier study, there comes a time in most manufacturing companies when the line of products, advance of technology, or spread of operations transcends the capacity of strictly functional executives to meet their full responsibilities. Another closely related occasion is brought about by acquisitions or mergers. An expanded product line may or may not be the impelling factor, but enlarged operations and additional management personnel necessitate a revamping of the organization structure. Whenever such occasions prompt a major reorganization, the sound and usual practice is to devise a structure that will readily accommodate future developments and plans to the end that subsequent organizational changes are infrequent or minor of character.

Companies in the third group—those who make frequent changes— are exceptions and involve only a few. The underlying causes for frequent modification are several in number, usually occurring singly rather than jointly. Failure to gear organization planning to the long-range company plans is the most common cause. It can and does happen that while the "music" for future operations is well composed, the plans for organization are "played by ear." This practice, of course, is counter to that discussed in Chapter 3 where long-range planning embraced companion long-range projections for organization structure and manpower.

A secondary cause for modification can occur when there are changes in top command. It is an accepted prerogative of a company's chief executive to have the pattern of organization that he wants and in which he believes. If the new head is brought in from the outside, he may have ostensibly good reasons to make modifications, one of which may well be an ineffective or inadequate plan of organization.

Still another cause, and one with some relevance to the preceding one, is the need to find an answer to an unsatisfactory or worsening situation. A possible cure is to change the organization structure, and if the new plan does not produce the desired results, try another one. Because of the disruptive effects of major organizational changes, it is fortunate that this third category is small in number and, where applicable, will undoubtedly attain a stabilized situation as the underlying causes disappear.

The single case that created a fourth category was a change from a basic decentralized structure to a highly centralized one with vertical functional direction. While this concept goes counter to general practice, the determination to make the 180-degree turn was a result of appropriate study and deliberation by top management, including final approval by the company's board of directors.

Aside from the attendant problems of adjustment, two disadvantages were recognized: (1) elimination of multiple profit centers and concentration on profit responsibility at one point—the chief operating officer; and (2) loss of the natural and built-in mechanism of developing executives with a general management orientation. The latter disadvantage can be overcome to some extent by providing multifunctional exposure at a fairly early period in the careers of promising young executives. On the plus side of the reorganization, several distinct benefits were contemplated and ultimately realized, as reported by the company: (1) improved coordination of long-range planning, (2) easier communication, (3) elimination of duplicated staff, (4) better facilities engineering, and (5) removal of two levels of management.

SPAN OF CONTROL

The number of people supervised by company officers has been a topic of interest for years to students and practitioners of organization. It has been surrounded by dogma in some circles. If corporate practice, currently and over a long period of time, may be accepted as a criterion, there most assuredly is no magic or immutable number of subordinates that should report to an immediate superior.

The appropriate span of control depends upon such variables as: similarity or dissimilarity of duties supervised, capacity of superior and capacity of subordinates, degree of decentralization and concomitant autonomy, age of the company and stability of the business, extent to which corporate objectives have been established and made known, and extent of policy coverage and promulgation.

If reference is confined to the position of chief executive officer, a highly varied situation is found among the companies in this study.

The span of control for this topmost post ranges from one to fourteen, with ten being both the average and median.

A historical review of this organizational feature reveals a similar lack of uniformity for these same companies. In one instance, the span of control for the top officer has been as limited as three individuals and as extended as fifteen. In another case, the spread has been from a low of five to a high of twenty. There is, of course, nothing surprising or extraordinary concerning this variability. It simply points up the fact mentioned in the preceding paragraph, that the span of control can be and is far from a fixed figure and still represents desired practice by a given top management.

MULTIPLE EXECUTIVE VICE PRESIDENTS

In earlier years, the position of executive vice president, if such were present in an organization, had ordinarily just one import—the incumbent was the heir apparent to the presidency and held the second most important job in the company. Thus there was a single executive vice president as there was a single president.

The advent of the practice of having multiple executive vice presidents is of relatively recent occurrence, perhaps a decade or two ago. Despite its comparative newness, this organizational device has had wide acceptance among the companies studied. The application would be universal if the position of group vice president may be considered as virtually synonymous. The title of senior vice president, found occasionally, is not here regarded as comparable. The full connotation of "senior" often carries the implication of honorary.

Although the more common use of the title of "executive vice president" or "group vice president" pertains to a line position with jurisdiction over two or more product divisions, these same designations are occasionally applied to a position with supervisory responsibility over a number of central staff departments. In both instances, the organizational purpose is the same; viz. to decrease the administrative load of the chief executive officer and the chief operating officer or, as stated in the preceding section, to reduce the span of control for the two top executives. An obvious additional objective is to have several potential successors for the presidency rather than one.

One of the participating companies has for many years followed an unorthodox organization plan for the role of its two executive vice presidents. This has been done deliberately. The organization chart shows these two positions reporting to the president but with no specific assignment of functions or areas of responsibility. Traditionally these positions have been filled by incumbents with long company experience and with strong capability in functional areas complementing that of the president. The only authority attached to the two executive vice presidents is that of being authorities. They not only serve as advisors to the president but are an integral part of his office, and when traveling they represent and speak for the president. When the president is away, one of the executive vice presidents is always in residence.

VICE PRESIDENT FOR ADMINISTRATION

In the preceding section mention was made of an occasional instance of an executive vice president or a group vice president having a number of staff departments reporting to that position. This organizational scheme is quite prevalent among the cooperating companies, but the more common title designating the position is "vice president for administration." One company, several years ago, actually used the title "vice president and chief of staff."

There are several interesting questions arising from the actual use of this organizational device:

1. What would be considered a somewhat typical group of staff departments constituting the package of the vice president for administration?
2. For a given company, does the package remain reasonably stable insofar as contents are concerned?
3. What purposes are served by the device other than reducing the span of control for a chief executive?

It is not surprising to find that there is no typical package. The nearest approach to an answer is that the number of staff departments in the group is predominantly six, and the specific departments appearing most frequently are: employee relations, public relations, secretary, treasurer, and legal. Beyond these two measures of similarity the contents of the various packages are as unlike as if drawn from a grab bag. All in all, 28 different staff agencies were found in one or more groups. The makeup of a few groups would lead one to suggest that the executive in charge should be designated more appropriately as "vice president for miscellaneous!"

The answer to the second question in the preceding group is the typical one—yes and no. About one-half the participating companies have retained essentially the same group of staff agencies as a package under the vice president for administration. The opposite situation is true in the other half; the only difference within this second category is the frequency of change. In one company the package changed substantially five times during a ten-year period. An analysis of the organization charts reveals that where changes have occurred, the incumbents have also changed, which suggests the natural conclusion that to some extent at least an attempt has been made to tailor the position to an individual.

Beyond the obvious move to reduce the number of individuals reporting to a chief executive, the grouping of a number of staff departments under a single executive, by whatever title he is given, serves some additional purposes. Improved coordination between certain functions is a definite objective. Examples would be long-range planning and organization planning, purchasing and traffic, patent department and research and development. Another objective could be to provide a temporary home for a newly created department until a more permanent organizational arrangement is established; an example might be an operations research activity. Others might be giving administrative strength to a department until that requirement is met from within, a condition that might occur with a change of incumbents, or providing a home for an activity known in advance to have a short-lived mission. Finally, service as a group executive of the type under discussion can be, and is, used as a means of management development and evaluation.

OTHER DEPARTMENTAL GROUPINGS

Somewhat related to the preceding discussion are several interesting and rather new departmental groupings found among the cooperating companies. Under the title "director of marketing services," one company includes the following activities: product planning, advertising, pricing, sales financing, market research, parts depots, service, visitor services. The functions thus assembled are available to the worldwide operations of the company and provide the global marketing effort with a closely related support package.

In three other companies a deliberate attempt to focus on and accentuate the interface of the technical and commercial forces is achieved by assembling under a high-level executive the central corporate-wide functions of research, engineering, marketing, and market research. To this core group one company adds its patent department, another includes advertising and economic research, and two companies include manufacturing.

MANAGEMENT INFORMATION SYSTEMS

This term is used somewhat generically to embrace such corporate activities as electronic data processing, operations research, mathematical programming, quantitative analyses, and so forth. The broad subject area will be treated extensively in a subsequent chapter, but it is introduced here to take cognizance of its organizational implications and to underscore the fact that it is an exciting new field of top management involvement occurring since the prior study of more than twenty-five years ago.

Among the participating companies there was not a single instance where the advent of the computer resulted in any change or modification of the basic organization structure. Therefore, the only consideration at this point is the location in existing organizational arrangements of the hardware and software components of the management information systems.

Because most of the companies are divisionalized, either on a product or geographic basis, the predominant practice is to have a central computer center with lesser installations at the divisional or even the plant level. In one-third of the cases, the central computer center falls within the finance-accounting area. No other pattern prevails. There were several instances where jurisdiction over the computer center resided in an independent department reporting directly to either the chief executive officer or the chief operating officer.

Quite a different situation is found for statistical and mathematical applications. Only rarely are those individuals involved in such activities organizationally a part of the computer center. Operations research activities are often fragmented, but if centralized in a single group, they are often found in a central research or engineering department and located physically at a technical center.

What the future holds concerning the place of the management information systems function in corporate organization structure will be explored in Chapter 9.

PRODUCT MANAGERS

Significant organizational developments or innovations do not occur with notable frequency, but when they do there is manifest interest and, if applicable, a willingness by top management people to adopt or adapt. One such development is the position of product manager. Somewhat akin to but not identical with this position are others designated as project managers and program managers. There are certain similarities in the nature and scope of all three positions but some differences as well.

The *product manager,* as found in several of the participating companies, has essentially the role of planner, coordinator, and promoter of a single product or closely related family of products within an operating division producing and selling a range of products. His reporting relationship is to the divisional general manager. In most instances the product manager is held accountable for the profit of his line.

There is an inherent anomaly in the situation in that the product manager has no direct authority over the research and development, manufacturing, or sales personnel involved. His primary responsibility is relating his line of products to its market, and in that connection he usually has a strong voice in the nature and amount of advertising pertaining to his area of interest. He is expected to maintain a watchful eye on quality and service. One company characterizes the product manager as the customer's representative in the manufacturer's environment.

The *project manager,* on the other hand, although product- and market-oriented as is the product manager, is involved with an embryonic rather than an existing or ongoing venture. His assignment is ordinarily established when a product of research and development effort gives promise of worthwhile potential and may or may not be related to any division's current sphere of activity.

The project manager is placed in charge of a task force composed of research and development, manufacturing, and marketing people to carry the project forward to a point of proven viability or a justifiable decision to abandon. If the undertaking is successful, the project manager and his team may be taken over by a logical division, or a new division may be created. As one company expressed its experience with the project-manager concept, briefly described above, it has been the means of saving newly developed products from becoming "dropouts."

The *program manager* is an outgrowth of defense work and, in fact, is virtually a prerequisite to obtaining a contract of any appreciable magnitude. He is the principal contact with his counterpart in the procuring agency. Like the project manager, his involvement begins early, and if all goes well he continues his assignment until the contract is completed. Like the product manager, he reports to the head of his division and may be only one of several program managers in the division.

If, as is usually the case, the program is of substantial size and duration, he will carry a vice-presidential title and be supported by a small personal staff. He works through the functional organizations of his division, but has no authority over them. In essence the program manager is responsible for the successful completion of his program on schedule, within budget, and in accordance with required performance. The assignment is one with heavy responsibility but without direct concomitant authority.

To clarify this situation and establish a workable arrangement, one company has delineated the program manager's task as follows:

1. Approves plans covering program requirements, schedule, work tasks, and costs. This approved plan is, in essence, a contract between the program manager and the functional organization.
2. Approves program letters, as needed, defining major events or tasks, assigning responsibility and completion dates for accomplishing the events or tasks.
3. Establishes program priorities and policies. When these conflict with other programs, he seeks resolutions with other concerned program managers.
4. Participates in and approves all major technical, cost, schedule, and performance decisions.
5. Participates and concurs in the selection of major make or buy items and the selection of suppliers for those identified as buy.
6. Establishes report requirements and reviews reports and controls necessary for the evaluation of all phases of program performance.
7. Detects potential problems and determines or recommends corrective action.
8. Assists in establishment of program budgets and controls the allocation and reallocation of company resources assigned to him.
9. Periodically conducts program review meetings and issues action minutes.
10. Refers to a functional head for resolution of matters that should be decided by the functional head, even when such matters are specifically brought to him by functional personnel.

11. Is the prime contact with the customer's counterpart and other major representatives of the customer.
12. Establishes a relationship with the customer's representatives that will permit him to know the customer's plans, needs, ideas, and thinking on matters relating to the program. Keeps such representatives fully informed on the program.
13. Establishes and maintains an effective communications network of program information and progress with appropriate personnel.
14. Follows up branches, subcontractors, and others to assure that program events and tasks assigned to them are being satisfactorily accomplished within cost, schedule, and specification requirements, and, when necessary, that timely corrective action is effected.
15. Leads and motivates all personnel assigned to the program by the functional organizations to maximize program team effort.
16. Is alert to new contract requirements, government regulations and directives that might affect the work, cost, or management of the program, and initiates timely responsive action. Is alert also to competing products, programs, and companies that might affect the program.

Even with the foregoing "bill of rights" established and made known, to be successful the program-manager concept demands much coordination and understanding. Otherwise the lot of the director of manufacturing, for example, would be something less than utopian if he were involved constantly with several aggressive program managers.

ORGANIZATION PLANNING DEPARTMENTS

Over the past twenty-five years, the organization planning department as a top-level staff agency seems to have moved full cycle. When the prior top management study was made, there were only a few—four out of thirty-one, to be exact—participating companies that had established organization planning departments, and without exception the reporting relationship was to the chairman or to the president. Among the companies cooperating in this current study, only five have organization planning departments, and in no instance does the agency enjoy a top-level reporting status. In three cases, the agency is an adjunct of the personnel department; in one company it is under the direction of corporate planning; and in the fifth case it is attached to the office of corporate secretary.

During the period intervening between the two studies, most of the companies had at one time or another instituted organization planning departments. Why have these departments, to a large extent, disappeared? There are several reasons: (1) As corporate organization structures became relatively stabilized and were able to accommodate growth and diversification, the need for a full-time group of organization specialists no longer existed. (2) As companies decentralized operations, considerable autonomy was granted the product or geographic divisions, including the freedom to organize the division as the division manager saw fit. (3) If at some time there arose the necessity to change the basic corporate organization structure in any material way, the chief executive assumed the role of architect himself, perhaps calling upon outside consulting counsel. (4) Executives who attain high-level positions, including divisional general management, are well grounded in the principles of good organization practice and hence are not dependent upon staff service in this area.

The continued existence of a few headquarters organization planning departments prompts inquiry as to the justification. The most obvious reason is that the company's organization structure has not fully shaken down and is therefore still in a state of change. Then, too, some of the organization planning departments perform other functions such as manpower surveys, salary administration, and consulting services to divisions and subsidiaries, particularly foreign ones.

CENTRALIZATION VERSUS DECENTRALIZATION

Most large industrial enterprises in the United States operate on what might be termed "controlled" decentralization and have been functioning on this basis for many years. Decentralization takes the form of product divisionalization in those companies that produce and sell a diversified line of products. Regional divisionalizaton is the common practice for those companies with a single or quite limited range of end products but widespread geographic operations. There are frequent examples of a combination of these two basic types, such as oil companies with a substantial petrochemical involvement and doing business on a national or even global basis.

Participating companies whose organization structure is of the divisionalized pattern were asked what functions or activities were centralized. The response was unanimous as to the following items: setting corporate objectives, strategic planning, determination of basic policies, finance, accounting systems, basic research, consummation of mergers or acquisitions, approval of capital expenditures over pre-scribed limits, setting of executive salaries and bonuses above certain levels, and selection of individuals for positions down to specific eche-lons in the organization.

For the last three items there is complete acceptance of the need for centralized control but an absence of unanimity as to the dollar limits or position levels. The widest range occurs in the matter of capital-expenditure approval. A division general manager in one company has authority up to $10,000; in another company this same level of execu-tive has authority up to $1,500,000. Usually there is a series of approvals and dollar amounts up to the chief executive officer. Equally wide is the range for capital expenditures when the executive com-mittee or the board of directors exercises control—from $100,000 to $5,000,000.

The salary level at which the approval of the chief executive is required, while somewhat varied, is in general about the $20,000 figure. This would appear to be low and to deprive a divisional general manager of a natural prerogative, as in a large company there would be hundreds of individuals at or above this annual stipend. This rather widespread practice is simply a reflection of the interest and concern of the top executive in gaining and maintaining cognizance of the exist-ing as well as the potential high-level management people in his com-pany. In no instance did a chief executive feel that this involvement imposed any undue burden. Rather, it is universally regarded as a major obligation.

In most but not all cooperating companies a few additional activities are highly centralized. One of these is the setting of wage and fringe benefit guidelines for the decentralized bargaining that generally pre-vails. Were it not for this preventive or precautionary action, a whip-sawing situation would develop in dealing, as some of the companies do, with up to as many as 80 unions. Similarly, in the matter of con-tributions and donations, limits or guidelines are established centrally both as a means of exercising appropriate control and of providing protection from local pressures on divisional managers. These limits or guidelines are in addition to the customary budgetary provisions.

Although in a number of the companies each division has its own public relations specialist, there is considerable influence, direction, and control residing in the central public relations department. An increasing awareness of and sensitivity to the external factors bearing upon corporate performance and actions has dictated this degree of centralization. In several instances it even includes tight surveillance over speeches given or articles written by an employee if the subject has any connection with the company's affairs.

With this rather broad recounting of the general practices of companies regarding the functions or activities carried out on a centralized basis, several questions appear germane. Is this a change from earlier practice? Has there been a substantial erosion of the divisional manager's autonomy? Does the fact that in several areas the pricing function, for example, no longer falls within the purview of the divisional manager make an anachronism of realistic profit and loss accountability? Does the present situation indicate a disenchantment with the concept of decentralization of operations? Has the computer been a factor in shifting the decision-making level upward in those specific instances of recent centralization of authority? What is the probable future trend?

Based on extensive interviews with top executives in the companies included in this survey, the following answers to the above questions represent a consensus. Current practice does reflect something of a change as environmental factors have had a definite impact on the need for more central responsibility. In addition, growth, complexity, and greater interdependence of divisions have accentuated the problem of coordination leading therefore to more action at headquarters.

Although there has been a gradual trend toward increasing control of certain activities on a centralized basis, there is no confirmation that the divisional manager's autonomy has been lessened to the extent that he has lost effectiveness. In prior times, when the division manager had more authority than is sometimes the case today, he never enjoyed a completely free hand, as most of the functions mentioned have always been centralized.

The top managements of those companies that have long operated under a divisionalized organization structure manifest no disillusionment as to the practicability of this concept. Whenever and whatever further centralization has developed, it has been a recognition of and accommodation to different conditions. In no instance was there acceptance of the idea that the computer has influenced this situation, nor is it expected to in the future. In other words, the levels of decision making will remain as at present.

Finally, what is the future outlook regarding centralization versus decentralization? Decentralization is unquestionably here to stay, at least as far ahead as any top executive cared to predict. Those companies operating under a divisionalized organization structure intend to continue with that pattern, and some of the companies not now operating in this fashion feel it is quite likely that they will move in the direction of decentralization.

INTERNATIONAL OPERATIONS

It has been mentioned that there is a high degree of stability in the organization structure of most industrial companies, including those participating in this study. One exception was found in the area of international operations. A review of the organizational arrangements for handling foreign business reveals that over the past decade or two quite drastic changes have occurred.

This reflects underlying causes which essentially are: a marked increase in the volume of foreign trade; a probable continuing trend in this direction; an ever-widening spread of foreign business geographically, that is, on a more global scale; the growing practice of establishing production and distribution facilities abroad through acquisition, merger, or original installation; and the impact of such environmental factors as competition, tariffs, trading blocs, governmental constraints, and greatly improved economic conditions in most industrial nations.

Chapter 8 will be devoted entirely to a discussion of international operations developed from visits to the headquarters of the fifteen corporations in this study. Suffice it to state at this juncture that there is every likelihood that further developments will occur in the organizational treatment of foreign business.

COMMITTEES

Over the years no organizational feature has been as controversial as committees. Their faults and virtues have been discussed and debated with amazing persistency. This situation existed at the time of the earlier study of top management organization and control practices, and it is evident in the current study. The principal difference found between the two studies is that today there are fewer standing committees and a greater use of ad hoc task forces. Nevertheless, in virtually every one of the current participating companies high-level committees are in use. The number of such groups runs from one to six, and it was made quite clear that these agencies are fulfilling a genuine purpose.

The most common committee is the executive committee composed generally of inside directors of the company. The executive committee is invested with most of the authority of the entire directorate and is a powerful administrative body. In some instances it is a decision-making agency, although in other companies it is regarded as an advisory group to the chief executive officer on whom devolves the final responsibility for decisions. It could be reported that even under the latter condition decision making is by consensus, as only rarely would a chief executive officer go counter to the preponderant opposition of his top executive group.

In those companies having an executive committee composed, in part, of outside or nonofficer directors, there is usually a committee of top executives exercising extensive authority for direction and control of the enterprise. These committees frequently have the term "policy" in their designation, for example: policy committee, operations policy committee, operational policy committee. These committees, while lacking certain prerogatives of the board of directors, are frequently reported, like the aforementioned executive committees, as the agency that runs the business. This characterization is supported not only by the matters that come before such committees, but by the frequency of their meetings — usually weekly.

The value of committees as communication devices is well recognized by many of the cooperating companies. Variously termed administration committee, management council, executive council, operations review committee, these agencies have memberships considerably larger than the committees discussed in the preceding paragraphs.

In one company there are 36 top people who constitute its management council. As stated by one chief executive officer, "Our administration committee meets monthly, at which time actions taken at the last board of directors meeting are reviewed and reports are made by group vice presidents and staff vice presidents; the committee is essentially a communications device and a medium for passing policy information to the organization."

The executive council of another company meets twice a month "to discuss general corporate problems, to review what happened last month, to evaluate where we are now and to take a look at the immediate future; the council has no power, records no minutes, but does follow an agenda for each meeting; it is purely a communications device."

In a third company the management council meets monthly, at which time the chief executive officer reports on the last board of directors meeting and invites discussion of major changes, plans, and problems; the council is used as a means to encourage two-way communication.

A fourth company has 23 officers on its planning committee which meets weekly to review the current situation of its several product divisions. In the words of the company's chief executive officer, "We use this, as well as several other committees, for communications purposes, as there is a man present who will have to make the decisions."

The vital importance of the research effort and the magnitude of the budgetary support involved have been responsible for the creation of another top-level committee in a number of the companies in this study. These committees are composed of representation from top management (usually the chief executive officer), operating management, research management, and sometimes engineering and financial management.

These committees often have a fourfold mission: (1) establishment of policies and broad guidelines to provide direction to research and development programs, (2) coordination of the viewpoints of line management and technical management, (3) bringing to bear a wide range of judgment as to the wisdom of embarking upon a specific undertaking, (4) periodic review and monitoring of ongoing programs with a view toward recommending or even deciding to continue or abandon certain projects.

Although, as mentioned earlier in this section, the occurrence of committees is less widespread than a quarter-century ago, they still are considered to be a valuable, if not indispensable, organizational device. When they are set up to obtain collective judgment, to provide mature advice, to permit of an interchange of ideas and opinions, or to serve as a medium of communication, committees fulfill a purpose not so well met by any other means.

BOARDS OF DIRECTORS

A board of directors, although in every sense of the word a committee, is not subject to the polemical treatment that attaches to committees in general. The role of this organizational element in governing the conduct of an enterprise varies in substantial degree among companies, including those participating in this study. A critic of American business practice once opined that the average board of directors has about the same control over the direction of its company that a streetcar motorman has over the direction of his vehicle.

The implication of this allegation is quite clear, that is, this topmost agency often endorses the program laid out by the chief executive and his management team without serious debate or challenge. There can be little doubt that this "rubber stamp" characterization is true in some measure in most companies, but complete dominance by the operating officers (unless it is an inside board) is, to say the least, not common practice. If the streetcar analogy may be carried a bit further, the board as well as the motorman can always apply the brakes or can exercise control over acceleration and deceleration. In short, full abdication by the board of its trustee obligation is rarely, if ever, to be found in publicly owned corporations and those with nonofficer directors.

Interviews with the chief executive officers of the participating companies elicited such broad statements concerning the use of boards of directors as the following:

Our board is used primarily for soundings on policy.

We regard our board as an "advise and consent" group. It is recognized as a sounding board. The outside members provide a detached viewpoint that is not possible for inside members. The outsiders have greater objectivity, more completely represent stockholder interest, and do not lose sight of the need to declare appropriate dividends.

The board of directors must have perspective and the courage to speak up and suggest but should not be used as a crutch for management. If a company relies on its board to manage, then the company needs to obtain some new management people.

Our board is anything but a rubber stamp board. I, as chief executive officer, would be stupid to take highly controversial matters to the board of directors without prior discussion with individual board members. When you face people like we have on the board, you better have your homework done.

The most important function of the board is to ensure continuity of able management and to keep management productive and fully responsive. If the board of directors abdicates this to management, the company will come a cropper.

Any time a board of directors tries to run a company you have trouble. We believe the board should review, evaluate, and set policy. The officers should operate and run the business. It is the function of the board to see that the company is run right, and if it isn't the board should change management.

The main function of the board of directors is to monitor the performance of the chief executive.

The foregoing candid comments reflect some rather wide differences of opinion among top executives as to the role of the board of directors. It is obvious that the companies cited all had nonofficers on their boards and in most instances a preponderance of outsiders.

In somewhat similar vein, a few of these chief executives gave expressions to the qualifications looked for in outside directors.

In obtaining outside board members, we want people of outstanding character and stature from various parts of the country and the world. We like to have people of real competence in such fields as finance, science, marketing, and international trade. We do not care about their holding company stock—they should represent all stockholders. We want a board that is constructively critical and not given to *pro forma* action. That would be dangerous for me.

What we look for in outside directors is an independence of view and a willingness to protect the company from its management. This attitude and potential position is as important as the knowledge and experience they contribute.

In addition to demonstrated ability and broad business experience, we seek geographic representation in our outside directors. We also look for wide diversification of business connections. The principal difficulties we have in attracting the kind of outside directors we desire are availability of time, absence of a conflict of interest, and age—the latter because we have a retirement age of 72 for directors.

Regardless of the actual extent of board influence in company affairs, there are certain fundamental determinations that generally reside with the full board of directors: approval of basic policies; declaration of dividends; changes in the financial structure; approval of capital expenditures over predetermined limits; setting of salaries, bonuses, and other financial benefits to officers; approval of mergers, acquisitions, and joint ventures; and its own plan of organization, particularly board committees.

In the book that presents the findings of the previous study of top management practices, an extensive discussion of boards of directors was included. This discussion dealt at length with the composition, duties, compensation, committees, and other aspects of corporate boards. There would be no purpose in duplicating that information, as in many respects the situation today is little different.

Boards are about the same average size (fifteen) with much the same proportion of inside members (40 percent) having duties of similar nature, and with many of the identical committees that were then part of the board organization; viz. executive, finance, audit, investment, salary and bonus.

In the area of board compensation, however, considerable change has occurred. Fees are much higher, and the practice of having outside directors on an annual retainer is widespread. Another significant and growing change is the establishment of a compulsory retirement age for directors, whether former officers or nonofficers. Still another change is the practice of holding one or more board meetings each year at important divisional headquarters or technical centers of the company so that outside directors may obtain a better understanding of company operations and can meet at firsthand key executives in the field.

Regarding the future of boards of directors, there appears to be no desire or intent to alter the status quo. In a few cases it is likely that the proportion of outside members will be increased. This obviously would apply to those companies that now have a preponderance of board representation from the full-time executive ranks. Also, more companies may reduce the number of full board meetings to four per year instead of the more common twelve. Two reasons underlie this potential move: the better opportunity to attract the caliber of outside talent desired, and the volume of board business taken care of by board committees. Aside from these modest changes, no evidence was gathered that would indicate any probability of radical change in the posture of boards of directors.

MANAGEMENT OF
RESEARCH AND DEVELOPMENT

5

In the quarter century since the original *Top Management Organization and Control* was published, tremendous changes have taken place on the technological front. The body of new knowledge has perhaps advanced more during this period than in all our previous history. Expenditures on industrial research and development have increased fourfold during the past fifteen years, and the rate of growth of the research effort is likely to accelerate at an even faster pace in the future. Today every major industrial company throughout the country is engaged in the exciting race of innovation and new product development.

The management of research and development in today's dynamic and changing society has captivated the interest and challenged the ingenuity of top management of every major manufacturing corporation. When the previous study was made, many companies made little or no effort to control research and development. In effect they acquired competent technical organizations and turned them loose with the hope that future profits would result. This situation has changed materially. In the present study the top executives of every participating company expressed their vital concern for and interest in all aspects of the research and development activities of their corporations.

Since World War II top management's interest and involvement in research and development have been particularly noticeable. The nature of this involvement and the most significant changes that have occurred in research and development, as reported by the participating companies, are described in this chapter under the following headings:

Establishing objectives and a research philosophy
Organizing, directing and controlling
    the research and development effort
A look ahead

Under each of these topics are several questions that top executives indicated were of primary concern to them and to their companies. The past, present, and future policies and practices of some of the participating companies are described as they relate to the questions that concerned the top executives. Selected examples of research and development practices of three companies are also included in this chapter.

ESTABLISHING OBJECTIVES AND A RESEARCH PHILOSOPHY

The most important factor in the successful growth and development of a corporation is the establishment of corporate objectives and strategies. Closely related to the corporate purpose and strategies are the goals, philosophy, and scope of the corporation's research and development program. Although there is considerable variation in the degree to which different corporations spell out their specific research and development objectives, the corporate research philosophy normally indicates the magnitude of the research effort desired and the degree to which the corporation will engage in the various types of research and development activities. Broad product, discipline, or customer need areas are frequently identified for primary attention; however, top management never appears to lose sight of the importance of change and flexibility as vital ingredients in a successful research and development program.

In every corporation that participated in this study, the president and/or chief executive officer recognized the importance of becoming personally involved in the establishment of realistic corporate research objectives and in the creation of a dynamic and far-reaching research and development philosophy.

Typical questions of concern to the top executives of the participating companies are:

1. *Nature of corporate growth.* What should be our pattern of growth? To what extent should we grow through acquisitions as compared to growth from internal new product development? How can we ensure optimum coordination between our research and development and our acquisition plans?
2. *Unity of approach.* What is the most effective way to ensure that the research and development plans and programs are tied into the corporate objectives and long-range plans? Are communication channels being kept open between central research and development personnel and line operating personnel to ensure effective teamwork?
3. *Competitive position.* What magnitude of research and development is needed to maintain or improve our competitive position on new products? What are our competitive areas of strength and weakness?
4. *Our corporate image.* Are we leaders in our industry on the research and development front? If not, what can we do to change our image? Are we attracting top-level scientific and professional talent?
5. *Research and development balance.* What kind of balance do we have between short-term and long-term research and development? Are our efforts being divided effectively between fundamental and applied research? How do we determine areas for primary and secondary consideration?
6. *Outside contract research.* To what extent should we engage in government research contracts? Should we take on research and development work for customers? For noncompetitive industrial

organizations? Should we subsidize research contracts at universities and/or private research institutes?

7. *Keeping up with the state of the art.* How can we best capitalize upon new knowledge coming out of universities and professional research institutes? To what extent do our scientific and professional personnel participate in professional meetings and publish articles in professional journals? How much, if any, time is allocated to research personnel for "free and uncontrolled research"?

8. *Profit orientation.* To what extent are our research and development activities profit-oriented? Do we have an effective balance between "the management point of view" and the "scientific point of view"? What is being done to bring these points of view closer together?

Answers to all the preceding questions were not found in each corporation that participated in this study; however, most of the top executives interviewed were concerned with these questions as related to the establishment of corporate research objectives and the creation of a corporate research philosophy. The following expressions from top executives indicate the extent to which they recognized the importance of the research and development activities within their corporations:

My greatest worry is keeping our technology bank filled.

The most important parts of my job are in the areas of new product and people development.

Additional growth from acquisition and merger has been stopped by the Antitrust Division. Our future, therefore, depends upon how successful we are in our research and new product development program.

Real innovation is the recognition of relevance.

The only excuse for a business to do research and development is to get something into the cash register. Making a research study is merely a ticket to the game. The game is the important thing.

Our previous concept of corporate research was that it should be given a fairly free hand because top management didn't really understand it. We tried this approach for a few years, but nothing seemed to happen. As a result we decided to engage only in the kind of research that would result in dollars in the marketplace within a reasonable length of time.

A few years ago we shifted the emphasis in our total central research effort. From 1956 to 1962 the corporate research budget had grown rapidly and considerable emphasis was put on fundamental research. The decision was made by top management to cut back on this type of research and to stress the product-oriented research which was based upon the needs of customers in the marketplace.

Obsolescence is a great thing if we do it ourselves. Our objective and challenge are to develop new products faster than we lose old ones. If we fail in this, we are dead.

This chapter has thus far focused attention upon a general discussion of the importance of research and development to top management. Consideration has also been given to the problems of establishing a research philosophy and of organizing for research. In the actual development of the research and development program, top management's involvement usually takes two forms: direct personal involvement, and indirect involvement through influence and direction in establishing a creative, participative, and productive research and development climate throughout the organization.

The top executives in all the participating companies are very much aware of the need for a flow of new ideas from all possible sources: general and divisional operating management; central research; operating research and development departments; operating manufacturing, engineering, and marketing departments; staff departments; customers; government; and universities. They recognize that a successful research program must have a constant flow of new ideas, plus an internal corporate environment that will nourish and develop such ideas into profitable products in the marketplace.

In the participating companies where the founders were inventors and are still represented in top management, or where their influence remains strong, the continuing support for research and development programs was usually evident. In one such corporation, a strong research and development program has existed since 1912, and today the chairman of the board and the president regularly attend the research and development and new product committee meetings. The vice president and director of research for this corporation commented as follows concerning the value of this top management involvement to the success of the research program:

The appreciation of top management for the value of research and development has made it unnecessary to try to put a price (or value) tag on the research and development effort. This would probably not be the case if top management were located far away. Frequent visits to the research and development labs, many face-to-face discussions, and detailed information on what is going on in research and development can easily be provided. It is believed the informal, personal relationships and the understanding they make possible could not be achieved by correspondence and occasional visits to the laboratories.

It is significant to note that when the chairman of the board and president of this corporation were asked to evaluate the importance of their various duties and responsibilities, new product development was number two on their list — preceded only by the selection and development of personnel.

With this kind of top management interest and involvement in the research and new product program over a long period of time, it is not surprising that the corporation has had outstanding success in building a creative climate internally and in establishing a reputation as an industry leader in new product development.

At every company visited, the presidents and the directors of research were clear and emphatic about the importance of a balanced, realistic, and profit-oriented research and development program. There was a general consensus that the most effective program is one that includes: (1) a range of activities from pure research through engineering and development to pure product modification, (2) active involvement by both operating and staff personnel, and (3) a composite of both the scientific and management points of view.

One company illustrated its balanced research and development program by a tree. The roots of the tree represented fundamental research in such basic disciplines as chemistry, physics, mathematics, and psychology. Research in the basic disciplines was depicted as providing nourishment for the trunk, limbs, and branches of the tree which, in turn, represented applied research and development, design engineering, and product modification as related to materials, component parts, and major products. Long-term, effective results, as indicated by this illustration, require both fundamental research and applied research and development.

Although most of the participating corporations referred to their research and development programs in rather positive and objective terms, there was little evidence of the existence of specific written goals and objectives. If research goals or objectives were stated, they were generally in very broad terms such as:

We desire a dynamic research program executed by a capable organization geared to our financial capability and compatible with our organization and its corporate objectives.

Research and development must be related to the present or anticipated product line. The relationship might range from present product modification and development to research on basic information such as "what happens in the atoms when a fatigue crack is getting started in metal."

About 50 percent of research and development normally goes into the development of existing products. The long-range work is on ideas and concepts, designs and models that will keep the company in business ten years from now.

Other corporations were more specific in stating their research and development objectives in terms of planned annual expenditures. These planned expenditures were frequently allocated on a percentage basis by types of research and development activities or between the central research organization and the research and development organizations within the operating divisions. As a percentage of sales, these expenditures ranged from a low of less than 1 percent to a high of 10 percent.

Considerable variation existed among the participating companies with respect to their definitions of the various kinds of research and development activities in which they were engaged: (1) pure, basic, or fundamental research and applied research; (2) unstructured and structured research; (3) exploratory, developmental, and new venture development; (4) fundamental, exploratory and early stage development, and late stage development; (5) fundamental, developmental, and engineering development.

A vice president and director of one of the participating companies which has a very effective research and development program expressed his opposition to the use of the terms "basic" and "applied" research. He described his corporation's research and development activity as follows:

Our first objective is to do effective *development* research. Most of this research, which represents 50 percent of the corporation's total research and development, is done in the research and development organizations within the operating departments. It is aggressive research—not defensive research. It is mission-oriented. The first thing we must do is to be sure our present products are in front of, or at least equal to, our competition.

If we don't do this, we are in serious trouble. We must continue to ask the question, "Is it relevant?"

Our second objective is to do *exploratory* research. This represents about 20 percent of the total research and development expenditure of the corporation. Each operating department normally distributes its research and development expenditure so that approximately 20 percent of the total expenditure is in exploratory research. This type of research is not tightly mission-oriented.

Any exploratory research that is being done in the central research and development organization is charged back to the operating departments on the basis of each department's total invested capital as related to the total invested capital of the corporation.

The third objective is to engage in *new venture development work*. Approximately 30 percent of the total research and development expenditure for the corporation is allocated to this type of research. This research may finally result in the building of a totally new manufacturing facility or in the formulation of a totally new marketing organization.

The top executives of this corporation explained that during the 1940s the central research department and the operating divisions that were doing research and development classified research as either fundamental or applied. There tended to be many subdivisions and classifications for types of research. Over the years there has been a tendency to group work according to the broad business purposes. In the words of one executive, "We don't keep books by basic and applied, so why should we divide our activities in that way? We constantly ask ourselves the question, 'Why are we doing this?' "

This variation in the definitions of research and development activities and the wide range in the amount of research and development expenditures for the various corporations are understandable in view of the different problems faced by each corporation and by each industry.

An analysis of the research and development expenditure of each participating corporation by types of research, however, indicated a tendency to concentrate maximum attention on development and applied research activities rather than on pure or fundamental research. The typical practice was to spend not more than 10 percent of the total research and development expenditure on fundamental or basic research. Discussions with top executives and with the directors of research indicated that there hase been a definite trend toward focusing more attention upon customer-oriented product research and development. This trend has brought about an increased marketing input at various stages in the research and development process. It has also been instrumental in improving the research organization structure and in producing a more effective system for directing and controlling the various research activities.

ORGANIZING, DIRECTING, AND CONTROLLING THE RESEARCH AND DEVELOPMENT EFFORT

Previous mention has been made of the differences in the basic research and development objectives and philosophies of many of the participating corporations. There was also substantial variation in the extent to which the president and other top executives became personally involved in the organization, direction, and control of the research and development effort. Specific policies, practices, and control techniques differed from corporation to corporation, although in some areas there were many similarities.

The following questions are typical of those which the top executives are asking about their research and development activities. Many of the questions are broad in scope, which is indicative of the level of involvement of top management.

1. *Centralization versus decentralization.* To what extent should the research and development effort be centralized at the corporate level? How much autonomy should the operating divisions have concerning their own technical activities? How much overlap and competition is necessary and/or desirable among the divisions and the central organization? Should the divisions be allowed to contract research and development outside?
2. *Type of organization structure.* What is the most effective way to organize the corporate research and development activity? By functions? By disciplines? By products? By customer groupings?
3. *Research projects.* To what extent should research and development activities be identified with specific projects? What is the most efficient organization plan that will ensure a smooth movement of projects from research through development and into production? What impacts will the use of the project technique have upon the regular line and staff departments? To what extent should top management get involved in project selection?

4. *Research committee.* What are the appropriate functions of a corporate research committee? Who should be members?
5. *Lag time.* What can be done to shorten the lag time between the idea stage and the production stage?
6. *Freedom versus profits.* How do we get maximum creativity? Is this accomplished best through "group think" or through individual effort? What is the most effective balance between freedom from controls and control for profits?
7. *Control tools and techniques.* Can we apply the basic principles of budgetary planning and control to research and development in the same way that we do in such functions as marketing, production, and engineering? If not, what are the differences? What kind of research and development control reports should top management receive? At what points should projects and programs be reviewed by top management?
8. *Evaluation.* How can we evaluate the effectiveness of our research and development effort? How do you successfully discontinue an unsuccessful product?
9. *New business ventures.* How can we best organize to produce the most effective results in development of new business ventures? What organization structure is most likely to provide the most effective guarantee of multifunctional inputs at various stages in the research and new business venture development?
10. *Use of quantitative tools.* How can new quantitative and mathematical techniques and tools be utilized most effectively in new product development?

Specific answers to each of the above questions is beyond the scope of this book. Because of the wide variation of the research and development needs and problems of the participating companies, it is impossible to provide answers that would apply uniformly to all companies. The questions are far-reaching and symbolic of the complexity of managing the research and development functions. A review of the policies and practices of a few of the participating companies should, however, suggest effective answers to some of the questions listed above.

Fourteen of the fifteen companies studied have central corporate research centers or laboratories which range in size from less than a hundred individuals to several thousands of scientific and technical personnel. In the fifteenth corporation, a vice president and chief scientist, with a small staff, report directly to the corporate president. In this corporation a large research laboratory of approximately 4,500 individuals is located at one of the major subsidiary companies of the corporation.

A summary of the reporting arrangements for the vice presidents and/or directors of research for the companies studied is shown below.

Companies with vice presidents or directors of research	*Report to*
2	Executive committee or board
4	President
4	Executive vice president
1	Chairman of board and chief executive officer
3	Senior vice president or vice president
1	President of subsidiary company

It is clear from the above reporting arrangements that the research and development functions are regarded with high esteem by the top executives of all fifteen companies. There was considerable variation, however, in the way the research and development activities were organized and in the amount of autonomy given to the central research and development organizations. In one company, for example, the central research and engineering organization functioned as an outside research institute. The operating divisions were responsible for their own research and development activities, and they had complete freedom to contract for research work either from the central research and engineering organization or from an independent outside research organization. This company was heavily oriented to the concept of divisional profit responsibility based upon return on investment.

In most of the companies studied, the central research organization exerted considerable influence in coordinating the total research and development activities of the corporation and in preventing unprofitable overlap and duplication of effort. In almost all instances, the fundamental or basic research activities were located in the central research laboratories. The coordinating and/or control functions normally were performed by the use of formal committees or through participation in operating divisional meetings by representatives of the central research organization.

The percent of the total research and development expenditures allocated to the central research organizations ranged from a low of 4 percent in one corporation to a high of 50 percent in another.

The following are typical comments concerning the degree of centralized control of research and development, plus the allocation by types of research:

We normally spend about 5 to 8 percent of sales in all research and development. Approximately 95 percent is spent by the operating divisions.

We spend about 8.5 percent of sales on research and development in the operating divisions, and about 1.5 percent of sales on research in the central corporate research organization.

Of the 3.5 percent of sales that is spent on research and development, 75 percent of this is spent within the operating divisions.

Approximately 50 percent of our research and development expenditure is for existing products. The remaining 50 percent is on new products and new ideas.

At the central research center we divide the research and development expenditures in the following manner:
1. *Fundamental* — 17 percent of budget. This is knowledge-oriented, similar to what you find in universities.
2. *Exploratory research* — 40 percent of budget. This research is understanding-oriented, studying new chemicals, uncovering new things, learning how to use the knowledge if it is to be successful.
3. *Early stage development* — 13 percent of budget. This establishes technical feasibility.
4. *Late stage development* — 30 percent of budget. How will this be converted into a product?

We have given a good deal of thought to the possibility of setting up a central research organization at the corporate level, but we decided against it. We feel that we will get better results by having the research tied into the various divisions.

Research and development used to go its own way, and if the line organization could not use the output, that was too bad. Now the individual division managers meet with the research and development people to discuss new products and ideas. Projects that are product-oriented take about 75 percent of the research and development budget.

The technical directors are technology specialists under the director of research. Each technical director also has a second hat as the research advisor for a particular market group. This group is selected as one that has a great deal to do with the technical director's area of specialization. The technical director goes to staff meetings, division meetings and plant visits of the market group and is expected to look after its research interest and projects in the research laboratory. This has the effect of broadening the experience and background of the technical directors by forcing them to look into related technical areas concerned with research projects of the assigned market group. The second hat also makes the technical director very familiar with the research problems and needs of the market group. As a result of this "two-hat" system, the technical directors get good experience and breadth of view that is good training for the job of director of research.

One of the participating corporations feels that major attention should be given to applied research and development and that most basic research should be left to the universities or to nonprofit research organizations. As a result of this philosophy, all research and development work is done in the various divisions of the corporation. The overall corporate coordination is accomplished by a research council made up of the vice president and chief scientist at the corporate level, plus the vice presidents and/or directors of research at each of the several divisions.

The research council meets every three months — usually at different division headquarters — at which time the total research efforts of the corporation are reviewed. In addition, the research council meets with the various divisions to review the long-range divisional plans. The council also meets with faculty members of leading universities to learn about new breakthroughs and knowledge that may be applied to problems of the industry and corporation.

Each division of this corporation has considerable freedom in organizing, directing, and controlling its research and development activities. One of the divisional research and development laboratories, for example, employs approximately 4,000 individuals with about 85 percent of the people engaged in developmental and product-oriented research. The organization structure of the research and development activity for this division was changed materially a few years ago. The change involved setting up, within the main laboratory, a number of sublaboratories such as physics, chemistry, mathematics, materials, and so forth, similar to departments within a university. Managers are selected as heads of each sublaboratory on the basis of their professional reputations and capabilities as researchers.

When a new project originates within the research laboratory, a number of scientists are assigned to the project. As work progresses, development engineers from the engineering department are invited to join the project. At a later stage, when the project is moved to the engineering department, a few research scientists may move with the project on a temporary basis.

In a similar manner, when the project moves from engineering to manufacturing, a few key engineers may follow the project. This movement provides a continuous flow of technical knowledge from the idea stage to the production stage. Approximately 90 percent of the program or project managers are engineers. They are more accustomed to working against schedules, whereas the scientifically oriented men are not.

The vice president in charge of this laboratory commented upon one of his major problems as follows:

> The real problem is getting scientists to communicate with the engineers. The research laboratory has to be scientific enough to attract scientists from academia. The laboratory then has a responsibility to make these scientists practical and realistic so that they can operate successfully in the industrial profit-centered organization.

Two of the major concerns about the research and development activities, as expressed by the top executives of the participating corporations, were (1) that potentially successful products would remain in the research and development laboratories too long because of the operating divisions' reluctance to accept them or because they would not fit into the product line of existing operating divisions, or (2) that potentially unprofitable items will remain in the laboratories too long because of the natural tendency for scientists and researchers to insist upon absolute perfection before releasing them to the operating divisions.

To eliminate these concerns, several of the participating corporations have provided multiple routes by which a new product can be advanced to the marketplace. Providing a variety of paths for development greatly reduces the prospect that some worthwhile innovation will be blocked which, in turn, means increased productivity and return on investment for research expenditures.

Among the new routes opened up, the most distinctive are the product transition organizations established by a number of firms. These new organizational units have the responsibility to carry the new products from the research laboratory stage to the point where they are new, fully tested products in the regular sales line of a product division. These organizational units may be labeled the new development department, the new venture department, or the transition engineering laboratory. They perform the vital function of making realistic analyses of technical engineering costs, production costs, and market potentials, and normally speed up the development of the new product.

Corporations that have introduced these new "in-between" departments are very enthusiastic about the results being obtained. A more detailed description of the specific function of these departments will be given later in this chapter.

Several companies have been successful in bringing about a better understanding between the research personnel and line management by including both in discussion sessions which deal with the selection of specific research projects and with the allocation of funds to different areas of research. The practice of having research personnel follow projects into the engineering and production stages of development has also tended to make the researchers more application-minded. In turn, this close association between line executives and research management has resulted in line management's more sympathetic understanding of the researcher's point of view.

The above statements and descriptions are indicative of the wide range of opinions among the top management of the participating companies concerning the most effective organization structure and/or the most desirable way to allocate research funds. There is, however, general agreement by the top executives in all the participating companies that a successful research and development program should place relatively heavy emphasis upon product- or customer-oriented research, but at the same time attention should be given to advancing the state of the art and to working closely with satellite "centers of excellence" at universities.

Perhaps one of the most significant changes in the organization, direction, and control of research and development activities during the past decade has been in the area of getting line management deeply involved. This involvement has taken place though improved profit planning, through service on research and development committees, through participation as project leaders, and through group efforts on new product business ventures.

A LOOK AHEAD

It was pointed out earlier that when the first study of *Top Management Organization and Control* was made by Holden, Fish, and Smith, it was generally believed that the most effective way to manage research and development was to give the professional researchers all the freedom they desired and to leave them alone. This attitude has changed significantly during the past decade. As previously indicated in this chapter, top management has become increasingly concerned with research and development activities and their impact upon the future success of their corporations. Most presidents and/or chief executives of corporations came up through engineering, manufacturing, sales, or finance, and therefore they have had little firsthand exposure to research as it is viewed today. It is only natural that they should look at the research function in terms of profitability, return on investment, and increased sales. Although this manner of behaving at times may have been frustrating to scientists and professional researchers, perhaps it has had a wholesome effect upon the future of the research and development activities in most companies.

There is tremendous pressure upon top management today to provide the necessary leadership to keep their corporations ahead of competition on the technological and new product frontiers. Many of the largest corporations are restrained by the Antitrust Division from growth through acquisition and merger. They must look, therefore, for growth through research and new product development. At the same time, business is becoming increasingly competitive because of tariff reductions and the aggressive practices of multinational companies.

With full recognition of the dangers involved in forecasting what is likely to happen in the management of research and development over the next few years, the authors would like to make the following predictions:

1. Corporations will continue to place major emphasis upon applied and developmental research geared to present products and customer needs. This does not mean that basic fundamental research will be eliminated. An appropriate balance between basic and applied research will be maintained, but the major thrust will be on applied and developmental research and development.
2. Corporations are likely to establish more effective liaison relationships with "centers of excellence" at major universities to ensure a constant flow of new knowledge. This will take the form of increased scholarships, fellowships, and internships. More use will be made of visiting and consulting arrangements with outstanding scholars.

3. With the growth of nonprofit research institutes, corporations will likewise devote more time to working closely with these institutes.
4. Research and development objectives, plans, and budgets will be coordinated more effectively with those of the entire corporation. The past tendency of considering the research function as "untouchable" will disappear.
5. More attention will be devoted to getting multifunctional inputs at various stages of the research and development process.
6. Line management's participation in planning, controlling, and evaluating research projects and programs is likely to increase rather than decrease. This is in focus with the increasing emphasis that is being put upon the concept of "management by objectives."
7. Greater emphasis will be given to the special problems of international research and development.
8. New quantitative tools and techniques will play a much more important part in engineering design, sales and economic forecasting, project and product control, and new business venture development. This is likely to result in a much more sophisticated selection of projects and new products.
9. There will be a closing of the communications gap between the scientific and management points of view. Because of recent changes in educational programs for management, future managers are likely to enter the business world with an improved background in the behavioral sciences. Likewise, scientists and engineers are becoming more understanding of and sympathetic toward management's profit-oriented point of view.
10. Controls over research and development activities are likely to become tighter. New advances in information and control technology are likely to result in more effective control through budgets, long-range plans, specific objectives and targets, an increased number of "look and see" evaluation points, and more rigid time limits on specific projects and programs.
11. There is likely to be a more effective use of research and scientific personnel because of improved supervision and the better use of supporting services. Top management has recognized that one of the most serious shortages in industry is the supply of top-level creative personnel. Every possible effort will be made to obtain maximum productivity from this scarce commodity.

12. In all probability, an increasing number of companies will resort to the use of interim departments such as new product development departments, new venture departments, or transition engineering departments with a view toward shortening the gap between research and the commercial introduction of new products.

Without doubt, there will be many other changes in the management of research and development in the years ahead. Interviews with top management and top executives in charge of the research and development functions in the participating companies, however, tend to support the predictions listed above.

EXAMPLES OF RESEARCH AND DEVELOPMENT POLICIES AND PRACTICES

Company A. This corporation has had a long record of success with its research and development program. Research and development activities are carried on in a large central research organization with several specialized laboratories, in a separate development or new venture department, in research and development organizations within the various operating departments, and under certain circumstances through contracts with outside research organizations or universities.

The atmosphere at the central research laboratories is much like that found at a university campus in that the personnel in the various disciplines of mathematics, physics, chemistry, and psychology are located in separate buildings at the center. When one visits the central research center, however, it becomes very clear that the academic atmosphere is charged with a feeling that successful research should be relevant to the corporation's long-term goals and objectives.

During the past five years the corporation has devoted major attention to the development of new products through experimentation with a "new venture development" approach. Top management recognized the need to develop the same kind of entrepreneurial spirit, independence, eagerness, and dedication to new products and projects that are found frequently in smaller business organizations. It was felt that the best way to accomplish this objective was to assign full responsibility for the new venture to one of the operating departments or to the development department. In either case the person in charge of the new venture is given authority over all aspects of the new venture, including technical development, production, market development, and sales. Ideally, this individual should have had multifunctional experience and he should possess a combination of optimism, enthusiasm, flexibility, pragmatic realism, and hard-headed analytical reasoning based upon facts, figures, and return on investment.

The independent development department performs a vital function of accepting and developing those products or projects that the operating departments are unwilling to take on either from a high-risk standpoint or because they do not fit with the other products of the department. When the new venture has proven itself to have satisfactory long-term potential, it normally is assigned to one of the present operating departments or it is spun off as a new department.

Quantitative analysis techniques are used extensively by the personnel working on development department ventures. At an early stage the project people, through computerized data processing, make detailed analyses of present and future market potentials for the product involved. At a later stage in the development process, quantitative analysis techniques are again utilized to aid top management in evaluating alternative choices and in determining the financial impact of decisions required at various stages in the development of the new product.

In addition to the large central research organization and the new venture development department, the corporation has strong research and development organizations in each of its operating industrial departments. These organizations have considerable autonomy in initiating new products or projects and in developing their product lines. If a new product comes from the marketing organization within an operating department, it normally goes to the department's research and development organization; however, it might alternatively go directly to the central research center.

Projects that start in central research can be advanced in four different ways: (1) The research and development organization of an operating department may take it over, (2) the development department may take it, (3) central research may make it a venture and continue to work on it, and (4) central research may contract it to an outside research organization or a university.

In commenting upon the problems of developing and evaluating new ventures, a top executive of this corporation said:

> We have experimented with every possible method of identifying or qualifying "new ventures." We finally decided that the best way is to

rely upon the judgment of the general managers of the particular divisions. When a general manager is willing to identify and accept a project as a new venture, the costs of the venture will be charged to his department. When the general manager makes his annual report to the corporate executive committee, he must show the results of the new venture separately so that the executive committee can get a look at where it is and where it is going.

Normally, when a general manager "buys" a venture, he transfers many of the people who have been working on the venture into his division. A general rule at this corporation is that "the people should go with the project" until it is in manufacturing.

All patent attorneys are in the legal department, but they are assigned to work with the operating divisions and with the research and development organizations within these divisions.

The coordination and control of research and development activities for this corporation are carried out in the following manner:

1. Each operating division makes periodic reports to the corporate executive committee. The committee thus discovers duplication and also evaluates progress on major research efforts.
2. The general managers of the operating divisions are held responsible for the coordination and control of their program, and they are expected to keep informed on what is going on in other divisions and in the central research department.
3. A specified member of the executive committee serves as advisor on all activities of the corporation. He gets reports on all research and development activities, gives advice and asks questions, but he has no authority except as a member of the committee.
4. The reports of each divisional research and development director are sent to all other divisional research and development directors, as well as to the central research department and to the research and development advisor on the executive committee.
5. The research and development directors and key members of the central research department meet monthly to exchange information.
6. In the central research department there is a steering committee that decides what broad areas should be researched. (One of the top executives expressed the opinion that they should probably have some kind of a "senate" made up of representatives

of the operating divisions to give advice to the central research department.)

Company B. In this corporation a recent organization change was made so that an executive vice president of operations and business development has the following reporting to him: vice president of corporate engineering, vice president of corporate research, and manager of corporate development. It was felt that having these three functions under one person would increase the effectiveness of the total new product and new business development program.

The vice president of corporate research supervises the central research personnel and serves as the landlord for the divisional research and development laboratories which are located at the headquarters research center. About 75 percent (650) of the research personnel are in the division laboratories. The divisional research managers have considerable autonomy. They can do their own research, hire central research to do it, or go outside the corporation.

Ordinarily the central research department test-markets totally new products that it develops. If the divisions are not interested in the new product, the corporate development department may make additional studies of the product potential and attempt to sell the new product to a division. If the division is still not interested in the product, the central research department may take the matter directly to the chairman of the board and chief executive officer. If approval is obtained at this level, it is possible for the central research department or the corporate development department to market the new product through brokers or through some other distribution method outside the corporation. In this corporation the research and development costs of the central research department for a particular product are not charged back to the divisions that take on the product.

The steps in the development of this corporation's annual research program are given below:

1. Key corporate and divisional research personnel have an annual meeting in September to discuss past accomplishments, present status of projects, and what to expect during the balance of the year. At this meeting six groups are formed with a mixture of corporate and divisional research people as members of each group. A division research manager serves as chairman for each

group, and a representative of the corporate research department serves as secretary for each group.

2. In January the proposed corporate research program is reviewed with the senior divisional research personnel. This program is then presented to top management for approval.

3. In April the corporate research program which has been approved by top management is presented to the divisional research personnel. This final program is presented by the technical heads of corporate research. This gives the technical heads a more practical view of research and provides a flow of information from the divisions to central research.

4. Each quarter during the year, the corporate research program is reviewed by subject area, but not by individual projects. Divisional research personnel attend. The purpose of this review is to provide an interdisciplinary perspective.

5. Twice a year the vice president of corporate research reviews problems and progress of each division research group with each division research manager.

Company C.   The management of research and development at this company has been altered materially during the past few years. Formerly the central research and development organization had considerable authority, whereas the line organization had very little to say about the development of new products. Now the individual divisions meet regularly with the central research and development people to discuss new products and new ideas. As a result, the projects are much more oriented to products and markets. The research people like this because they feel that someone is showing an interest in their work and they like to see their output used.

This company reorganized its corporate staff functions recently so that a vice president of operations services has the following functions reporting to him: manufacturing, engineering, marketing, market services, and research. One of the major objectives of this change was to obtain better coordination and broader inputs in the total research and new product development areas. From all reports of the top executives, this objective is being accomplished in an effective manner.

The other major change made was to get the group vice presidents and the vice presidents and managers of the operating divisions directly involved in research and development activities as part of their regular long-term and short-term profit planning programs.

Research and development is centralized for the most part. The central laboratory has about 550 professional people, of whom about 40 percent have Ph.D. degrees.

The total research program consists of several groups (one for each product group of the corporation), plus basic research, advanced technology, technical consulting assistance, and general corporation projects.

It is the policy of the corporation that the central laboratory will not fluctuate much in size. Primary attention is given to evaluating all projects and establishing priorities so that only those with the highest rating get into the actual research program for the year.

Each technical director in charge of a particular product group at the central laboratory serves as the coordinator with the operating divisions for his group of products. The vice president of research for this company commented upon the importance of careful evaluation and control of research in the following manner: "I refuse to accept the idea that basic research will always produce a serendipity. Science is so big these days, it can dissolve any amount of money. Thus, the basic research program must receive unusually careful scrutiny."

The cost of operating the central research laboratory is charged back to the operating divisions. The assessment is based one-third on each of three elements—profits, sales, and number of engineers. The central laboratory takes on outside research contracts on a selected basis with a view of keeping up with the state of the art or of utilizing available men and facilities. Consideration is also being given to establishing small "satellite laboratories" near major centers of learning.

One of the interesting features of this company's research and development program is the way in which the group vice presidents become involved in project evaluation and presentation. The proposed projects for each product group are arranged in "ladder form" so that relative priority is clear. These "ladders" are developed by discussion between the technical directors from the central research laboratory and the product line people. The group vice presidents play an important role in the selection of the projects and in establishing their positions on the ladder. When the proposed central research program is presented to the president's council, each group vice president presents the part of the program that relates to his product group.

A somewhat unusual feature of this company's research and development program is the transition engineering laboratory which is under the direction of the vice president of engineering. This laboratory is responsible for carrying products from the research laboratory stage to the point where they are new, fully tested products in the regular sales line of a product division.

The transition engineering laboratory makes analyses on several bases: product performance characteristics, production costs, and selling price. If it appears that the product will fail on any one of these bases, it is dropped. An economic or market survey is made before final development (or production engineering) work is done by the transition engineering laboratory. At this time, the research laboratory people assist in establishing what performance or physical characteristics the product can or will have. The line sales and marketing people assist in determining the price and potential sales volume. Production helps estimate cost. If these answers look good— including return on investment—then targets are set as to performance, cost, and price, and a timetable is set up. The transition engineering laboratory may carry out market surveys, test-marketing studies, and so forth, and has a budget to cover the costs of losses in the early part of a product's introduction on the market. If the product fails to meet the targets on performance, cost, and price at any stage while it is in the transition engineering laboratory, it will be dropped. Some products, therefore, never get to the point of having product introduction losses to absorb.

People in the transition engineering laboratory come from many related areas and may move again after a project is completed. The vice president of engineering said, "Engineers who feel away from real engineering work often enjoy these assignments. The transition engineering laboratory has the further advantage of giving research, engineering, and marketing people involved on a project a chance to broaden their perspective and learn more about the interrelations of the various functional areas."

PRODUCT LINE
DIRECTION AND CONTROL

6

In a competitive society geared to freedom of choice in the market-place, an effective product program plays a vital part in determining the success of the corporation's long-range plans. Typically, the over-all corporate strategies and the attainment of corporate objectives are directly related to the planning, direction, and control of new and present products. The following typical questions, which are of primary concern to top management, all have product line implications:

What kind of business do we want to be in?
How can we make the greatest contribution to society?
What are the requirements for success in our industry?
What is our distinctive competence or particular advantage?
How fast do we want to grow?
Where are the greatest opportunities for growth?
What has our past product performance been with respect to profitability, market share, quality, and price?
Are we leaders or followers on the technological front?
Should we grow through internal development or through acquisition and merger, or both?

Top-level executives of every company visited in this study gave recognition to the importance of having a continuous flow of new products, a positive plan for the improvement of present products, and an effective control system to ensure the weeding-out of unprofitable or obsolete items.

The chairman of the board of one company described his involvement in and commitment to product development in the following words: "We are not a 'me too' product development company. We continuously express the importance of having a creative and effective product program. Our main thought is, 'can we make a contribution?' The planning and control of the product line is my personal responsibility."

The president of another company commented upon the importance of having a continuous flow of new ideas and products in the following manner: "One of my greatest worries is in keeping up our 'technological bank.' We have spent approximately $19 million of assets from our 'technological bank.' This bank needs constant replenishing or we are in real trouble so far as our long-range plans are concerned."

In Chapter 5, attention was directed to the part played by top management in establishing and maintaining a creative environment for new ideas that, hopefully, turn into profitable products. In this chapter, primary consideration will be given to top management's concern for and involvement in planning the product line and in directing, coordinating, and controlling it through the stages of development, engineering, manufacturing, and marketing. In Chapter 7 consideration will be given to top management's involvement in the external growth of the product line through mergers and acquisitions.

PLANNING THE PRODUCT LINE

The top executives of the participating companies were all personally involved in planning the product line, although the degree and stages of their involvement varied considerably. Their points of view and their strong concern for salable and profitable products, however, permeated their organizations from top to bottom.

Balance and emphasis. Of particular concern to top management were such matters as: maintaining the appropriate balance between an engineering-oriented and a marketing- or customer-oriented product line; determining the most effective division of responsibility among the operating divisions, the corporate staff departments, and central research; obtaining the most effective use of computers and new information techniques to improve product line planning; and integrating new product planning into the long-range plans of the company.

A vice president and director of one company commented upon the dichotomy of marketing versus technology in the following terms:

> Over the years the basic philosophy of product line planning and control has changed somewhat. In the early years of the company, technology was the most important factor. Recently much more emphasis has been put upon marketing. At present some of our product lines are more clearly defined than others. Some argue that we should break the whole thing up and reorganize on the basis of marketing outlets. In fact, the movement within the operating departments during the past few years has been on the basis of markets. No longer can you depend just on the product. Marketing is becoming more and more important because of increased competition.

In almost every company visited top executives stressed the importance of obtaining effective marketing inputs at an early stage in the product-planning process. Two typical comments are given below:

> In the future, it is our hope that we can adapt our product more to the consumer and his needs. This does not mean, however, that we are interested in taking on any product merely to get a part of an already existing market. Merely the marketing of another indistinguishable product is not for us. The key points in introducing a product to the product line are: (1) Is it distinguishable? (2) Will it add value? (3) Is it consistent with our basic philosophy of being the leader in the field?

We have reorganized our total corporate effort around the needs of the customer. Each of the major groups of the corporation are given a certain "province of responsibility" so far as products and customers are concerned. In fact, we organized the corporation from the customer backward.

Under the "province" concept each division of the corporation has a written charter that spells out its responsibility with respect to product lines and product development. Separate sales and marketing research organizations within the respective divisions provide up-to-date information for product planning and development. This information serves as the foundation for developing the short-term and long-range plans of the corporation. In developing the divisional product line plans, other inputs from the central research organization on new products and from the economics research staff on economic conditions are considered and incorporated. A more detailed description of the "province" concept is included in the Appendix at the end of this chapter.

In most of the participating corporations, product line planning was decentralized to a high degree within the various operating divisions. This practice, of course, is in line with the decentralized profit responsibility and "management by objectives" concepts which the majority of the corporations advocate and practice. A few corporations, however, stressed the importance of centralized quality and product control to protect the corporate image and reputation. As one executive expressed it, "If there is any disagreement among central engineering, manufacturing, or marketing on a new product, central engineering has the final say."

Other corporations stressed the need for centralized control of engineering design, particularly where component parts were utilized by more than one division or where the product line image was involved.

Pricing and timing.   One of the most important functions included in product line planning is pricing. The authority for approval of prices— particularly on major products—usually rested with the president or chief executive officer, the executive committee, or a special top-level products committee. In a few corporations, which were highly decentralized on a divisional return on investment incentive basis, pricing responsibility rested with the divisional manager. In one corporation which manufactures heavy equipment the authority for pricing remained with the president and the chairman of the board of directors.

There was general agreement among the top executives of all companies visited that top management should become very much involved in product pricing as a means of maintaining competitive product line planning and as a means of guarding against possible charges of antitrust violations.

In planning the product line, one of the greatest concerns of top management is in the area of timing. Diverse pressures are built up in various segments of the corporation: Central research is reluctant to release new products which, in its judgment, are premature; the sales organization demands new and better products at lower prices; the finance organization wants sufficient lead time to supply needed funds for capital expenditures; and manufacturing vigorously argues for longer runs of the present products with a minimum of change. Providing a continuous flow of high-quality products at the right competitive price at the right time requires a high degree of skill in timing and decision making on the part of top management.

Use of management information systems. During recent years top executives have sought to improve their timing and decision making in introducing new products and in modifying present products. The expertise of top-level staff departments in the field of economic analysis and forecasting has been utilized with a modicum of success. A few top executives have also experimented with some of the new quantitative tools and techniques such as mathematical models, simulation studies, and decision-tree options in an attempt to improve their decision making in the areas of new product introduction, new venture development, and product line planning.

In the companies visited in this study, it was evident that computers and operations research techniques have been useful in improving the design of products, in reducing inventories, in improving the scheduling of manufacturing operations, relieving lower and middle management of considerable routine decision making so that they could spend more time in productive product planning, and in providing top management with more up-to-date operating information.

There was little evidence among the fifteen companies, however, that major product planning decisions had been made on the basis of operations research or computer simulation studies. A few typical comments by executives are given below:

> *A general division manager:* We have tried to develop an overall centralized plan to control all orders as well as the scheduling of the mills

and plants. We have been unsuccessful because of the inability to forecast or control the changes in the market.

We have experimented with simulation studies on a number of divestitures. In most instances, however, the studies merely confirmed our previous knowledge that we had some "dogs" in our product line.

A president: The real impact of computers thus far is that they have put decision making at lower levels. I formerly made decisions on levels of inventory, etc. Now these kinds of decisions are being made at lower levels.

A divisional manager: We are using computers to determine the best mix of 400 different kinds of models of products. We have been running parallel systems for several months. Our model gives us better results than previously.

Computer systems are designed to cover the last hair on the dog's tail. Sometimes we can't even find the dog!

A manager of information systems and data processing: The cost of taking a product through test market has gone from $250,000 to $1 million in twelve years. If this time can be shortened or testing results improved by simulation studies, the savings can be tremendous.

The following comments represent divergent views from four individuals within the same corporation. These differences of opinion between the technical staff and the operating staff are typical of those found in a number of the corporations visited:

The manager of the business economics department: The business economics department uses multiple correlation in sales forecasting. Linear programming has been useful only in assembly line balancing. Exponential smoothing has been used as an additional means of sales forecasting on product attachments. There are not enough people at the top level who understand them to justify application of any of these new techniques on a grandiose basis. The senior executives often do not even know how to ask good questions about the results.

The chairman of the corporate product committee: Computers have not been used in product planning or price and market analysis by production. Product committee members, with a total of 500 years experience in our business, want to keep the analysis of key product problems in their own hands. Asking the data processing people or the operations research people to make decisions puts the key assumptions and judgments in the hands of transient employees who have limited experience in our business.

The general manager of a division: Computers have speeded things up and have taken over routine things. Computers cannot anticipate the desires of customers three or four years from now. They do not have any emotional capability, which is the most important thing in this business.

The director of new product development: We have experimented with the development of a number of models in connection with the introduction of new products. We haven't come up with any practical solutions, however, which have been used for clear-cut decision making.

In spite of the differences of opinion between the technical staff personnel and the top operating executives, and the somewhat negative comments made about the productivity of the new quantitative tools and techniques in the area of product planning, a number of top executives indicated that their corporations plan to continue to experiment with these tools in the hope of improving product planning results in the future.

DIRECTING AND CONTROLLING THE PRODUCT LINE

Planning of the product line is only the first step in a successful product program. Implementation of the plans through effective organization, direction, and control is equally important.

In the fifteen companies studied, there was considerable variation in the types of organizations and in the administrative methods utilized in directing and controlling the product program. In those corporations in which a basic raw material or common process represents a major part of the total production, there was a higher degree of centralized direction and control. On the other hand, as would be expected, corporations that operate on a decentralized profit-center basis delegated a larger share of product line direction and control to the respective operating divisions.

The corporations that have a single family of related products tended to organize to obtain vigorous centralized direction and control at the corporate level in such functional areas as engineering, research, marketing, finance, and manufacturing. In many instances, this overall coordination was affected through one or more corporate product committees, or through special meetings of the executive committee or president's council. In these corporations, the responsibility for approving prices of products usually rested with the president and/or the chief executive officer. In some instances, however, the product committees were given the authority to establish prices. Corporations that utilize this concept of product line direction and control are described in the examples at the end of this chapter as Corporation A and Corporation C.

In the second category of corporations the major responsibility for product line planning, direction, and control rested with the various operating divisions. In general, each division manager was given considerable freedom to improve or delete present products and to add new products to the line. Problems of coordination among manufacturing, engineering, marketing, and research normally were handled within the divisions by divisional management. Any product problems involving other divisions were referred either to the group vice presidents, to a corporate products committee, to a central research and engineering committee, or to the president or chief executive officer. Nine of the fifteen corporations visited featured decentralized product line direction and control with a limited degree of centralized guidance and coordination. When the executives of these corporations were queried as to whether there would be more or less centralized direction and control in the future, the typical answer was: "If any change is made, it will be in the direction of more decentralization, which is in tune with the modern concept of profit responsibility at the lowest possible level." The decentralized concept of product line direction and control is illustrated at the end of this chapter by the example of Corporation B.

Use of product, project, and program managers. In Chapter 4, "Organization Structure," mention was made of the importance of the recent development in the use of product, project, and program managers. Approximately one-third of the participating companies indicated that they utilize this concept in their product programs. The general reaction of those using this concept of management was very favorable.

A group executive in one corporation described the functions of the product manager in the following words:

> The product manager is really a coordinator, not a little general manager. He has the market responsibility for the product, but on other

matters he is not a line executive but a planner and coordinator. I don't see how we could possibly operate without this or something close to it.

The vice president of product distribution in another company made the following comment concerning the functions of the product managers:

There are 29 product managers in the corporation. They are, on a small scale, vice presidents in charge of the sales of their products. The product manager must deal with the several plants around the country in determining what should be made and where it should be made, he must coordinate with the sales and marketing organizations which are set up on an industry-wide basis, and he must serve as coordinator in getting new products out of the research laboratory through production and into the appropriate distribution channels.

In this corporation the product managers are charged with the responsibility of watching their products on a national basis and, to a limited degree, on an international basis. The product manager has the authority to meet competition's prices on his products. Distribution planning is done by the product managers who work with the district sales managers to determine what volume will be sold in what territory and at what prices.

In the participating corporations involved in major construction projects or defense programs, project or program managers were utilized extensively. They were given considerable authority for the administration of their respective projects or programs. In a sense, these managers are general managers for their ventures and in this capacity they assume responsibility for coordinating the total efforts of the various line and staff departments to meet predetermined objectives and targets.

Project and program managers have been very effective in cutting through red tape to keep their projects or programs on schedule. Frequently this requires the use of shortcuts and the development of new information and communication channels outside of the traditional organization structures. New control tools and techniques such as PERT have been used effectively in monitoring the individual projects and programs.

Program and project managers have an opportunity to utilize the skills and techniques required of general management at a fairly early period in their professional careers. Program management, therefore, serves as a proving ground for future top executives. Frequently the project or program managers are required to work directly with the top executives of the corporation when critical problems arise. This arrangement provides an opportunity for the top executives to obtain firsthand evaluations of the performance of subordinate executives. In one of the participating corporations, the president described his involvement in program management in the following words: "I reserve the right to 'red line' [pick up the phone and call anyone at any time]. I do this frequently with project managers or program managers, and they understand that they can 'red line' me if the need arises."

In the corporation described above, some of the program managers and group vice presidents were asked about this "red line" practice of the president to ascertain whether it caused organization problems. None of them seemed to be concerned. They indicated that a certain amount of this practice is essential because of the amount of traveling done by many of the executives. When the president was asked whether the use of the "red line" technique had caused any organizational problems, he replied, "Not at my level!" There was no evidence that the president's use of this technique had caused any serious problems anyplace in the company's organization.

The product, project, and program concept of management has had a significant impact upon improving the direction and control of specific product programs. This technique has been particularly effective in the area of military projects and programs. Product managers have also made significant contributions in some of the highly competitive consumer goods industries where specialized sales promotion techniques are essential.

Control over inventories and spare parts.　During the past few years great progress has been made in improving the control over inventories and spare parts. Much of this improvement has been made possible by improved transportation, by the application of new operations research tools and techniques, by the availability of larger and improved computers, and by the development of more sophisticated information systems.

In every company visited in this study, there was evidence of progress and of future promise for additional improvements in the control of inventories. Typical examples of changes in this area of product line control are described below.

One corporation has centralized the control of 80 percent of the standard products in its consumer products division. The central computer automatically reorders on repetitive routine decisions. Field stock control has been centralized for eight field warehouses and 25 small distribution centers.

Another corporation, which has 22 different inventory lines with 140,000 separate parts, has established a central computerized inventory control system for fifteen of the inventory lines. This has resulted in a 20 percent reduction of total parts inventory. The vice president in charge of inventory control indicated that they invested 50 man-years in planning for the introduction of the IBM 360. At present the computer automatically adjusts inventory control levels unless the change is over 15 percent. Then the data are printed out for review by an analyst. He expressed the opinion that the corporation would soon have a central parts inventory control system that will control both the corporation's and the dealers' parts inventory on a worldwide basis.

The improvements in the control of inventories and spare parts have been significant, but the surface has only been scratched. Looking ahead, we can expect that the rate of change and improvement in these areas will be greatly accelerated within the next few years.

Product authorization.   In all the fifteen corporations visited, additions, deletions, or major modifications of products or product lines required the approval of top management or general management of a division. In some instances, approval of the president or of the chief executive officer was required; in other cases, approval of a top-level product committee, the executive committee, or the president's council was necessary. In those corporations with highly autonomous operating divisions, the general divisional manager often had considerable authority to approve product additions, deletions, or modifications subject to higher approval of his total profit plans, capital expenditures, or long-range plans.

Product safety.   During the past few years top management has become increasingly concerned about product safety. This concern has been particularly noticeable in the automotive, tire, and aerospace industries where inadequate product quality control or poor design may result in accidents involving the loss of lives. The government has also shown an increasing interest in this area.

One of the corporations studied recently established a special senior safety review board to review the adequacy of the safety phase of the corporation's products. The board's findings are reported to the responsible program, project, or product manager, to his vice president or general manager, and to the president of the corporation.

TYPICAL QUESTIONS ASKED BY TOP MANAGEMENT

The following list of questions represents the authors' summary of typical questions that chief executives are asking themselves and other members of top management concerning the evaluation and improvement of their product line programs. The questions are grouped under the separate headings of planning, organization, and direction and control.

Planning

1. What kind of balance does our product program have in relation to the present and future needs of our customers? Are we keeping the company "future-oriented"?
2. How effective are the new product research projects in terms of the company's specific goals, opportunities, strategies, natural resources, and competitive threats?
3. Are we investing our available capital resources in projects and products that will produce the maximum rate of return?
4. Do we have specific short- and long-term goals by product lines? Are these goals high enough?
5. Does our strategy for growth include allowances for the natural economic growth of the world economy? Does it include full exploitation of present products in new markets?
6. Do we give adequate consideration to prices and customer value judgments at the time we plan a new product or modify a present product?
7. Should product prices be computed from the customer level down? From the cost base up? Or as incremental business?

Organization

1. Does top management become sufficiently involved in the planning, direction, and control of the product lines?

2. How can top management delegate authority to achieve the most profitable mix of research and development projects? To what extent should research and development personnel select the projects on which they work? Should the projects be chosen as a result of the integrated viewpoints of the company as expressed by representatives of the major operating and functional divisions?
3. Are multiple channels available for the development of new products?
4. Are there clear-cut definitions of responsibilities and authorities at each stage in the development of new products? In the modification of present products? In the deletion of unprofitable products? Are these allocations understood by all parties concerned?
5. Does our technology transfer system fit the company's organization structure and philosophy of management?
6. Do we have sufficient organizational flexibility so that we can delegate multifunctional authority to a top executive to move a major "crash" program or project from the idea stage to the market stage?
7. Where should final responsibility for product design decisions rest? To what extent should there be multifunctional inputs in making this type of decision? How early should marketing and production engineering become involved in projects that are in the research organization?
8. What is the most effective way to utilize product committees?
9. What degree of authority should the product managers have in such areas as pricing, advertising and sales promotion, design, and inventory control?
10. Is our present product program organized to take full advantage of anticipated growth on the international front?

Direction and control

1. Are we doing a skillful job in evaluating capital investment proposals for new products and business ventures? Do we have specific objectives such as a 15 percent return on investment, and do we adhere to these objectives in our evaluation process? Are discounted cash flow techniques used in evaluating all proposed projects?
2. Are we a questioning company — a hard-to-satisfy company that is unwilling to accept anything but top performance? Do we in-

vestigate why particular product development projects fall below, or exceed, their forecasted return on investment?

3. To what extent is the creativity of the entire organization being tapped to improve the product line? What are the sources of new product or improvement ideas? Are there suitable incentives? How are new ideas screened?

4. How price-sensitive is our company? Have we succumbed to the myth that volume increases alone will cure all profit ills? Do we objectively explore the true impact and relationships of price, profit, and volume increases and decreases? For example, what result would a 1 percent price increase have on overall corporate profits? What is our "track record" on profits from the sale of "package or combination deals"?

5. To what extent should the authority for pricing be delegated to the operating divisions? How do we get divisional and field sales personnel to sell value, performance, quality, and service rather than price?

6. Is there a clear-cut assignment of responsibility for product cost improvement? How effective is our program for making detailed cost analyses of competitor's products? What is the evidence of tangible results from this program?

7. Have we identified and eliminated all factors that tend to inhibit the transfer of new technology from research to operations?

8. How effective is our multifunctional and multistep design review system for new and modified products? What specific tools are being used to get timely action?

9. To what extent can raw materials, finished goods, and spare parts inventories be reduced through improved distribution systems management? Will our company benefit from the establishment of a separate materials or distribution management division?

10. What are we doing to improve our product line control through the education and training of our dealers and/or distributors? Through the vertical integration of information systems?

A LOOK AHEAD

There was a consensus among the top executives interviewed that the development of new products and the improvement of present products will become increasingly important and that top management will be required to devote a larger portion of time to opportunities and problems in this area.

When the top executives of the participating companies were asked to give their views on possible future changes in product planning, direction, and control, they were in general agreement that the rate of product change will accelerate in the next few years and that substantial improvements will be made in the management of both new product development and product line control. The authors' summary of these views is presented below:

The "needs in the market" concept will play an increasingly important role in determining the product line. Improved marketing inputs will make significant contributions at various stages of product research, development, engineering, and manufacturing.

In almost every corporation visited there was evidence that top management was not satisfied with the quality, quantity, or timing of present marketing inputs as related to both new and present products. Many corporations have already taken specific steps to improve these inputs through the establishment of better information systems and/or through changes in organization structure. Others have indicated the desirability of future moves in this direction.

Top management will become more involved in the overall coordination and direction of the research and development program.

In the past, many top executives succumbed to the myth that researchers were different and that they must be isolated from the realism of engineering and manufacturing and from the high-pressure environment of marketing. As a result, central research organizations were created in an atmosphere of academic freedom with a minimum of outside control. In the discussion on research and development (Chapter 5), it was pointed out that the corporations which have had the most successful new product programs during recent years were those that were able to maintain an effective balance between fundamental research and applied product development. The top management of these corporations has recognized that with certain modifications, managerial tools and techniques such as long-range planning, budgets, management by objectives, accountability, and progress reporting can effectively be applied to the area of research and new product development.

Looking ahead, top management is likely to play a more aggressive part in the establishment of research and product development goals and in the creation of an atmosphere of urgency in the maintaining and control of the entire product program.

Corporate short- and long-range plans will be improved through better product line planning.

Improvements are likely to be forthcoming in the areas of sales and economic forecasting techniques due to the availability of more sophisticated computers and information systems. Improved information and distribution systems should also make it possible for more product decisions of a technical nature to be made at lower levels of management. This change, in turn, will free the time of middle and top management for overall planning and coordination of the corporate product program.

There will be more effective teamwork and cooperation among the functional organizations of research, engineering, financial control, manufacturing, and marketing.

During the past 25 years many corporations have experienced internal conflicts between, on the one hand, the traditional finance, engineering, and manufacturing organizations and, on the other, the rapidly expanding research and development organizations. Organization changes and realignment of responsibilities and authority for new product development often resulted in mistrust, passing the buck and resistance based upon the "N.I.H." (not invented here) concept.

In most of the corporations visited in this study, these conflicts and disagreements have disappeared or are disappearing. There was general acceptance by top executives interviewed that an effective product development program requires dedicated teamwork and cooperation among all segments within the organization. There appeared to be a telescoping of the scientific point of view, the engineering point of view, and the marketing point of view into a more mature corporate and managerial point of view.

This new managerial maturity of viewpoint, marked by increased responsiveness to change and to differences of opinion, is likely to be more prevalent in the years ahead as young executives with broader education, training, and experience than that of their predecessors assume positions in top management.

There will be an increase in the use of new venture departments or new product departments to provide a smoother, faster, and more effective transition from central research to commercialization.

The corporations that have utilized separate organizational units to perform this function were enthusiastic about past results and optimistic over future opportunities and prospects. Transition departments or laboratories for new products offer many advantages. An outlet is provided for new products that operating divisions may be unwilling to accept. Authority for the success of the new product can be assigned to one individual who can assemble a team of experts from different departments within the corporation. Faster decisions will be made at various stages in the development of the new product. There will be a minimum of interruption with the regular activities of the engineering, manufacturing, and sales organizations. The new venture or new product manager concept provides an ideal atmosphere for the development of entrepreneurial-minded general managers.

The use of product managers and/or project managers is likely to increase in the future.

The corporations that have used this technique of management generally feel that the advantages of faster action, improved coordinated control, more effective profit responsibility, and broad-gauged managerial development far outweigh the disadvantages related to organizational conflicts. In the future, the project manager concept, which has been used extensively by corporations with defense business, is likely to be applied more frequently in nondefense projects.

New quantitative managerial tools and techniques will be used to a greater extent in the future to improve the direction and control of the product line.

The full impact of the application of new tools and techniques, such as computers, operations research, discounted cash flow, PERT and other control systems, has not been widely felt as yet in the area of product line direction and control. Although considerable progress has been made on this front, substantial additional improvements will be effected when a new generation of management, educated in the use of these new tools and techniques, assumes positions in top management.

Value analysis programs and competitive product cost comparison programs are likely to receive greater attention of top management in the future.

Continuous wage increases, accompanied by growing competition in the marketplace, will produce additional pressure for improved product line cost control. Some corporations have already launched extensive value analysis programs to reduce costs of present products. One corporation has created a central product cost control laboratory under the joint responsibility of the corporate engineering and manufacturing executives. The laboratory functions in a service capacity to the operating divisions which have ultimate responsibility for product costs. Product cost improvement teams include representatives from corporate engineering, manufacturing, and marketing, as well as representatives from the divisions that submit products to the central laboratory for detailed analysis and comparison with competing products. The corporation reports that 80 percent of the cost improvement recommendations of the product cost improvement teams have been put into effect. The top executives of this corporation predict that this joint-effort approach to product cost improvement is likely to be expanded in the future.

Product life cycles will be shortened at an accelerated rate.

There was general agreement among the top executives interviewed that the speed of technological obsolescence will increase during the next decade. The reasons for this increase are many. Because of antitrust restrictions, many of the largest and most successful corporations have been prevented from expanding their present product lines through acquisition and merger. Consequently, they have focused their efforts upon internal growth through a more aggressive research and development program. In many instances, this growth has been in completely new product areas, producing increased competition across the traditional industry boundaries. At the same time, many products are becoming obsolete through the increased use of new materials such as plastics and new synthetic fibers. The reduction of working hours and the concomitant increase in leisure time will result in changing demands for certain present and new products. Tariff reductions, the changing patterns in foreign capital investments, and increased worldwide competition have had, and will continue to have, an increasing impact in shortening the life of present products.

EXAMPLES OF PRODUCT LINE PROGRAMS

Brief descriptions of three product line programs are included below. Corporation A is representative of a corporation with a fairly high degree of centralized control over its product lines; Corporation B is illustrative of more decentralized product line programs; and Corporation C represents a combination of the two philosophies.

Corporation A. This corporation manufactures and sells heavy earth-moving and construction equipment on a worldwide basis. It is organized on a functional basis, with a high degree of centralized direction and control. The vice president of engineering and research has the major responsibility for the development of new products and the improvement of present products. The director of research, who reports to the vice president of engineering and research, has a staff of approximatly 750 engineers and scientists. They spend approximately 50 percent of their budget in improving present products and the remaining 50 percent on new ideas and products. Budget charges of $25,000 or more must be approved by the vice president of engineering and research.

Every three years, the corporation holds a major "product conference," which is attended by the top 25 executives of the corporation. During the meetings all present and proposed products are reviewed, detailed quality, design, and price comparisons are made with competing products, and anticipated customer needs are discussed.

The corporation has a top-level product committee with membership consisting of the assistant to the president as chairman, two executive vice presidents, the vice president of engineering and research, the vice president of marketing, the vice president of industrial products, and the director of economics. The committee studies the total market and reviews specific opportunities for improving the corporation's market share for different product models. It reviews all products and projects periodically and establishes priority ratings. In essence, the committee is a filter for all product development ideas and proposals. It makes recommendations, establishes target dates for stages of development and production, and monitors progress through periodic review.

All recommendations of the product committee are submitted to the president who makes the final decisions or approvals. The president and chairman of the board frequently attend meetings of the product committee.

Before new products or product modification proposals are submitted to the product committee by engineering and research, inputs are obtained from sales, marketing, research, business economics, finance, and manufacturing. The presentation to the committee includes detailed product specifications; estimated dates for design approval, release of production prints, and final production; estimated engineering, development, and tooling costs; estimated industry and corporation sales; and price, total cost, and profit estimates. A presentation summary sheet is shown on the following page.

Corporation B. This corporation manufactures and sells a wide line of heavy industrial products and consumer products on a worldwide basis. Its basic management philosophy is geared to a high degree of profit responsibility within the operating divisions, coupled with a minimum amount of top-level corporate policy control. Each operating division has considerable autonomy with respect to product line planning, direction, and control, which is spelled out in the corporation's market province concept. There are written product charters of responsibility for each division or group of divisions.

The addition or deletion of major product lines or major changes involving substantial capital expenditures or possible acquisitions are cleared through the group and executive vice presidents for consideration at a meeting of the president's advisory council (membership includes the president, two executive vice presidents, the vice president of finance, and the vice president of corporate staff departments). The president, however, makes the final decisions prior to referral to the board of directors.

The respective divisions initiate the sales forecasts, proposed pricing schedules, and cost and profit estimates for each product line as part of their annual and long-term divisional profit plans. Each division establishes sales, profit, and return-on-asset goals and targets which are incorporated in the corporate overall long-range plans.

Each division manager's performance is measured upon his success in achieving sales and return-on-asset goals that measure up to those established by the corporation. The division managers are also expected to make full use of the central staff departments such as engineering, manufacturing, marketing, finance, and research.

The top executives of this corporation appear to have been very successful in achieving profitable growth by creating an atmosphere in which the various operating divisions work closely with the central

PRESENTATION SUMMARY SHEET

Model

Product committee meeting

Date

	Presented to product committee (estimate)	SCHEDULE OF REVIEWS			
		Prove design stage	Release of production prints	First production	Post introduction
Proposed date of review					
Actual date of review					
Specifications					
Horsepower					
Weight					
Capacity					
Other					
Dates					
Prove design release					
Production release					
Production					
Engineering & research development cost					
Spent to date					
Future expense					
Total					
Tooling cost					
Capital					
Expense					
Total					
Estimated annual sales					
Units					
Industry					
Corp. A					
Dollars					
Industry					
Corp. A					
Price					
List price					
Net price					
Cost, price setting					
Cost, variable					
Dollar profit					
Percent profit					
Annual dollar profit					

121

research laboratories and a new product transition department in developing new products and improving present products. There was also evidence of a very effective product cost improvement program which was coordinated on a corporate-wide basis, with the major responsibilities for cost improvement resting with the operating divisions. Value analyses and competitive cost comparison programs have been used with considerable success. A detailed description of the "market province" concept of this corporation is included in the Appendix at the end of this chapter.

Corporation C.   The product program in this corporation has many interesting aspects. It possesses an effective balance between decentralized planning and centralized coordination and control; it typifies a maturity of viewpoint drawn from over 55 years of experimentation and aggressive leadership in the area of research and product development; and it reflects a recognition of the intricate product-related problems challenging the top management of a corporation that has established itself as a worldwide leader in a technical consumer products field.

This corporation, which allocates approximately 6 percent of sales to its research and development budget, is oriented to both research and marketing. Its research orientation is rooted in the fertile soil of its creative founder who possessed an insatiable appetite for change and product improvement. Its marketing orientation was molded in the rugged competitive environment that exists in the consumer products market.

The domestic marketing organization is divided into five major divisions by class of trade. Each division has its own budget and operates like a separate marketing company. Major functional departments within each division include: sales, advertising and customer services, product planning, and information and analysis. Sales departments serve as the apex for the marketing divisions in implementing approximately 50 detailed marketing plans.

The corporation formerly operated under a product manager concept, which was abandoned about five years ago because it was felt that more productive team effort was needed to produce maximum results in the complex worldwide markets. The present product planning managers possess a more specialized type of responsibility. They are no longer responsible for advertising and selling, and therefore are able to allocate more time to product designing, planning, and development for their respective divisions. By devoting major attention to product planning, the product planning managers have been able to inject timely and customer-oriented marketing inputs into the corporate product development programs.

Top-level coordination and control of the product program is accomplished in this corporation through the use of a central research and development committee and multiple product planning committees. A core group of top executives are members of the research and development committee. They include the executive vice president as chairman, vice presidents of finance, manufacturing, marketing, and research, and the vice presidents and general managers of the major operating divisions. The executive vice president devotes a major portion of his time serving as chairman of the research and development committee and as chairman of twelve separate product planning committees.

The core members of the research and development committee attend the meetings of the twelve product line committees. A typical product line committee meeting has representatives present from manufacturing, marketing, research, international, and finance. Overlap in committee membership and flexibility in selecting members for each committee has resulted in improved coordination of the total worldwide corporate product program. The function of the product committees in this corporation, however, has been strictly advisory in nature. Key decisions on the introduction of new products and on deletions from the present product line remain the responsibility of the president.

The corporation also has a finished products committee which includes many members who also serve on the research and development committee or on one or more of the product line committees. The finished products committee establishes estimates on future sales by products, considers present inventories, and makes recommendations for future production schedules. These recommendations are submitted to the president for his approval.

APPENDIX: THE MARKET PROVINCE CONCEPT

General. The "market province" concept is a plan to explore and develop new and broader markets for the company's products, systems, and services. It involves the designation of special areas or "provinces" in which the company's strengths and skills can be applied. A "province" is defined as a designated area of a market or technology in which to apply the abilities and skills of the company and its people.

Within this broad corporate province, specific provinces have been identified and assigned by the executive vice president to group general managers. Plans for development of these assigned provinces will be prepared at the group level. Such plans will be coordinated within particular groups or between groups so that all appropriate company strengths are enlisted in managing the profitable growth of each province.

In addition, charters for each profit center will be maintained so that responsibilities of these units will be clearly defined.

Policy. It is the company's policy to identify broad market areas or provinces which the company is best equipped to serve, and to enlist and develop strengths, skills, and abilities throughout the company in profitably serving these areas and meeting customers' identified and anticipated needs.

Responsibility. Group general managers have overall responsibility for the profitable development of their assigned provinces. They may break down these provinces into separate categories of products, systems, or services for assignment to profit centers within their groups. They may also arrange for assignment of parts of a province to profit centers outside their particular groups. If assignment outside a product group is required, the group general managers involved should reach agreement on the specific assignment and obtain approval from the executive vice president.

Procedure for establishing provinces. Steps taken in defining established provinces, and which should be followed in establishing new provinces, are:

1. Appraise the skills, facilities, and resources available.
2. Identify the broad market areas in which the company is best equipped to operate.
3. Define the province in terms of: (a) class of customer or market served; (b) function to be performed, such as environmental conditioning; or (c) product line, such as scientific equipment.

Suggestions for new provinces may be sent to the director, new products services, research laboratories. New product services will make the required study of the proposal for a new province, utilizing corporate staff departments as required, and make recommendations for final screening by the planning committee. Recommendation of a new province designation and its assignment to a group general manager will be reviewed by the executive vice president and approved by the president before becoming effective.

Objectives.   The broad intent of the province concept is to encourage and facilitate the profitable growth of the company and its organization units. Specific objectives are:

1. Identify the business areas to which the company's efforts should be directed so that its basic strengths are employed most profitably.
2. Provide focal points of responsibility for broad areas of business opportunity.
3. Develop plans and techniques for selling and accepting responsibility for the end result required by a customer, rather than emphasizing individual products.
4. Attempt to sell and receive adequate payment for consulting, application, and systems engineering as part of complex equipment negotiations.
5. Explore all possibilities for profitably selling service, installation, continuing maintenance, and replacement.
6. Consider leases and rentals as a means of obtaining plus business or extra profit.
7. Develop coordinated marketing plans for broad groups of products that serve an industry or class of customer.
8. Utilize purchased components or products to round out a line, complete a system, or expand a service, where desirable.
9. Consider the advantages of entering into license agreements in areas where the company does not have potential design leadership.

Working relationships.   To assure the success of province marketing and, at the same time, preserve the authority and responsibility of profit-center managers for their own operations, there must be close cooperation among the company's various organization units.

Assignment of province responsibility does *not* establish a new layer of corporate authority within the organization. Province assignment involves the obligation of group general managers to develop soundly conceived plans that will encourage voluntary, enthusiastic participation of all organization units to meet customers' defined needs.

If plans are soundly conceived, all participants will benefit. Province marketing plans, therefore, must incorporate advantages to customers and to the company as a whole.

Each profit center within its charter is expected to use all appropriate company strengths in developing its business. A group may wish to enlist from other parts of the company such strengths as research and development, specific products and components, cooperative marketing, cooperative engineering applications, systems design, and other available services.

In the case of conflicting interests among divisions, adequate consideration must be given not only to the effect of the decision on the future profitable growth of the profit center, but also to the obligation of all to act in the company's interest. In working out solutions to such problems, the best interests of the company should be paramount.

The following rules, which recognize the interests of profit centers and provinces, are expected to be interpreted from both the long-range and the short-range points of view:

1. Divisions are free to refuse to develop or provide components that are covered by their charter when, in their judgment, it is not to their advantage to do so.
2. In the event of such refusal, the requesting division may:
   (a) Offer to underwrite the development or excessive cost.
   (b) Develop and produce the needed component for incorporation in its product or system (but not for outside sale as a component).
   (c) Purchase the development or component needed from an outside supplier.

Some province marketing situations will develop where it is desirable to approach a customer on a corporate basis. This permits taking advantage of the wide range of the company's products and services to simplify the purchasing problems of the customer. It allows offering such services as coordination of product design, programming of scheduled deliveries to a construction site, corporate-wide financing or leasing plans, and arranging for blanket maintenance service. Advantages in selling on a corporate basis may also arise in certain trade relation situations.

The degree to which it is desirable for a province marketing unit to perform the selling function for products, systems, or services of other profit centers will vary with different marketing situations. It is important that province marketing be reconciled with the normal marketing plans of each profit center involved, and it is equally important that profit centers whose products or services are offered as part of a corporate proposal agree to the proposed marketing plan.

Systems selling. Systems selling will be stimulated by the province approach. With a rapidly changing technology, systems are becoming increasingly important and are expanding in complexity and scope. Customers, therefore, will tend to rely increasingly on organizations that are knowledgeable about systems and can supply them to the customer's advantage. In the marketing of systems, the company should accept responsibility for the end result. Rather than using the "bill of material" approach, the company's selling efforts should concentrate on the economic benefits to the customer from a guaranteed performance.

The marketing of systems requires close cooperation between marketing and engineering. Through their joint efforts, they must:

1. Develop an intimate knowledge of the customer's system needs.
2. Design a system to fit the defined need.
3. Determine that the system is economically sound.
4. Stimulate product development to permit improved systems.
5. Formulate practical plans for providing the needed customer services.

Evaluating performance.   Under the province concept, group general managers have a responsibility not only for supervision of the divisions that report to them, but also for management of the corporate profitable growth in their provinces.

Total corporate profitable growth within a province is the primary objective of the province concept. Sound market position is essential, but it should not be achieved through a loss of total dollar profit. Group general managers are expected to exercise balanced judgment as between market participation and realized price in order to maximize total dollar profit.

Charters.   A charter is a written description of the specific responsibility of a profit center for supplying products, systems, or services. Although most charters will be built around product responsibility, it is possible for a charter to include the entire scope of a designated province.

A charter description should be based upon the present product line responsibilities of the profit center, but should be broad enough to provide opportunity for new product development. A charter responsibility may include design, development, manufacturing, and marketing.

A charter description should include the following elements:

1. General description of the market or class of customer, function, system, or product lines included
2. Specific products included
3. Closely related products excluded
4. Specific markets or classes of customers served
5. Marketing channels utilized

Initial preparation of charters will be done at the profit-center level. Tentative charter descriptions will be reviewed by group general managers to ensure complete coverage of the provinces assigned to their groups and to eliminate duplications among profit centers of the group.

The executive vice president will review and approve all charters in order to eliminate duplications and omissions among groups.

MERGERS AND ACQUISITIONS

A manufacturing company may expand its existing product line or diversify its product line by internal development, by mergers or acquisitions, or by both methods. Two chapters, "Management of Research and Development" and "Product Line Direction and Control," deal at length with the internal development route. The discussion that ensues will treat solely the merger and acquisition route.

This method has been widely followed for many years, but antitrust action of more recent time has created almost insurmountable roadblocks for some enterprises. An exploration of this corporate practice among the participating companies reveals a situation somewhat as follows.

Virtually all are precluded from enlarging their existing product lines or adding a closely related product line through merger or acquisition. Greater freedom, however, is felt when such ventures are in the foreign field. For product line diversification, most of the companies have more legal room in which to maneuver. Those companies already highly diversified and not dominant in the industrial areas of which they are a component part are quite active and aggressive in pursuing compatible affiliations. This situation also applies to most of the companies that, although leaders in their respective industries, seek through merger or acquisition to move into completely unrelated products and markets.

TOP MANAGEMENT INVOLVEMENT

The merger or acquisition process consists of six steps: identification, initiation, evaluation, negotiation, consummation, and integration. How do companies go about this process? In various ways, if the practices of those involved in this study are typical.

The first stage is actually the pinpointing of specific prospects. To avoid aimless search and needless deliberation, some companies have developed guidelines to give meaningful direction to this phase of the process. These criteria may be broadly and briefly stated; one company merely said, "An eligible candidate is one that fits our engineering, manufacturing, and distribution capabilities." Another company prepared a more extended statement of objectives:

1. Our divisions will consider the acquisition of manufacturing companies not competitive with existing operations.
2. A proposed acquisition should be compatible with our capabilities to the extent that benefits can be gained from our technical, manufacturing, and marketing strengths in one or more of the following fields [here eight different industries were mentioned].
3. Even though it is outside our presently established product and market areas, a potential acquisition may be of interest if it has unusual growth possibilities. If the business is quite unrelated to our present knowledge and experience, the candidate company must have competent management willing to continue with the operation.

4. A possible acquisition should have sales in the $10 million to $60 million range and a demonstrated record of profit growth. This size stipulation is important in the conservation of the time of top management as it requires about as much effort to acquire a small enterprise as a large one.

5. A company having annual sales of less than $10 million or in a distress situation will not be considered favorably unless its product lines are clearly compatible with at least one division's operation, thereby permitting effective integration.

Which management personnel are involved in step one? In several of the operating companies a high-level vice president is given the principal responsibility of identifying likely prospects. In other companies — particularly if divisionalized — the divisions are encouraged and expected to nominate appropriate candidates. In virtually all the companies, the chief executive officer assumes some responsibility and takes some part in this initial step. Participation by an outside director might occur, but no company held such action to be a part of a board member's duty.

Step two, initiation, is the exploratory stage of the process—the making of formal or informal overtures to a candidate company. Here company practices are similar. Because of the strategic factors attendant at this phase, tight procedural control is generally followed. Moreover, it is at this stage that the chief executive officer and others in top management are "calling the signals."

One company has a diversification committee composed of the six top executives who screen all candidates and make recommendations to the board of directors for a decision to pursue the venture further or to drop it. In another company, the chief executive officer used these words: "I get into the act as the opening curtain goes up. If there are valid reasons why the project is not feasible, it would be unrealistic to waste time and effort on further consideration." A third company, which has successfully followed the merger and acquisition route for many years, permits no overtures whatever until the three top officers are informed and decide what action to take. This company also requires the chief executive officer to make the intial contact to demonstrate sincerity of interest and overcome any resistance to discussion.

Step three is the fact-finding stage. It involves the assembly of all the pertinent data that can be obtained. This is done in some companies by an ad hoc committee created for the specific purpose; in other companies one of the qualified staff departments is assigned the task. To provide sufficient information for evaluation and to ensure comparability if more than one candidate company is under consideration, one of the participating companies equips its fact-finders with the following check list:

1. Complete product literature.
2. Brief summary of the company's sales organization and method of distribution.
3. Copies of the balance sheets and income statements covering the past five years. Explanation should be provided regarding any unusual expenses reflected in the statements: large salaries and bonuses, nonrecurring profits or losses, and so forth.
4. Current order backlog with comparable past figures.
5. Breakdown of dollar and unit sales by products or major product groups, including gross margins.
6. List of significant competitors in each major product line. Estimate of the market size and the percentage held by the subject company and by each competitor.
7. List of issued patents and general indication of any new product developments nearing successful completion.
8. Indication of the seller's basis for valuing the company and degree of ownership influenced by the seller.

An extended version of the above check list is shown in the Appendix at the end of this chapter. Data thus developed and analyzed become the basis for proceeding with the next phase.

The fourth step, negotiation, is the confrontation between the principal executives of the two parties. Usually the chief executive officer, either alone or supported by appropriate members of his top-level team, occupies the key role. The end result of these deliberations is the mutually agreed-upon plan that forms the basis for the next step.

The fifth step, consummation, is the final wrap-up of all that has gone before. If steps three and four particularly have been carried out in a sound, thorough, and equitable manner, and if the boards of directors have been kept fully informed during the various stages, step five can be virtually a *pro forma* validation even though stockholder approval is necessary.

The last step, integration, may turn out to be the most troublesome stage of the entire process of merging or acquiring. An affiliation may be brilliantly conceived, may present undeniable advantages, may give every promise of success, but, because of failure to plan properly for the assimilation, it can be fraught with disappointment and frustration. Reconciliation of policies, disturbed morale, and human inertia are but a few of the inherent problems.

The smooth consolidation of operations and personnel requires, as already indicated, an awareness of the intrinsic problems and a well-thought-out plan to resolve them. One company with long and successful experience in the process of merging and acquiring sums up its philosophy with respect to absorbing a new entity as follows:

> We never acquire a company unless it has good management. Our strategy is to disturb the new operation as little as possible. We try to standardize accounting and financial reporting at the earliest practicable time. We then give attention to the industrial relations area with a view to making whatever adjustments are necessary. Of course, before final consummation of the acquisition, the future status of key personnel will have been agreed upon, and basic policies, such as pricing, will have been made consistent with those of the parent company.

A LOOK AHEAD

The urge to merge and the desire to acquire are not new corporate objectives nor, despite the constraints imposed by antitrust actions, are they hopeless ones. As pointed out earlier in this discussion, the present attitudes and future outlook of top executives in the participating companies run the full gamut. One company's position was tersely expressed as follows: "As far as acquisitions or mergers are concerned, we might as well forget them. The door is closed, locked, and bolted." At the opposite end of the scale, the following quote epitomizes the position of another company: "We have done a lot of screening and currently are looking at 40 to 50 companies. The top ten or twelve of them will be given major consideration. We expect to be very much involved in the area of mergers and acquisitions for at least the next ten years."

So, a forward look at corporate growth and product diversification through mergers or acquisitions is for some companies a dead issue, while for others it is a positive and planned way of business life.

APPENDIX: CHECKLIST USED BY ONE COMPANY TO DEVELOP INFORMATION FOR EVALUATING AN ACQUISITION POSSIBILITY

Personnel

1. Brief résumé including title, age, year employed, background, and experience of key management personnel available to continue with the business. Similar data, if practical, for sales and engineering personnel.
2. Listing of annual salary, bonus, and any other compensation received by the foregoing key management people.
3. Tabulation of overall company employment showing number of personnel in each principal department on fixed salary, indirect hourly and direct hourly wages. If practical, develop an organization chart to show scope of executive and departmental responsibility.
4. Summary outlining any management bonus, salesman's bonus, general profit sharing, medical and life insurance, or retirement programs covering the company's employees. Copies of contracts, if available.
5. Listing of union contracts showing name of union, number of employees represented, wage schedule, contract expiration or reopening dates, and principal fringe benefits covered. Copies of contracts if available.
6. Average shop wage rates by work centers. Hourly or piece rate? Comparison of these rates with competition and with other industries in the community.
7. History of labor relations. Frequency and severity of work stoppages. Has there been any unusual turnover of personnel? Has there been any difficulty in obtaining labor?

Financial

1. Copies of audited balance sheets and operating statements for past five years with interim statement to date.
2. Current order backlog with comparable figures for at least one prior year.
3. Breakdown of dollar and/or unit sales for at least two years, preferably five, on the following bases as appropriate:

   a. By product or major product groups including parts and service
   b. By geographical territory
   c. By method of distribution
   d. By month
   e. By principal users accounting for roughly 80 percent of sales
   f. By market

4. Breakdown of gross profits by products or major product groups for at least two years, preferably five. If on standard costs, outline standards procedure and obtain variance analysis for the two-year period.

5. Breakdown of cost of sales for at least two years, preferably five, to clearly indicate direct labor, material, factory overhead, and any other charges that are normally made to cost of sales. Detail on factory overhead is desired.

6. Breakdown of charges under selling and advertising, engineering, and general administrative expenses.

7. Brief statement on depreciation policies, bad debt write-offs, and inventory obsolescence practices. Date of latest physical inventory. Obtain the amounts of write-offs during the past five years.

8. Schedule of insured value of buildings, equipment, and inventories.

9. Comment on any unusual charges such as royalties received, interest payments, capital gains, and so forth, under other income and other deductions.

10. Schedule of all company loans or debentures outstanding including name of lender, interest payments, payment requirements, and restrictions. Comment on any warrants or stock options outstanding.

11. Statement of preferred and common stock authorization as well as the date and state of incorporation. Review directors' meeting minutes as well as corporate charter and bylaws for items of significance.

12. Distribution of key stockholders constituting at least 85 percent of the voting shares outstanding.

13. Statement on the latest year for which statements have been reviewed by the Internal Revenue Service. Include the settlement amounts paid during the past five years. Statement of existing tax credits, losses, and so forth. Summary of state and local tax situations.

14. Schedule of any important contractual agreements not elsewhere covered, such as employment contracts, material purchase contracts, or any other commitments that may be of continuing obligation to the company.

15. Brief summary of all litigation during the past five years which resulted in any substantial loss or gain to the company. Include all litigation still pending.

16. Management's best estimate of annual sales and operating profits during the next five years. Indicate any new products that are expected to contribute significantly to the company's sales volume. Include estimate of major capital requirements for equipment and facilities that will be needed to realize management's forecast of future operations. Also indicate any industry indices that have some correlation to the company's general business activity.

17. Extent of management control techniques used—budgets, and so forth.

Marketing

1. Outline of sales organization and methods of distribution.
2. Salesman's compensation arrangement and outline of field expense policies.
3. Tabulation of geographical sales coverage showing territorial coverage; number of sales, service, or other personnel assigned; and names and addresses of manufacturers' representatives, agents, distributors, jobbers, and dealers.
4. Copies of standard sales agreements used with manufacturers' representatives, agents, distributors, jobbers, or dealers.
5. Schedule of discounts extended to various levels of distribution.
6. List of major competitors with estimate of the market portion held by each.
7. Complete set of current product catalog literature with price lists covering the past five years.
8. Recognizable advantages that the company and its products have over competitors, and comparable advantages of competitors.
9. Long-range market forecast for the company's industry and product lines.

Engineering

1. Brief résumé of the name, title, age, service, and technical training of engineering department personnel.
2. List of principal company products that have been contributed by this engineering group.
3. Market introduction date of each important product line.
4. Outline of any significant development programs underway.

Patents

1. Listing of issued patents and applications including number, expiration date, and identification of product covered.
2. Brief summary of the significance of these patents.
3. Name and address of patent counsel and clearance for our attorney to contact if necessary.
4. Schedule of all royalty agreements including name of licensor or licensee, royalty rate, prepayments made, term of agreement, and product covered. Copies of agreements, if appropriate.

Asking price

1. An indication of the asking price and preferred method of payment.
2. Seller's basis for valuing the company.
3. Seller's reasons for considering sale.

Manufacturing

1. Description of plant facilities, including office and engineering, machinery, and equipment, to include amount and condition of auxiliary equipment such as tools, patterns, and materials handling equiment.
2. Layout or sketch of physical factory arrangement. Availability of transportation facilities, adequacy of water or power supplies, and possibilities for plant expansion.
3. If significant, indication of the source and tonnage of raw steel supplies, as well as iron, steel, and nonferrous castings and forgings.
4. Data on all outside subcontract manufacturing being done, including amount, types of work, material furnished, and so forth.
5. Copy of any recent appraisal report on plant and equipment.

INTERNATIONAL
OPERATIONS

8

In the past decade international operations have provided a tremendous opportunity for American business, according to the experience of the companies participating in this study. In a number of cases, the return on investment has been higher overseas than at home, and many of the companies have found that sales abroad grew at a substantially greater rate than in the domestic market.

The long-term prospects for further growth in international operations are impressive, for several reasons. Abroad, the development of the Common Market in Europe will open a substantial market for trade without tariff barriers. This development, of course, will provide a great stimulus for American firms to establish or enlarge manufacturing plants in Europe and thus protect their production for the Common Market from the tariff barriers to outsiders. Another factor favoring the growth of international operations is the economic advancement taking place in many underdeveloped countries. As the economies of these nations develop, they will become both better suppliers and more attractive markets. The years ahead will see millions of people added to the effective market potential in numerous overseas lands.

In view of these prospects, it is not surprising that the director of corporate planning for one of the participating companies said, "Our growth and investment opportunities are greater abroad than in the U.S." A member of the executive committee of another firm commented, "In 1965 our international sales were $150 million, and by 1970 we are forecasting international sales of $400 million." This is an annual growth compounded at a rate of more than twenty percent each year.

FACTORS INFLUENCING INTERNATIONAL OPERATIONS

In the earlier study primary attention was given to organizational problems and structure related to international activities. Because of the increased importance of international operations today, several additional factors that affect foreign operations have been included in this study: cost, government policies, market characteristics, and changing conditions.

Cost.   Manufacturing, transportation, and distribution cost considerations have a substantial influence upon major decisions in the field of international operations. Top management in the participating companies is deeply concerned with comparative cost studies of labor, materials, transportation, and distribution when determining where new facilities should be located or new markets opened. Changes in labor costs in certain countries, improved transportation equipment and facilities, and more sophisticated inventory control and information systems have had tremendous influence during recent years upon top management's decisions in the area of international operations.

Executives in the participating companies made frequent references to savings and cost reductions resulting from shipping domestic parts to assembly plants overseas.

Distribution costs are also of vital importance to top management. The executive vice president of one of the participating companies pointed this out: "It's fine to be a low-cost manufacturer, but to be competitive you also have to distribute at a low cost." In a number of the firms studied, this objective was accomplished at low-volume levels by having the international division serve as manager of certain foreign activities until the market or product line could support the expense of a separate sales and distribution staff in the area concerned. The importance of such an arrangement was alluded to by a consumer products executive: "If we've made mistakes, it's in buying companies that were too small to throw off enough profit to establish a good distribution system." Of course, distribution costs are also important at the high-volume end of the spectrum. One of the firms studied plans to use huge ships that can go into very few ports because of their draft. At a port in Ireland, these ships will transfer their cargo to smaller vessels for delivery to various ports in Europe.

Another, even more important area of influence on international operations lies in the various aspects of government policy.

Government policy. Both at home and abroad government policies are of primary concern to top management. Such factors as tariffs, political climate, foreign currency risks, tax policies, local content policies, investment participation policies, antitrust policies, and balance of payment policies enter into all major decisions in international operations.

Tariffs. Tariffs are an obvious way in which foreign governments can influence the location and organization of international operations. In many of the companies studied, tariff savings were a major reason for locating manufacturing plants abroad.

Political climate. Even if tariffs are favorable, a hostile or unfavorable political environment can be a serious deterrent to successful operations within a particular country. The risks range all the way from expropriation of capital facilities to minor inconveniences such as delayed customs inspections, sabotage, and damages resulting from careless handling of materials and equipment. Political pressures of one sort or another may result in decisions that are not to the best long-term interests of the company.

The president of one of the participating companies described the impact of political climate in a foreign country upon top management decisions as follows:

> All the economic factors and the various financial alternatives have been carefully analyzed with respect to opening a large new production facility in a certain foreign country. Everything looks very favorable except for one factor—the political situation in the country. Our final decision on this proposed project will, in all probability, be made on the basis of our best judgment as to what is likely to happen politically in this country during the next five years.

Tax savings and currency risks. Taxes and foreign currency risks are significant factors in determining the nature and structure of international operations. A major industry supplier may find that the tax preference available is a major reason for establishing manufacturing facilities as subsidiaries in various foreign countries. Or the company may find that serious inflation, such as that experienced in Brazil in the early 1960s, may more than offset any possible tax advantages. Most of the participating companies with foreign plants give considerable freedom to the local management on such matters as financing accounts receivable, inventories, and such matters. However, major decisions on capital expenditures are usually reserved for top management.

Local content policies. Many countries have adopted policies that are intended to encourage foreign firms to establish manufacturing operations in the market country. The goal of these policies is to increase the local content or value added within the foreign country. In some cases the proportion of local content is raised over the years so that the operation is converted from a minor assembly activity to a complete manufacturing process. South Africa is an example of a nation that has used this approach for several years to implement its policy of increased economic self-sufficiency. As a result, automobile manufacturing operations in that country are probably far more elaborate than they otherwise would be.

Investment participation policies. Constant pressure is being exerted by many foreign governments to obtain a larger local ownership share in United States companies with operations abroad. Most of the firms studied prefer to maintain sole ownership of the overseas operations; however, several companies have accepted foreign stock ownership in their subsidiaries as a means of obtaining a more favorable business and social climate. In most instances the joint ownership ventures have been very successful. However, executives in a few companies expressed strong preferences for worldwide ownership of the parent company's stock. The chairman of the board of one participating firm commented: "If we are to have a truly international company, the stock investment of foreigners should be in parent company stock rather than in subsidiary stock." This company has been very aggressive and successful in retaining sole ownership of its foreign subsidiaries.

A different and intriguing approach to this problem is under study by one of the participating companies. It plans to make management contracts with foreign companies in which it holds a minority interest. These contracts are expected to be attractive to the overseas stockholders of the foreign companies, and to give a wholly owned subsidiary of the parent company full authority to run these minority ownership foreign affiliates. Two advantages are foreseen: (1) avoidance of controversy and friction about foreign stock ownership in overseas subsidiaries, and (2) a leverage opportunity to exercise control over far greater assets than are owned. This plan and its implications will be discussed at some length later in this chapter.

Antitrust policies. Recent antitrust decisions in the United States have also had an effect on the organization and development of international activities by the firms studied. After the Imperial Chemicals case and the General Motors court decisions, both relating to marketing agreements with overseas firms, a member of the executive committee of one of the companies participating in this study stated that he would not seriously consider a major acquisition abroad.

Balance of payments. At every company visited, top management was very much aware of the United States government's concern over actions that may affect the country's current trade balance. It was quite evident that executives recognized and accepted the need to cooperate with the government in attempting to maintain a favorable balance of trade for the United States. The vice president for international operations of one company explained that his big problem was how to export American capital and still keep peace with Washington. This company had $350 million available in the United States for overseas investment. However, because of United States government pressure, it was expected that most of the new overseas investment that year would have to be financed from foreign borrowing at 8 to 10 percent interest rates, and/or from the profits generated by the current activities abroad. This situation was typical of those described by executives in the other companies.

From this brief review, it seems clear that government policies provide many restrictions on the freedom and decision alternatives of top management in companies engaged in international operations. It is also clear, however, that the executives in the companies visited recognize the challenge and opportunities that exist in international operations.

Market characteristics.   The overseas market for a product may differ from the United States market in a variety of ways. Determining these differences, and deciding how to deal with them, is a key problem area for executives engaged in international operations. These market differences are especially noticeable in product preferences and requirements, distribution patterns, and need for interchangeability.

In photographic work, for example, some overseas markets prefer dull prints and object to the glossy prints so common in America. In publications, too, the market differences are important. In Europe, the sepia shade in rotogravure is preferred in newspaper picture sections, whereas in the United States this type of picture has almost disappeared.

Even more significant are differences in consumer tastes and habits in things as fundamental as food. Differences in eating habits are, in many cases, quite independent of availability, nutritional values, or cost of the food products. Such differences are almost purely a matter of taste and custom.

A particularly difficult problem of market differences is illustrated by the experience of the agricultural equipment and earthmoving equipment industries. In this case, the acceptance of standard United States equipment for earthmoving is virtually worldwide. However, in agricultural tractors, even machines that are technically well suited to the job may be unpopular because of established preferences as to horsepower. As a result, American manufacturers are likely to sell lower horsepower farming tractors in Europe than in the United States, but exactly the same horsepower bulldozers in either market, for the same kinds of jobs.

With these differences in mind, it would seem easy to anticipate the market requirements for other farm machinery. However, fresh complications rise to plague the marketing executive. A combine that performs well in the United States will be unsatisfactory in Europe. This time, the problem is the result of physical differences — the density of grain per square foot is greater in European farming than in American. Differences may also exist on purely nationalistic bases. Fiat wants to use tires made in Italy, and Volkswagen prefers tires made in Germany. Tastes as to the interior trim of automobiles have differed enough to make this a favorable factor in determining to build manufacturing plants abroad. The size of the typical European automobile is a clear example of a difference in product requirements between the United States and the overseas market. There, the higher tax on gasoline and vehicles has produced a strong demand for small automobiles and motor scooters. Some other product choices are related to experience and information. For example, many European trucking firms prefer the radial tire because it is cheaper than the conventional tire, in cost per mile. In the United States, where the knowledge and use of tire recapping is greater, trucking firms find that the increased ease of recapping conventional tires gives them a lower cost per mile. In the field of electrical appliances, the voltage and frequency of the current available set certain operating requirements for products.

In terms of organization for international operations, product preferences and requirements can be controlling factors. Thus, it may be desirable to organize manufacturing and sales by market areas rather than by product line to permit better adjustment to particular marketing needs. Where national feelings are important, separate subsidiaries may be required for each major country. This need in turn can impose special problems on the parent company for direction and coordination of its overseas subsidiaries.

Speaking of distribution patterns, the president of a large consumer products company said, "Product division integration on a world basis does not make sense because the companies which have been acquired outside the United States are in many different kinds of products." To use a product division type of organization abroad in a situation where each overseas subsidiary handles several different product lines would mean that many of these overseas subsidiares would have two or three bosses within the parent company. The executive vice president of a large, diversified manufacturing company described a firm, acquired in Spain, whose product lines cut across corporate groups as well as product divisions. In these several illustrations, the problem might have been avoided by simply expanding abroad through the existing product line organizations; however, this may not be the best way to develop a market promptly, and it may not be the most profitable approach to international operations in particular cases.

Even where product divisions are not involved, differences in distribution systems may be necessary. The president of the international company of a large American manufacturer stated, "There are significant differences in distribution patterns and methods between United

States and overseas. There is little franchise trading around the world. Overseas, even when the corporation operates its own outlets, it may have to carry other manufacturers' products as well as its own. There's a practical limit as to how much business you can get."

Here again, the emphasis for organization is on the market characteristics. What organization pattern is best adapted to the overseas situation, and are the advantages of this type of organization worth the problems it creates in coordination and control for the parent company?

The need for interchangeability obviously depends on the nature of the product and its use. Where a product varies substantially between United States and various overseas markets, as in automobiles, there is not much need for interchangeability of parts. However, where a product is nearly standard throughout the world markets, such as 35 mm camera film in several speeds, substitutability becomes a marketing essential.

This feature of interchangeability can also apply in the field of spare parts. The executive vice president of a large equipment manufacturer commented, "Our international operation is vitally affected by the fact that the company decided to build the same products at home and abroad." In this case, the equipment manufacturer does not try to produce identical parts for its equipment around the world, but it does make sure that the parts for particular units are interchangeable regardless of the country of manufacture.

The two examples of substantially uniform products seem rather simple in their organizational implications. For these products, the organization structure abroad must be set up to assure a high degree of control and coordination. This is made easier by the fact that product preferences and requirements appear to make little difference in the market acceptability of these particular items around the world. But what of the company whose product lines must be different to sell in various major markets? Until such time as the various product lines generate an overseas volume sufficient to support separate manufacture and distribution, they will pose a continuing problem for the parent company. It must attempt to devise an organization structure that will best meet the special needs of its international operations at an acceptable cost.

Changing conditions.   Adapting to change is important as the overseas markets grow. The impact of a changing foreign market on organization was well expressed by one executive in the following terms:

When the international organization was set up, the determinants were not product oriented, but rather government, tax, people, customs, and area oriented. By 1960-62, however, competition became more sophisticated and product problems became more important than area problems. With the increasing demand for technical competence in the marketplace, it became quite clear that it would be better to have the international operations under control of the appropriate product divisions.

This clearly illustrates the need to shift from an area type of organization to a product type of organization as a result of changes in the overseas market.

Changes in organization structure may also arise from developments within the supplying company itself. This situation was described by the vice president for international operations of a large basic industry firm participating in this project:

Sequentially what happens internationally is: (1) Creation of an export department. (2) Establishment of a new company in a foreign country—provision of controls, auditors, acounting, and management—in 3 to 5 years. (3) Regional man reports to executive in parent company. This man is American but he speaks the foreign language and he serves as a liaison man. (4) Appointment of a technical man for the overseas area who reports to executive in parent company, but provides the technical capability needed. (5) Full integration with domestic division.

In contrast, the executive vice president of another company anticipates a change from a product division organization abroad to an area organization. He puts it, "Ultimately, maybe in ten years, if we have a lot of plants in Europe, we may go to a vice president for Europe, who will have charge of both manufacturing and sales in Europe."

Another strategy was explained by an executive from a consumer products company. He indicated that the growth at the international level had been largely to establish "beachheads" which would provide the opportunity for the company to enlarge them by adding other products from its existing lines.

MANAGEMENT FUNCTIONS ABROAD

As international operations of United States companies have developed, the changes have affected the problems and scope of several major business functions. These include top management direction of marketing, manufacturing, research and development, finance and control, long-range planning, and personnel management. As indicated previously, organization structure also has been significantly affected. In general, these changes reflect the increasing size of overseas opportunities and the tailoring of operations to fit these opportunities as managements develop a better understanding of them.

Top management direction. One of the cooperating companies with extensive world-wide operations has taken special measures to provide coordination and guidance by the parent company board of directors. Each member of this board is designated as contact director for a specific geographic area and/or for particular corporate staff departments. The contact director becomes the specialist on the board for the regions and functions assigned. He is expected to keep fully informed and to provide guidance and counsel for the overseas executives and the corporate staff officers concerned. For example, a member of the parent company board may be the contact director for South America and also may serve as contact director for one or more corporate staff departments such as transportation, purchasing, and so forth.

The contact directors serve as executive aides to the chief executive officer of the corporation. According to one senior officer of the company, in many firms the contact directors would be shown on the organization chart in a single box labeled "office of the chief executive." In the company discussed, the contact director is usually the sponsor of proposals coming from the operating companies. Sometimes the contact director may oppose a venture but nevertheless would introduce it before the board or the executive committee. On occasion an operating company may make its own presentation to the board. Officially, the president of an operating company has the authority to go directly to the president or the chairman of the parent corporation; however, this formal approach is rarely used.

The role of contact directors bears a striking resemblance to the functions of the individual members of the executive committee in another large firm. In this case, the executive committee members serve as counselors and coordinators for the various product divisions with their important world and domestic markets. This similarity in organizational roles is not surprising since it results from the same need—to find an effective means of top management coordination in a large, far-flung enterprise. As United States firms continue to grow and to expand their overseas interests, this pattern of coordination by top management appears likely to be used more widely.

Marketing. "The biggest problem in the international area is marketing," according to an executive vice president of one large, multidivision United States company. Understanding the market and what will appeal is one of the major difficulties, and it is made more confusing by the fact that American tastes, advertising, and promotional ideas are sometimes transferred to foreign countries with great success and at other times find little acceptance overseas.

Marketing difficulties in international operations involve a wide variety of factors including product design, operating conditions, and customer appeals. Several examples of these problems were discussed earlier in connection with product preferences and requirements. There appears to be no better answer than to get a detailed understanding of each major market. To obtain this detailed understanding, the firms participating in this study have tried a number of ideas:

Key headquarters jobs concerning overseas marketing are filled by men with substantial experience abroad. As yet, there are few foreign nationals in these positions. However, as executives from other countries continue to advance in United States companies and their subsidiaries, it seems certain that foreign nationals will occupy various key jobs in the parent companies.

Key jobs in overseas operations are being filled by qualified nationals or Americans with substantial experience in the overseas market.

Boards of directors of foreign subsidiary companies might appear to be a fine source of market "know-how" overseas. However, the companies that have developed their international operations to the point of running subsidiaries abroad often have already developed a considerable number of parent and subsidiary company management personnel who are well qualified to analyze overseas problems or offer recommendations. In addition, the board of directors of the overseas subsidiaries is often a legal formality and little else. In such cases, it is not likely to provide the kinds or numbers of executives needed to give expert advice on the problems of international operation.

Overseas advertising agencies have grown substantially in recent years. These foreign agencies and American advertising firms with offices abroad have provided another way in which the American businesses studied have been able to get a better understanding of foreign markets.

Market surveys and pilot projects have also proved useful. Recognizing that foreign markets can be unexpectedly different, some of the American firms studied have placed great emphasis on a detailed analysis before entering. In several cases, this careful market survey has been followed by a "pilot project" and then a series of further developments based on the results of the earlier experience.

This strategy is particularly appropriate when a substantial amount of innovation is involved in the marketing techniques, and when the magnitude of the potential market is not clear. In addition, this approach suggests that the competitive situation permits adequate time for utilizing a step-by-step development. On the other hand, if important rivals are firmly established in the foreign market, or if the marketing techniques and product lines are already well accepted, a more direct approach may be desirable. Such an approach would probably involve an accelerated investment and development program to establish a strong position as early as practicable.

Manufacturing. The scope of responsibilities in manufacturing operations abroad is often greater than is involved in similar assignments in the United States. An executive from the international division of a participating company gave two reasons for this: (1) The overseas plant will handle a great many more models of the company product, and (2) the overseas manager has to handle a wider range of problems, without headquarters staff assistance, in areas such as labor relations, financing, real estate, and so forth. It seems likely that this disadvantage will be reduced as the overseas operations grow in size and are able to justify their own specialist staffs.

In another way manufacturing abroad has had some advantages, at least for certain companies. The vice president and general manager of a large manufacturing division in one firm explained:

> Rebuilt machines can be sold at half the cost of latest automated equipment. This allows my division to replace its present machines faster. It gives overseas plants excellent machines at a minimum cost. Since overseas labor costs are lower than in the U.S., the rebuilt machines may be actually lower unit cost producers overseas than would be the latest automated machines at the full price. This policy also makes the international operations division a tougher competitor overseas because it gives that division lower investment and lower production costs.

Although these two examples may appear to offset one another, the difficulties of overseas manufacturing seem likely to be encountered far more often than the advantages. It appears that, for a long time to come, manufacturing abroad will involve some special challenges for managers beyond those faced by their counterparts in United States manufacturing plants.

Research and development. The scope of overseas research and development activities by the participating companies has varied greatly. In some cases, the differences are simply reflections of the fact that the parent companies' international operations are at different stages of development. In other cases, the differences in research and development activity appear to result from products or from management approaches.

Several levels of research and development activity can be distinguished among the companies studied. Perhaps these differences are best presented by comparing statements from some of the executives contacted:

Minimum research and development activity abroad. "Design and modification problems would funnel through international division offices and would then go to the appropriate operating domestic divisions. The solution would then be reported back through the international division to the customer." (From an executive in a multidivision manufacturing company.) In another company, the vice president for operating and technical services said: "When corporate research people are overseas, they do not, at present, look for areas of technical development the company should get into. They are looking at new developments in their assigned areas of research."

Some research and development facilities abroad. The president of the international company of a major United States manufacturing firm described its research and development activities overseas by explaining that most basic research (on raw materials, for example) is purchased from the parent company. There are two technical centers in the international division — one in Europe and one in South America. They do a lot of testing, product development, and research on components. Most of the research is applied — "it's more development than research." The vice president for international manufacturing in another large company described a similar situation very briefly: "Product innovation abroad is encouraged but not much is spent on it so most of the research and development *work* is done in the United States, and overseas operations mainly contribute ideas." The vice president and general manager of one of the divisions of this same firm put it this way: "Some new product research and development goes on overseas. The fellow who gets the idea usually has a chance to go further with it. Later, the work may be divided among several groups or plants. Duplication of effort is often allowed, to see who will get the best results."

Extensive research and development activities abroad. Greater emphasis on overseas research received strong endorsement from an executive vice president in one of the participating companies when he said, "Up to now, new product development has been primarily domestic. This must change." A number of ideas have come in from the international groups in this firm and greater emphasis on new product development abroad is expected. It is believed, however, that the international division of the company will also continue to handle some of this work for the overseas markets. An additional reason for this approach was cited by the executive vice president for international of a major basic materials company: "Foreign countries are concerned about the 'brain drain' and therefore there is pressure to encourage more research being done in foreign countries."

Finance and control.   The philosophy on finance and control in international operations is quite permissive in a number of the firms studied. A fairly detailed statement of this approach was given by the executive vice president for international of one company when he said, "Each overseas venture is expected to stand on its own feet and work within the appropriation provided. Each venture has an annual budget which is proposed to, and reviewed by the . . . board of directors, even if it is a 51 percent French company. . . . As long as the overseas venture is running within its budget, the overseas management can do pretty much as it sees fit." Further inquiry revealed that long-range plans and new facility proposals are carefully reviewed in the United States.

In another participating company, which prides itself on the autonomy of its divisions, an executive vice president explained that the largest overseas subsidiary "is operated very much like a . . . division. This would be quite different if the parent company had only a partial interest in an overseas enterprise."

In one of the leading "light manufacturing" companies, there was a philosophy of informal control but still a good deal of participation in the management of the overseas activities by the executives from the parent organization. The vice president for corporate international operations expressed the approach in these terms: "The top officers want as few things as possible to come to them, and they expect others to get the job done. One of the top officers preaches, 'If you are so cautious that you never make mistakes, you are not doing your job!' " The vice president continued, "We allow the people in charge of the foreign divisions considerable freedom in the determination of the product line. For example, the local manager in charge of our German operations may get together with the European marketing manager and they may decide that it is no longer economical to continue to manufacture a particular item. If so, they would then negotiate with the appropriate domestic division manager."

The executive vice president for marketing of an equipment manufacturing company explained that their policy "is to manage by getting around and visiting operations." He had been to Europe three times in six months and also once to Japan. The question "Does this apply to the world?" was frequently used in considering new ideas and policies.

Regardless of policies and procedures for coordination and control, it seems likely that the vice president and general manager of a division in a major consumer products company went to the heart of the matter when he said, "We get cooperation and coordination because people want to make it work, not because there is a system for making it work."

In contrast to the permissive philosophy on management control in international operations, financial control appears to be very definite in many of the participating companies. For example, the president of the international company of one firm said, "In essence, the decision on financing any place in the world is made here. . . . We are not about to make the subsidiaries more independent. . . . In a word, I think we will see more centralization, not less centralization." An executive in the international operations of another company said, "Plant managers are responsible for production and sales, but the financial responsibility goes through the treasurer and to a top-level committee to headquarters." These comments are reinforced by statements from other corporations indicating that the profit-center concept is regarded as an effective way to provide financial control. As a senior executive at one large equipment manufacturer put it, "We all like the profit-center concept and try to work at this whether we are thinking domestically or internationally."

One of the special features of international operations is the handling of foreign currency problems, which appears to be done centrally in most of the companies studied. Here are statements concerning the practice at three of the corporations with large overseas business: (1) "Foreign currency problems are handled largely by the vice president for finance of the international division but the corporate vice president for finance helps him worry, too." (2) "Local plant managers do not have authority to speculate in currency devaluation. This is done at headquarters." (3) "The treasurer's office handles all money transactions for all worldwide operations."

A very specific picture of a more decentralized way of handling this problem was provided by the vice president for finance of still another company involved in the project: "Protection against inflation in manufacturing and sales overseas is the responsibility of the management personnel overseas." The vice president for finance and his staff offer advice and assistance. A special committee has been set up for this. It includes:

Vice president for finance (chairman)
Vice president for overseas divisions (two of them)
Vice president for corporate planning
Treasurer
Controller
Corporate economist
Assistant to the president

This committee meets monthly, or more often, and goes over the situation country by country. Results of discussions and recommendations are submitted to the executive committee.

Pricing is another important aspect of finance and control. Here again, for various reasons, central control or coordination is often provided. An executive vice president and director of one of the participating firms explained: "The need for protection from political pressure is so great that, in spite of differences in production costs, all affiliates adhere to the same price list on transfers among themselves." A producer of less critical products has the policy that, "Price control is handled through the international marketing organization. The theory is to make prices equitable throughout the world. The Common Market has more or less forced a common price in this market." The vice president of international manufacturing for this firm added, "Overseas prices are nearly uniform and are basically a result of coordination among various manufacturing plants and the international markets division. A distributor doesn't take action to raise the price without consultation because this would simply shift the demand to another company source."

The pattern for finance and control of international operations may be summarized as central authority or coordination, and participation by the overseas management in consideration of specific problems. As we shall see below, this pattern is similar to that developed on long-range planning relating to overseas activities.

Long-range planning. In many cases, the management function of planning ahead for overseas operations did not receive attention until current problems were brought under control. Speaking of his own firm, the assistant general manager of the international division of a consumer products company indicated that "in the past the international division has been so busy in acquisitions and in getting the operations going that there has been no time to do long-range planning or to establish criteria for future growth." Of course, as United States companies have become better established in the various overseas markets, increased attention has been paid to long-range planning.

In general, United States firms can be divided into three categories in terms of their long-range planning for overseas activities: (1) Some firms doubt the value of attempting specific, comprehensive plans. (2) Some concentrate on operating plans for about five years ahead. (3) Some survey trends and facilities requirements ten to twenty years in the future.

An example of the first category is provided by the statement of the executive vice president for international of a leading basic materials corporation: "The international division has long-range planning of a general nature. It is difficult to put dollar figures for X number of years. Rather, you look at specific proposals and time of opportunity."

The second category is illustrated by comments from several of the companies studied. From a large, multidivision manufacturing company: "We run a five-year program by quarters. This includes projected profit and loss, personnel plans, new product schedules, and gross margin by products for every product." The vice president for corporate international operations of a participating company explained, "On the international front we had done very little long-range planning until 1965 when we established a five-year plan. We made a five-year forecast for each of the three manufacturing companies. We tried to make a sales forecast by products. On an area basis, we have done a fairly good job of forecasting sales for a one-year period. We have forecast within 5 percent of actual." A similar approach is taken by another large company. The head of the international operations indicated, "We make a seven-year forecast of automobile registrations for every country in the world. This is converted to a forecast for *our* products over the next seven years. This is necessary to develop a five-year financial forecast."

The third category, firms that make projections for ten to twenty years ahead, is illustrated by one of the largest manufacturing companies studied. It has a group of about twenty headquarters people concerned with ten-year projections. They look ahead on particular projects, possible acquisitions, and so forth. This group handles matters on the economics side and has nothing to do with finance. The long-range planning group works with the line organization and consolidates the total for all the overseas divisions. The data are then presented to the overseas policy group. Another example of these longer-range plans was found in a large consumer products manufacturing company, where, according to the vice president for international operations, long-range planning goes twenty years ahead on basic facilities overseas.

It seems likely that more and more American firms will do long-range planning for about five years ahead on their overseas activities. This may be simply a by-product of similar development for their domestic operations. Firms with major overseas investment prospects probably will take a good look at really long-term projections of their facilities and capital requirements. The trend of development in long-range planning is likely to be an increase in the number of firms that follow the medium and long-term planning steps already taken by some leaders in international operations. Since there appears to be little justification for going more than twenty years ahead in projections, even for capital equipment, the leading firms probably will perfect their techniques rather than increase the time periods covered by their projections. Long-range planning will almost certainly be another area in which international operations will benefit from developments on the domestic scene.

Personnel management.   A number of companies have made it a point to arrange for personnel regularly assigned in the United States to get some familiarity with overseas operations. The executive vice president for marketing of a major equipment manufacturer described the policy of his company: "Our home office personnel have heard many detailed presentations and management questions on overseas matters. The company has also 'travelled people' on a frequent and casual basis. This improves their perspective on, and understanding of, overseas matters. All the officers have been abroad many times on company affairs." He added that practically all department heads (below officer level) had been to every overseas manufacturing location of the company. He felt that this also rubbed off on their associates through office and other discussions. A similar approach was taken last year by the chairman of one of the large consumer products companies. He sent the directors who were not full-time employees of the company to various European countries — primarily for their education in the overseas business of the company.

With this kind of interest in the international orientation of non-overseas personnel, it is not surprising that even more attention has been given to the special requirements and features of overseas duty assignments. These are briefly discussed below.

Recruiting and selection. The practices of one large company with extensive overseas activities provides a useful illustration of changes that have taken place in the area of personnel recruiting and selection. In this firm, personnel recruiting was once aimed at getting domestic *or* export people. It was formerly thought that business school graduates were all right for domestic assignments but that an engineering degree was necessary for export jobs — partly because of the nature of the work and partly because of the prestige some people abroad attached to the title "engineer." Now the company recruits with the intention of using the employees anywhere in the world.

This same company formerly staffed overseas operations by taking an excellent number two man from a domestic operation and sending him abroad to take charge. It is now felt that it is far more difficult to start a small new operation, particularly abroad, than to keep a big one going. For this reason, the company now picks the best man for the overseas job and promotes an excellent number two man to replace the executive sent overseas. In spite of emphasis on getting the best man in terms of job performance, however, the company has learned "the hard way" that personal adaptability of the man and his family is far more significant in overseas assignments than in domestic jobs.

A somewhat different policy on overseas selection was described by a vice president of a major consumer products company: "People are not required to go abroad nor are they penalized for not going. In staffing a new plant every case is reviewed separately. There are no rigid rules on sending an assistant manager from an existing plant (or a manager). . . . The company tries to find a rationale for each situation, not just to apply some established policy."

The significance of timing in overseas assignments was emphasized by the president of another international company: "The penalties, in many cases, are just as great for being too far ahead as they are for being too far behind. Anytime we take a man who has been around a while, has had say ten years experience domestically, and put him overseas, 99 times out of 100 it doesn't work." He indicated that the same results seemed to occur when men who had received their major experience abroad were brought to the United States.

It is clear that the recruiting and selection of men for overseas assignments is not an easy task, but what about the requirements for the wife? A director of one company commented on this point as follows: "Wives must be suitable for living abroad or a man shouldn't go into a foreign assignment. . . . The company tries to learn about the wife's attitude on these things by discussions with her. You can't be sure about the adjustment of either the man or the woman unless they have been abroad before. After a man has served abroad, if he liked it, he's a good bet for another overseas assignment elsewhere."

Problems of living abroad. Language difficulties are one of the most obvious problems in overseas assignments. And language ability is important, according to a member of the executive committee, because, "Translators are never entirely satisfactory." This firm, like many others active in overseas operations, is trying to build up language skills in its domestic personnel. Here again, the role of the wife deserves special attention. The executive vice president for marketing of a large equipment manufacturer said, "Foreign language knowledge is more important for the wife than for the husband." The company feels that speaking the foreign language is polite and often useful for the man. It is considered vital for the wife for two reasons: to get her involved with the foreign setting, and to help her feel that she is assisting. To aid in acquiring the foreign language skill, many corporations provide free instruction for families bound overseas.

Another important problem in overseas assignment has been named "cultural shock," a result of sudden change from familiar surroundings to completely different conditions. The problem is greatest for the wives, and the remedies have been to provide additional information, to organize overseas staff to help new arrivals with their problems, and to provide as much advance orientation as practical.

Health and children's education also create difficulties in certain areas. These matters have led to company support of local schools and provision of additional medical service for families accompanying husbands on overseas assignments.

Overseas benefits. The most obvious personnel benefit from overseas assignments, in many of the companies studied, is the increased pay. For example, one company provides a 20 percent addition to base salary, plus an allowance for quarters, education, and other things, to assure that the family can maintain its United States standard of living overseas. Of course, the other major benefit from serving abroad is the greater management opportunity and experience often involved. This may be of special importance in giving a man a chance to show a wider range of abilities than he could demonstrate on his United States job. Thus, an overseas assignment can lead to better future advancement prospects than an equivalent job at home.

Assignment patterns. There appears to be a substantial difference of opinion among the participating companies on how best to utilize executives who have had some experience abroad. The companies that handle their overseas activity as an extension of a product division or of a functional department are likely to move a man back and forth between foreign and domestic assignments as the problems require. Firms that are organized for international operations along geographic lines often tend to move a man from one overseas assignment to another and rarely return him to domestic operations. There seem to be at least two reasons for this scheme: (1) A man who has had overseas experience may appear to be more valuable to the company if that overseas skill is used in another foreign assignment; (2) bringing men back from overseas and placing them in suitable jobs is a complicated problem often involving coordination and scheduling of transfers among several divisions. To offset these problems, and to make the best use of the management talent in the organization, one giant firm maintains a record of men considered outstanding for their age and experience. Executives serving overseas appear on this record along with the others so they are not overlooked when new assignments and career patterns are being considered either abroad or at home.

Foreign nationals. Although the American companies studied have substantial manufacturing and sales activities abroad, they typically are operated with a relatively small proportion of Americans. In a large consumer products company, for example, the assistant general manager of the international division indicated that, "The seventeen foreign companies are managed at the general management level by about 50 percent nationals and 50 percent American managers. Most people below the plant-manager level are nationals." In another large consumer products firm, there are only 60 Americans out of a total of about 7,000 employees abroad. In this case, there are several countries in which the firm is represented but have no Americans employed. Finally, in a major manufacturing company with about 15,000 salaried personnel in the international division, there are only about 250 Americans. Of them, perhaps half are in executive jobs and the rest are in specialized jobs or are trainees.

If Americans are rare in the international operations, foreign nationals are even more scarce in the domestic operations of the parent company. However, by their rise to top positions abroad, foreign nationals have demonstrated their management ability and it seems only a matter of time until they are significantly represented in United States activities as well. For example, the president of one large equipment manufacturer said, "We are hopeful that we can use nationals as much as possible. We have been abroad for only thirteen years. Our hope is to put the best man in the job without regard to nationality." This view was echoed by the vice president for international manufacturing of a major consumer products company with the statement, "A few foreign nationals have become a part of the parent company. More are desired and expected in the future."

If these trends continue, it appears that there will be greater interchange of personnel around the world and within American business organizations in the future. There is also the prospect that increasingly, on the basis of ability, foreign nationals will be represented in the top management of American corporations. An executive of one of the largest companies studied expressed the hope that twenty years from now nobody will be invited to join the executive committee of his firm unless he has served a tour of duty with an overseas operation.

APPRAISING PATTERNS OF ORGANIZATION

It seems clear that the characteristics of the market are the controlling factors in the organization for international operations. The fundamental decision is based upon whether the technical or the social aspects of the market are more important.

For example, the organization for international operations may well be centralized and product-oriented when:

The product is substantially uniform throughout the world.
It is bought on specification.
Performance, cost, and delivery are the only significant features in competition.
The product is distributed separately from other items.
Distribution costs are of minor importance.

On the other hand, the most suitable organization for international operations is likely to be decentralized and oriented to national or ethnic areas if conditions differ significantly from these criteria.

Because it is rare for the market characteristics of a product to be entirely technical or entirely social, management is usually faced with a problem of weighing the relative importance of these two aspects of the market for the product in question. The answer is seldom simple and clean-cut. The most appropriate answer may also change over the years. The desirability for change in the organization pattern of international operations may result from shifts in the balance of technical and social characteristics of the market, or from substantial changes in volume. Since conditions are rarely static, it is important that management make its decisions concerning organization for international operations in the light of current conditions *and* the apparent direction of changes that are taking place.

On the following pages, a number of different organization patterns for international operations are appraised in terms of the circumstances for which they appear well suited.

Foreign agents and representatives. A fairly simple arrangement, common in the past, involves the selection of dealers abroad or the designation of selling agents to call on overseas customers. Such an arrangement may work well when (1) selling a domestic product abroad, when (2) the specific product is not manufactured overseas, and when (3) the sales volume and prospects are not sufficient to justify establishing a marketing organization for international operations.

This distribution arrangement is normally under the direction of an export manager or an export department in the marketing organization of the company. For consumer items, it seems to have little appeal. Only one of the firms studied used agents and foreign representatives in the distribution of consumer products. In this case, they functioned primarily as wholesalers. They are an historical feature and are not part of the current preferred distribution pattern of the United States company. The volume of sales makes them unnecessary now. The foreign subsidiaries of the parent company handle all the manufacturing abroad. However, the distributors were there first, in many cases, so they continue as a part of the firm's international operations and are bought out as the opportunities arise.

International division.   A variety of roles have been assigned to the international division by various companies studied. The division may (1) direct several national subsidiary companies abroad, (2) direct sales efforts of overseas distributors handling products from several different manufacturing divisions of the parent company, and (3) provide for sales of product lines not able to "go it alone" in terms of sales volume in one or more overseas markets.

In one of the companies studied, the international department developed a concept of joint responsibility with the domestic departments for various overseas ventures. The product and process knowledge is supplied by the domestic departments and the geographical and special marketing knowledge comes from the international department. Another variation in the role of the international division was noted in one of the vertically integrated companies. Here, most of the operating companies have their own ships, but "international runs the swing fleet." It takes care of the changes in shipping requirements of the operating company fleets. It also handles overseas sales in large volume lots, and coordinates scheduling of raw product movements and certain international sales that affect more than one operating company. In another company, the international division controlled several foreign manufacturing and marketing subsidiaries.

From a different industry we have the statement: "It is a service unit to the operating divisions. . . . our international division handles all products for all divisions in Japan." And for a diversified manufacturing and research company we find: "Recently, the product divisions were given the responsibility for overseas operations for their major products. For small lines, however, the central international division is responsible."

Generally, the international division is located in the main office of the company. The status as a separate division indicates that the company regards the international market as a significant part of its total opportunity. Obviously, as the quotations indicate, a substantial volume of sales is implied by the decision to establish a separate division and the expectation that it will be an economical way in which to direct all or part of the international operations of the company.

Because of the flexibility of the international division in size and functions, it can adjust, or be adjusted, to changing conditions without much trouble. This should ensure its existence as a part of the international operations structure for many firms for years to come.

Foreign subsidiaries. A separate company is sometimes established overseas to handle all or part of the business abroad. Because of the overhead involved, a foreign subsidiary usually requires a considerable volume of business to justify it. Circumstances that seem to offer greatest advantage for use of a foreign subsidiary include the following: (1) The foreign market requires a product different from that produced for the United States market. (2) Manufacturing operations are to be conducted abroad. (3) A chain of company stores or supply points is to be operated overseas. (4) Coordination of manufacturing and sales activities is needed in a foreign country or area. (5) A regional foreign subsidiary is needed to coordinate several national foreign subsidiaries.

The foreign subsidiary may be wholly owned, majority owned, or the parent company may have only a minority interest in the firm. Most of the companies participating in this study had a clear preference for 100 percent ownership of foreign subsidiaries, but showed varying degrees of willingness to accept lesser degrees of control. Some advantages and problems of different degrees of ownership are discussed below.

Wholly owned subsidiaries provide ease of control but require full investment of the amount required and provide the maximum potential for national friction. Majority owned subsidiaries require less investment, may create less national friction, and provide greater ease for understanding the customs and attitudes of the people and the market situation; however, effective control may be awkward at times because of the attitude of minority interests. Minority stock ownership by the United States firm in a foreign enterprise appears to offer the maximum in ease of understanding, the least prospect for national friction, and the least investment, but it also provides a proportionally reduced income and may offer the least control. Since control is often believed to be necessary to assure satisfactory profits, lack of control is considered by many as a disqualifying factor in overseas ventures. One of the companies studied is seriously examining the minority interest investment as a possible advantage, however.

Years ago, the railroad managements in the United States made use of several devices to provide effective management control with only a minority interest in the stock of another carrier. One method was to obtain a long-term lease on the physical property of the railroad to be controlled. Another technique was to secure a management contract to operate the other carrier. These arrangements, and others like them, may be helpful in international operations. Some of the advantages could be full control, greatly reduced investment, reduced prospects of national friction, and possibly leveraged earnings. If the majority stockholders of the foreign enterprise received a reasonable guaranteed income for the management contract, earnings above the established level would accrue to the management, the minority stockholder firm. For example, if the United States firm owned 20 percent of the stock in the foreign company, arranged a management contract for a guaranteed return of $5 per share, and was able to earn $7 per share, the result would be $15 per share return on the equity of the United States firm. Of course, this places a premium on the ability of the management to produce improved results, for if less than $5 per share is earned the leverage works against the United States organization. Nevertheless, the prospect may be attractive when the United States firm is contributing technical know-how, management skill, or coordination opportunities that were not available in the foreign country. It seems likely that these "minority interest plus" arrangements will get careful consideration in the future since they offer the chance to overcome important difficulties with foreign governments and investors, with a reduced investment, and possibly at an improved return on the investment.

In a discussion of foreign subsidiaries, the coordinating subsidiary deserves special attention. This is an organization set up to provide central direction and coordination for several national subsidiaries. The coordinating subsidiary provides guidance without the delays that would be involved in referring plans and questions to the parent company headquarters, and executives from the coordinating subsidiary can be physically located so they can easily visit the national companies or trouble spots. A coordinating subsidiary also permits, for example, the Common Market coordination that may be required without disturbing government relationships, national pride, or the personal prestige of the executives in the national subsidiaries. It accomplishes the effect of a merger, insofar as policies and direction are concerned, but without the difficult legal and political problems that an actual merger would entail. As the scale of operations grows with developing technology, and as market areas expand, the need for coordination among "sister companies" is certain to increase. The establishment of the coordinating subsidiary as a holding company for the foreign subsidiaries under its control offers a neat and effective way of dealing with the problem. It is expected that the use of foreign subsidiaries for coordination of related firms abroad will find increasing favor in the years ahead.

World marketing by product divisions. Many companies are discussing the idea of world marketing by product divisions. For some, it is looked on as the next step in a series. The president of one company described his firm's experience as follows: "We went through several steps: From export department, to foreign trade group with its own president and vice president, to merging these activities into the company so that overseas problems got the same administrative handling as domestic problems."

For the most effective use, this approach to international operations requires:

1. Standard products, with little difference between those produced and sold at home and those sold abroad.
2. Separate distribution of its products by each division of a multi-division firm, to avoid conflicts of jurisdiction in direction of marketing and distribution activities.
3. Few problems overseas requiring on-the-scene knowledge or speedy action by senior division executives.
4. Competence by division headquarters personnel in normal international operations.
5. A sufficient volume of sales to support separate distribution and selling organizations around the world for the several divisions. (This last requirement can be eased considerably if an international division is created or retained to handle distribution and sales activities for certain product lines in areas where they cannot individually provide the sales volume to justify direct handling by their parent divisions.)

Where the above conditions are substantially met, the concept of world marketing by product divisions offers an attractive opportunity to build an integrated "one world" manufacturing and selling organization, with a high degree of flexibility. However, meeting the requirements described will take years of effort in some organizations. It will be truly a process of development. In other organizations, because of the nature of the products and their market characteristics, the concept of world marketing by product divisions will be impracticable and undesirable for the foreseeable future.

Inquiries by management

1. *Long-range planning.* What is our long-range planning system for overseas activities? How are these plans evaluated and by whom? How is the development of long-range plans for separate overseas units coordinated, and how are the overseas plans coordinated with long-range plans developed in the parent company?
2. *Marketing.* What are the sales-volume trends in our individual overseas market areas for major product lines? How are our international markets distinctive from the domestic market and from one another? Is this pattern changing? What is the significance in terms of product design, merchandising, and pricing?
3. *Manufacturing.* How do we evaluate the desirability of overseas manufacturing for our various products? Who makes the decisions? By product groups and geographic areas, how is the desirability changing concerning the manufacturing of complete products, major components, or parts? How does this affect our customer service and competitive position?
4. *Research and development.* What are the problems and advantages of overseas research and development? Is there a trend in the relative importance of these factors? How do our practices compare with those of our rivals? How do we coordinate research and development activities? How do we evaluate our advantages from specialization or competition among the research and development groups? Who is responsible for reviewing and recommending changes in our policies and programs in overseas research and development?
5. *Financial control.* How is financial coordination and control achieved for our overseas operations? What changes are favored or suggested by our managers overseas? How do we evaluate the cost of delayed decisions overseas and the various advantages of our present arrangements for financial coordination and control?

6. *Management control.* If we had to change, what would be the best plan we could devise for holding only majority (or minority) control of our overseas subsidiaries? How would the feasibility and desirability of such a plan or plans be determined? What are the pressures for such a change in our various overseas marketing areas? What would be the impact of such a plan or plans on our competitive position overseas?

7. *Organization.* Should our overseas organization(s) be primarily area-oriented or product-oriented? How does the answer vary among our product lines? What is the best organization pattern for our overseas operations in low-volume market areas and in high-volume market areas? How do we achieve the desirable degree of coordination among our overseas units? How does our present organization for overseas activity match or differ from the features suggested by answers to the questions above? What do our headquarters staff organizations, domestic divisions, and overseas groups need to carry out their roles effectively in our present or improved overseas arrangements?

8. *Personnel.* How do we select personnel for overseas assignments? How do we evaluate the prospects for good adjustments by wife and family to overseas conditions? How do management personnel, in general, appraise the advantages and rewards provided for overseas service? What is our future goal in terms of the distribution in the parent company of personnel who have had overseas experience? What plans or arrangements do we have to provide for visits or short-term overseas experience for management personnel? How do present personnel policies and practices for overseas experience fit with our proposed organization for overseas activity?

MANAGEMENT INFORMATION SYSTEMS

9

Despite the relative recency of their arrival on the scene, management information systems already have had a major impact on business. They are probably the most important new management tool developed in the past generation. Under these circumstances, it is not surprising that there is considerable controversy about their role and potential.

The electronic computer, operations research methods, and many of the allied facilities and techniques that make up the management information systems had not been devised at the time of the earlier study,

Top Management Organization and Control. Thus, a review of the development of these new tools may be useful for exploration of other new techniques in management as well as for guidance on the probable further potential of management information systems.

PROBLEMS IN DEVELOPMENT

A basic problem is the limited understanding of computers and quantitative methods of analysis on the part of most senior executives. Unfortunately, this limitation is matched by the lack of understanding of the business and its problems on the part of many information and operations research specialists. The intellectual arrogance of some of these specialists has caused problems. It blinds them to their own lack of understanding, causes overselling of new techniques, and rebuffs many line executives who might otherwise display a genuine interest in computers and operations research.

Some of these specialists have resigned themselves to the view that, "We won't make real progress until another generation of top management arrives, trained in operations research and data processing." There is considerable validity in this attitude. However, the basic idea might also be reversed (although the specialists never expressed it this way) to say, "We won't make the progress we should until the information and quantitative specialists recognize their need to understand the real problems of business." As a vice president of one of the participating companies put it, "The big problem in computers is communication between the man with the problem and the computer specialist."

Fact and fancy. The tendency to oversell management information systems was indicated in a number of interviews. The director of the computer center of one firm described as "overdone on many fronts" an article in a major business magazine describing the functions and capabilities of his center. Presidents of other companies used such phrases as "Computers have been oversold," and, "Other areas have had similar waves of popularity in the past. . . . Today the new panacea is the computer."

In another case, claims about the results of an operations research study within a large company apparently were exaggerated. This study covered 33 different paper-making machines located in several states. A rescheduling of their output, following an operations research study, was said to have turned a $1 million a year loss into a $5 million a year profit. On further inquiry, it developed that changes resulting from the operations research study were only part of the total picture. During the period, price and demand changes had occurred, and following an organization study by a leading consulting firm, a new manager had been appointed and changes had been made in marketing and advertising plans. Clearly, it would be incorrect to attribute the entire savings to any one of these factors—or to the operations research study alone.

A still more impressive example of misinterpretation was found in another firm. Here, the operations research staff had made intensive study of the prospective market for a major new product. They were convinced that their study had been the principal factor in the top management decision concerning the new product. However, when top management officials were queried about the matter, they indicated that the assumptions made by the operations research team were so unrealistic that their market estimates had first been cut in half, and that the final decision had not been influenced significantly by the work of the operations research staff. Lacking specific information on how the decision actually was made, the operations research staff had confused their expectations with fact.

It should be noted that the executives mentioned above were favorable toward the use of computers and quantitative methods in business. They were simply trying to offset the misleading impressions sometimes obtained from enthusiastic technicians and exaggerated articles. All the companies studied in this survey made extensive use of management information systems, expected to develop them further, and anticipated substantial increases in their usefulness to the enterprise.

The reasons why. There appear to be at least three major reasons for the differences of "fact and fancy" noted above: (1) the impact of professional training, (2) rapid equipment development, and (3) the nature of management problems.

The line operating executive usually has had a variety of experience and understands at least a major segment of the business. He is oriented to problem solving in terms of the success of the enterprise, department, or division. By contrast, the operations research or computer specialist often knows little about the business. He has been trained in particular operations research and data processing techniques. He therefore tends to be technique-oriented rather than problem-oriented. Knowing a lot about new techniques and only a little about the nature and complexity of the business problems, he may easily mistake the significance of his contributions.

Rapid equipment development in the data processing and communications fields has been a fact of life for executives working in these areas. Similarly, new techniques and applications in quantitative analysis have obsorbed the interest of specialists in operations research. As a result, even when these men have been employed in a business for several years, their orientation is still primarily to equipment and techniques rather than to the problems of the enterprise. Certainly, when they have been hired as experts in these areas, it is reasonable to expect them to keep up with the developments in their chosen specialty. However, this tends to limit their time or incentive to really understand the problems of the business.

The nature of management problems adds a further complication. Frequently, management problems require careful diagnosis before their real identity and extent can be determined. After the problem is defined, various alternatives must be considered and the appropriate solution selected. Finally, the solution or program must be implemented. Sometimes this last step can be the most troublesome of all. By contrast, the management information systems specialist is likely to concern himself only with the second of these three steps. Someone has already defined the problem for him, and when he determines the optimum solution he often considers the problem solved. Under these circumstances, it is not surprising that the computer or operations research specialist may get an exaggerated idea of the importance of his role in handling management problems. In fact, he probably has dealt only with the middle step in a series of at least three and, unknown to him, his assumptions or limitations of information may produce answers that are not realistic.

The difficulty can be presented in another way. Management information systems work best when data are available in quantity, values are definite, and relationships are accurately stated. Unfortunately, many management problems are made more difficult because only limited information is available, values are indefinite, and relationships are vague. Working chiefly with the "easy" problems, or parts of problems involving comprehensive and accurate information, may cause the management information systems specialist to underestimate the complexity of the other problems of the firm.

In many cases, management must share the blame for these errors. Perhaps because they expected the technicians to understand the business, the operating executives often have not defined problems explicitly for the management information system specialists, or provided guidance to establish reasonable assumptions. Evaluating the reliability of information and setting realistic parameters for alternatives to be studied are other areas where management has frequently failed to provide needed assistance.

The natural result of these circumstances is to continue the lack of understanding between the operations research and computer specialists, and the operating executives. This makes the current working of management information systems less effective and retards the development of their full potential.

APPLICATIONS OF MANAGEMENT INFORMATION SYSTEMS

There have been so many applications of computers and quantitative analysis techniques publicized in the past few years that it may be useful to try to classify them, rather than to discuss a variety of illustrations.

Most of the management information systems applications can be described as: (1) record keeping, (2) problem solving, or (3) automatic control.

Examples of record keeping would be storing and updating payroll or inventory records. Problem-solving applications would include such things as calculating the optimum distribution of orders among a group of warehouses. Automatic controls are typified by the monitoring and adjustment of petroleum refining or other continuous process operations according to a computer program. As might be expected, very simple record keeping was the first application developed by most companies. It is an obvious opportunity and the advantages are easy to demonstrate. In recent years, however, the emphasis has shifted to problem solving and to automatic control. In general these developments, although more complex, offer greater prospects for management improvements.

Another way of classifying management information systems functions is by the methods or activities involved. Thus, we can distinguish: (1) information processing, (2) simulation, and (3) operations research. These are not entirely independent categories, but they serve to distinguish important methods underlying many management information systems applications. Here again, the progression has been from the simple to the complex. Current emphasis is on developments in simulation and operations research where the greatest profit appears to lie for many firms.

Storing, updating, and retrieving information are the primary activities in handling transportation rate tables by computer. If we include a bit of addition and subtraction, we can handle the accumulation and classification of sales information for a manufacturer, or the maintenance of customer checking-account records in a commercial bank. These are all a simple "keeping track" type of clerical operations.

Simulation involves a sequence of computer steps arranged to imitate the circumstances being studied. Thus, the simulation process is particularly useful in seeking answers to "what if" questions. A financial simulation for a firm might give us computer printouts of *pro forma* financial statements for a ten-year period based on various assumptions about costs, prices, sales, and so forth. Likewise, a simulation program for a distribution system might show us the build-up of product inventories and their locations under varying assumed conditions. A series of simulation runs may be used to seek, by experiment, the best combination of variables for a problem—the best answer.

The operations research methods are generally aimed at determining the best answer for a problem directly rather than by trial-and-error testing. The answer might be a matter of pump design to meet a particular job, or the best operating schedule for a fleet of trucks, or the lowest cost combination of earthmoving equipment for a major construction project. In addition, the operations research formulas can be used to produce simulation results for various conditions. Thus, the difference between simulation techniques and operations research is more a difference in emphasis or primary goal than a difference in capacity.

The significance of these various methods lies in their impact on management. Record keeping by a management information system can relieve people of many routine functions and give them more time to think about problems of the business and to develop opportunities. Properly used, simulation can permit executives to evaluate a much wider range of alternatives than the unaided mind could handle in a reasonable time. Operations research, or optimizing methods, may allow company officials to determine the best answer, within a given set of assumptions and conditions. In this expansion of management capacity lies the real contribution and prospect of management information systems. It is no wonder that so many top management people are concerned about how to use these tools more effectively.

PROVIDING THE SERVICE

As with any new activity, there has been considerable experimentation with management information systems in trying to find the best way to provide service. Some of these approaches are discussed below.

Typically, the management information system started as a part of the accounting or controller's department. This is quite natural since, in most businesses, the accounting functions were those to which the computer was first applied. In some cases, operations research developed separately in the engineering, production, or research and development areas. There has been a tendency to put operations research into the management information system group since the operations research specialists make extensive use of computers.

Data center development. Over the past ten years, there has been a definite trend toward centralization and independence of the management information system in large companies. This trend appears to result from at least four factors:

1. There has been a rapid rise in the volume of computer processing work.
2. Large computers are more economical per unit of work than small computers.
3. The availability of long-distance data transmission has made it possible to concentrate computer work at one or a few locations.
4. Rivalries and duplication of data processing and operations research services have sometimes arisen as simulation, problem solving, and automatic control applications have developed in various parts of an enterprise. This has highlighted the advantages of consolidation of service.

Under the impact of these developments, many firms have consolidated major data processing activities into one or a few centers, either inside the accounting and finance organization or reporting separately to top management.

The developments at a major divisionalized manufacturing company were described by the director of data processing in these terms:

Each division has had considerable autonomy to establish its own system. Central then established controls comparable to those existing in the capital expenditures area — to prove return on investment. These controls are still in existence. When the divisions had to justify return on investment, they soon saw that it was economical to centralize some of these services for the divisions.

In another company the controller indicated that data processing was set up as a service bureau reporting to the president, primarily because of conflict between finance and manufacturing.

A third company went still further. Not long ago it combined most data processing, operations research, mathematics, and engineering into a separate company. The magnitude of the activity is suggested by the computer rental bill of $18 million a year, and the staff of about 3,000 persons of whom approximately 1,100 are professionals. The new company is organized with a vice president heading each of the three major areas of activity: (1) coordination and planning, (2) research and technical services, and (3) accounting and information systems.

The pattern of change is reminiscent of the organizational changes within the U.S. armed forces as military aviation developed. Military aviation started out as a division of the Army Signal Corps, performing photographic and observation functions. Then other functions developed, other branches of the Army found applications, and the demand for the airplane increased. The Aeronautical Division of the Army Signal Corps progressed through several organizational changes to become the Army Air Corps, the Army Air Force, and ultimately the U.S. Air Force.

The growth and organization of management information systems seems to be following the same pattern of development as U.S. military aviation, which is not surprising since the same general reasons apply: an increasing variety of applications, a growing demand for the service, a rapid improvement of equipment and techniques, and the development of able and articulate leaders who see a brilliant future for the activity. There is even a parallel in the fact that the centralization is not complete in either the air services or in management information systems. The U.S. Army, Navy, Marine Corps, and Coast Guard all have their own separate air services, just as many plants, divisions, and departments in the corporations studied have retained or developed their own capability in computer and operations research activity. These capabilities are in addition to the services available centrally. The question for business is not whether there should be some centralization in management information systems, but how much centralization is best. Generally, large plants or division activities that have a specialized need and a substantial workload of computer or operations research activity will be provided with some independent resources to meet these requirements.

Scope of services. Although separate management information centers have been established within many companies, there is considerable variation in the functions they perform. All centers provide data processing facilities, and many offer some operations research service. In two of the firms studied, most of the long-distance communications facilities were also grouped with the data processing capacity. In one of these companies, several data centers were established, all reporting to a vice president for data centers headquartered in the accounting department. In this case operations research capacities were provided by the research and engineering department and elsewhere in the firm.

Customer freedom. Another important difference in organization for management information systems is the amount of choice available to the customers within the company. Here are two extremes.

The data processing center at the headquarters of one company will provide free programming and operating service on any project that is justified by potential cost reduction or company improvement. On the other hand, the data processing center maintains a monopoly on the corporation's digital computer service in that area. This monopoly has not caused much complaint since most of the corporate customers are getting data processing service "free" to their departmental budgets. Of course, this arrangement provides real advantages for the data processing center. Since no other group in the corporation has the expertise *and* responsibility to evaluate the center's cost estimates or equipment requirements, the latest equipment, and plenty of it, is ordered, and project cost estimates can be sufficiently generous to cover the increased overhead expense. The center provides good service. Unfortunately, some projects that might otherwise be undertaken may be "priced out of the market" by the system. The research laboratory has an analog computer which it directly controls, but even this machine is physically located in the data processing center. Convenience in maintenance support and in use of other computers apparently makes this an acceptable arrangement for the research laboratory.

The opposite extreme in customer choice is illustrated by the data center of another company. This center provides programmers, computer time, and related services for hire. Company departments may use any combination of these capabilities they desire, or purchase them outside the company, or provide their own capabilities. This policy is consistent with the company's general philosophy of decentralization of its major product divisions.

The advantages seem to be: (1) the benefits of vigorous competition to assure good service at reasonable cost, (2) the opportunity for divisions to get work done "outside" when the temporary workload at the company data center would otherwise delay projects, and (3) education of an increased number of operating people in the usefulness of computers.

Arguments against this degree of competition include: (1) the splintering of the staff with data processing skill so that no significant career ladder is provided for this specialty in any office, (2) use of many different machine languages and duplication of some data, and (3) difficulty in planning for future computer requirements by the company data center when the full extent of divisional activities and plans may not be known.

Obviously, other arrangements are possible and may be attractive. It is interesting to note, however, that the management groups in *both* of the examples cited above appear to be satisfied with the results. This fact suggests that management information systems may be an area in which differences in organization structures are far less important than the skill and attitude of the persons providing and using the service.

IMPACT ON THE ENTERPRISE

It is generally accepted that computers and operations research have made substantial contributions to management effectiveness and to the profitability of many enterprises. However, there is still a great deal of controversy about the internal impact of management information systems in terms of centralization versus decentralization, the importance of middle management, and the role of top management. Information from this study of fifteen leading companies provides some interesting insights on these topics.

Centralization versus decentralization. The computer, plus long-distance data transmission, permits information to be collected rapidly from many distant points and analyzed efficiently at a central location. This capability gives management at the central office the opportunity to review an abundance of facts and to make timely decisions about distant operations. These possibilities have led many persons to believe that the widespread use of computers would increase centralization in business. The incentive, of course, would be increased efficiency and profits by having more decisions made by the best decision makers and by reducing the total number of decision makers needed in the organization.

Specific inquiry was made to many executives in the participating companies as to whether the computer has, in fact, strengthened and encouraged decentralization rather than producing increased centralization. Typical of the responses was one from a chief executive officer who stated:

> Centralization of computers will not affect organization of the divisions. The general manager can get better information and faster, but this arrangement will not materially affect the divisions or their organizations.

A director of data processing from the automobile industry expressed a similar view:

> You can have a central information system and a decentralized system of organization. I don't think the two are inconsistent at all. The function of the central information system is to collect and put the right information in the right place at the right time.

In explaining why centralization had not resulted from the capabilities of management information systems, executives offered a variety of reasons. Their points included: (1) The price and competitive situations are so fluid in many major markets that central scheduling of activities would be impractical. (2) Handling of plant or division functions by a central headquarters would only reduce the time the central office executives had for headquarters problems and would make it difficult to hold the plant and division managers responsible for results at their levels. (3) Management information systems make decentralization more profitable and effective than before by providing better information for local decision making. As one executive put it:

> The focus of creativity and initiative is more important than the level or capability of management information system centralization in decision making and strategy of centralization or decentralization.

Impact on middle management. Another concern relating to computers and mathematical techniques has been their impact on middle management. Executives interviewed in this study commented on four significant aspects of this impact: the decision-making role, management focus, management training, and size of the middle management group.

The executives interviewed were unanimous in their opinion that the decision-making role of middle managers would not be reduced by the development of management information systems. There were, however, differences of opinion as to whether or not the decision-making role would be unchanged or whether or not some decisions would be pushed down to the level of middle managers. Production scheduling, warehousing, and transportation were areas specifically mentioned where the decision level had been moved down in the organization.

Not only did the executives visited seem in substantial agreement on the decision-making role of middle management, they also indicated similar viewpoints on the emphasis at middle management levels resulting from management information systems development. Here is a representative comment:

> The advent of electronic communication and computation has had its major impact on lower and middle management jobs and has had the effect of concentrating their attention on management rather than on clerical supervision.

To make sure that middle managers are prepared to make effective use of computers and operations research groups, many of the organizations studied are sending managers to executive programs or are running training sessions of their own. In addition, some are following up these basic orientation programs with specific discussions and meetings on applications in the company. The statement by one top executive is illustrative:

> At the next six monthly management meetings, we will spend two hours each meeting on computer applications to business. Last week we had all managers attend a special three-day program on applications of the computer.

Management information systems are expected to have little influence on the size of the middle management group in the future, according to the executives interviewed. Instead, there will be greater emphasis on problem analysis and planning using the information and capabilities of management information systems. One official put it:

If anything, the computers have increased the number in management because we give them much more information to analyze and consider .... The rising middle management people spend a great deal of their time on special studies. For example, there are more management people in the traffic department now than ever before and they are one of the most advanced in the country in terms of computer and mathematical applications.

To sum up, the middle manager apparently is in no danger of losing important decision-making functions, the nature of his work will place more emphasis on managing and less on routine supervision in the future, and the number of persons in middle management is not likely to decline as a result of the development of management information systems.

Let us now consider what the role of top management will be in connection with these developments.

Role of top management. Among the many executives interviewed, there was strong agreement that there would be no major change in the level of decision making by top management as a result of the growing use of computers and mathematical techniques. It was particularly significant to find these views expressed by both senior and middle management executives and by both general management and technical personnel. Here are the views of three executives from one of the participating firms.

A member of the executive committee. In terms of the computers changing the level of decision making, I have not seen any evidence of that, and I doubt very much that this will take place in the future.

The director of new venture analysis (who uses computers extensively). With respect to the contributions of computers and new information techniques, we feel that the amount of information that will be available will increase, and the time required to get this information will be shortened. This will be useful, but it will not change the actual decision making of executives or the level at which the major decisions will be made.

The manager of data processing. From a management point of view, I don't see where it [management information system] has greatly affected senior management or senior management decision making in this company. The reports and content are very much the same as before. A viewer on the desk doesn't change the value of the data.

Data for decisions by top management was another area explored with executives. Again, no change in the role of top management seemed indicated. The president of one company said, very simply, "I am aware of computers in that I can quickly get information that I want." The president of another firm was more specific and stated that he is now able to get the detailed operating results for the past month, plus the adjusted forecasts for each division and group, by the eighth of the next month. This was not possible before the development of the centralized system of computers. In addition, one of his vice presidents stated, "We have not done anything to move major decision making from the division to the group, or beyond, as a result of the computers." Apparently it was typical in companies visited that the development of management information systems had provided top management with better information and supplied it faster than before.

The president of one company, commenting on the use of new information and mathematical tools, said flatly, "We're not going to decide on more details up here than we ever have." A group vice president stated, "Even if I had a console on my desk, I wouldn't use it for plant and division detail matters. There just isn't time. Looking after these activities is the work of others." He went on to say that the president and key executives of his company were looking at less detail now than in previous years, in spite of the tremendous development of the computer in their firm. Possibly this development reflects the ability of the management information system to supply more specific, accurate, and timely information than was available before. This would make it possible to handle many decisions at a lower level, or to eliminate reference to a variety of estimates and cross-checking approximations about the same operations.

The president of one company was asked to what extent he utilized operations research and mathematical models in assisting him to make decisions on such things as location of mills or new plants, or in deciding on the nature of new facilities to optimize product mix. He replied:

> Really, not very much. We look at the result and it becomes one of many factors which we weigh in making our decision. There are so many indeterminable or unpredictable factors working in the marketplace, many of which are much more important than everything included in your model, the major focus of the decision making is on these marketing factors rather than on the model.

The importance of another "nonquantitative" factor was emphasized by the president of a different company:

> We do more talking about people than numbers. If I get the right leader in a division, the division looks good. It's true that we look at numbers, but when something goes wrong, we correct it through people.

IMPLICATIONS OF TECHNOLOGY

The rate of development in management information systems technology has been very rapid. Both the product demand and the rate of product improvement seem to be accelerating. Under these circumstances, it is likely that whatever forecasts of development seem reasonable to us today will be conservative in terms of the actual advances of the next decade.

Computer capacity and cost.   The information available indicates that we can expect further increases in the capability of computers in the future. This will result, in part, from the continuing work on microminiaturization and circuit design. These improvements are likely to be accompanied by a further reduction in the cost per unit of work with the new, larger computers. The speed, size, and cost changes will increase the use of computers by management. The capacity increases will permit larger problems to be run, or more problems to be handled simultaneously, and the reduced cost will encourage the application of computers to a variety of problems for which the savings did not justify computer handling in the past.

Computer speed and flexibility.   We can expect to see increases in machine capability. Increased speed will result from some of the same developments that are expected to increase capacity. Computer flexibility is concerned chiefly with the ability of the computer to perform a variety of operations at the same time, including work on several completely different problems. This capability is being marketed now under the name of "multiprogramming" and has particular appeal when combined with remote input-output stations that allow persons at widely separated locations to utilize the same computer facilities. Time sharing is an additional development in this area. It permits quick response interaction with various users by interruptions in work which are so short that most users are unaware they occurred.

Very small computers of reasonable capacity and cost are a recent development. For many "limited volume" management applications having limited data inputs, these small machines may ultimately become significant rivals of time sharing on giant computers. It will be interesting to watch the growth of these two nearly opposite patterns of development in computer technology. Either way, we are assured that computer capability choices of the users will be further increased in the years ahead. Developments in speed and flexibility will serve to increase the usefulness of the computer to business management.

Auxiliary equipment. Progress in the variety of auxiliary devices may be even greater than in the computer itself. Already one of the companies studied is using facsimile equipment to transmit orders to data centers where they are converted into digital form.

An area of great promise for managers is the increased use of graph-drawing machines (x-ray plotters) connected to the computer so that the information desired appears in diagram form as well as in numbers. This ability to get graphic presentations and comparisons of time series, performance records, and relationships among variables should be of great value to highlight the significance of the information displayed. Hopefully, it will allow the manager to interpret the computer information more swiftly and with greater insight. Combined with the flexibility of time sharing and remote input-output stations, the manager in the future will be able to get a graphic presentation or comparison of a wide variety of data, on demand, and tailored to fit his immediate information requirements.

Cathode ray tube displays for the presentation of information on a television-like screen are another development that will become common. For the general management executive, these tubes will provide a means by which the numerical or graphic results of computer inquiry are presented. This may be the display of a custom-tailored report produced in a few seconds, the presentation of up-to-the-minute data on some operating or financial activity stored in computer memory, or the results of the application of some formula or mathematical technique (via stored programs in the computer) to a particular problem posed by the executive. Engineers and designers are already using a "light pen" to draw diagrams on the face of the "picture tube." When the diagram, design sketch, or proposed circuit is outlined to the satisfaction of the user, the information is transferred from the tube face to the computer in numerical form. The information can then be analyzed, compared, stored, or revised, as desired. This use of the computer in basic activities seems destined to increase greatly the usefulness of the machines and the productivity of the designers, but these new applications call for a great deal of auxiliary storage and for increased speed in computer functions. Both the technical and general management executives may gain substantially from the developments in auxiliary equipment for computers in the decade ahead.

Communications facilities. The availability of dependable, long-distance electric communication has made the central computer practical for geographically dispersed organizations. Communication costs to the user will probably rise less in the future than most other business expenses for three reasons: (1) The alternative of private microwave communications systems is available for high-volume users. (2) The communications industry is concerned, already, with retaining volume customers. Last year, American Telephone and Telegraph carried to the U.S. Supreme Court a case in which it requested authority to provide reduced rates for four classes of volume users of its services. (3) New technical developments, such as the communications satellites circling the earth in space, may also reduce long distance costs as well as greatly increase the available capacity for transcontinental or intercontinental communication. All these developments point to greater convenience at low cost for users of far-flung management information systems.

Software. The term "software" is frequently used to designate the computer programs and applications instructions required by data processing installations. In recent years, the manufacturers of computers have placed increased emphasis on developing programs to increase the operating efficiency of their machines. They have also produced many different standard applications programs and are making these available to their customers, free or at nominal cost. This service is important because of the time and cost involved for each user in the independent preparation of the numerous programs required for any large computer installation. In discussing this development, the director of data processing for one of the participating companies said, "Actually, we choose our computer equipment by software rather than hardware capabilities." With computer applications becoming more numerous and more elaborate, it seems reasonable to expect that both computer manufacturers and users will further the development of standard or library programs. A particularly promising field for these developments will be the construction of a variety of programs permitting the user of the computer to request and receive special reports or summaries, custom-tailored to his instructions, from any part of the information network of the enterprise.

Mathematical developments. With the high degree of interest now being shown in application of mathematical techniques to the problems of management, new advances in this area seem certain. Some examples of ongoing work that could be of great benefit to management are (1) research in Bayesian statistics to improve techniques for combining best human judgments in complex situations with mathematical analysis, (2) improvements in linear programming to permit this technique to be used effectively when relationships among the variables are not constant (capable of being represented by a straight line), and (3) development of dynamic models to permit more extensive and realistic use of simulations for analysis of management problems.

A LOOK AHEAD

From the discussion above, it seems clear that the prospects in new technology all point to increased capability, greater versatility, and lower cost per unit of work for management information systems in the future. For business managers, the real challenge will be how to use these improved resources most effectively.

There will also be some specific machine problems. As computers are more widely used to process key management information, safeguarding these data (profits, production volumes, sales figures, and so forth) will become an increasing problem. This will be especially difficult if time-sharing methods are in use allowing many different persons or groups direct access to the computer. Identification codes are a promising means of dealing with this problem but currently are not completely secure. Another machine problem results from the fact that the more management data we put into the computer, the more dependent we become on the proper functioning of the computer machinery. With an increasing share of management information going into computers in the future, we will become increasingly vulnerable to machine breakdowns and to the accidental or intentional erasure or garbling of electronic records. A third machine problem is produced by the longer and more complex programs that will be involved in the advanced information system applications in the years ahead. Since each step or computer action involves a very small chance of machine error, as the number of steps increases, the probability of *some* error in the result also grows. Higher accuracy in machine performance or internal checking procedures will be necessary to maintain existing levels of accuracy as programs become longer.

It was generally agreed that an understanding of mathematical techniques and data processing would be vital for the executives of the future, although such understanding would be no substitute for management training and experience. The line or staff, generalist or specialist positions of the executives seemed to make little difference in their viewpoints on this matter.

The head of the operations research group of one company described in considerable detail the three categories of university training and personal orientation in mathematics that were useful in business:

1. The first group consists of those with a very high mathematical capability. These men are highly paid technicians who may work on major linear programming projects. They probably would be math majors with considerable technical work at the graduate level. Normally, they are conspicuous by not relating well to the real world. Individuals in this category are likely to end up working for one of the computer manufacturing companies.

2. The second group consists of operations research people similar to those I have working for me. These individuals are interested in working with business problems and in applying their operations research techniques. A Ph.D from a graduate program is an ideal person for this kind of activity. [When asked where he would expect the Ph.D type to be in five to ten years if he stayed with the company, the head of the operations research group replied, "He might become a staff man to a plant manager, but if he wants to go into general management, he would have to get out of operations research and get into line management."]

3. The third group I see as a somewhat different group. People working in this group will be working in areas where there is a very high percentage of input in human judgment. They will be required to get preferences from panels, and from sales managers and salesmen who will be selling the products. These men will be working on new business venture analysis problems and in a new and exciting area. I would select a man for this type of work who has had considerable

education and experience in psychology, selling, and advertising. It would be very helpful if he were to have an M.B.A.

We must recognize both the importance and the limitations of computers and mathematical techniques for management in the future. The desirable university training for management should provide the student with an understanding of the concepts and applications of these mathematical and information-processing techniques—but not specialization in those subjects. This perspective would be a part of a general educational program. Finally, the man who aspires ultimately to become a part of top management *must not* spend a long period in operations research and computer services during his business career, and he *must* acquire extensive, and hopefully varied, line management experience.

The previous discussion has indicated a variety of current applications for management information systems. That the future will involve "more of the same but better" is an easy inference. However, there are other prospects that seem to go beyond this. Some of the most interesting of these prospects are described below.

In the planning area the executives contacted saw great possibilities for developments. These included: (1) a better picture of the world market, both supply and demand, through the use of management information systems potentials; (2) improved sales forecasting by product market areas, product groups, and ultimately by product lines; (3) faster and more complete information for advertising media selection decisions.

In the area of product design, it is expected that computers will speed design work where many interrelated factors must be taken into account. An example cited for job-shop-type production was the use of the computer to determine the best combination of characteristics for a pump to meet particular performance requirements at minimum cost. It was expected that the field salesman would telephone his inquiry to the computer center and receive a prompt response, giving price and features of the pump most satisfactory for the job, which he could relay to his customer.

An executive vice president of one company expressed his belief that in ten years the central computers will be receiving all orders for his corporation and will schedule those orders, on a lowest-delivered-cost basis, to the appropriate plant. The manager of the plant would, however, have the responsibility of running the plant and changing schedules according to his needs. He would then notify the central computer section of the changes.

For periods when prompt delivery is critical, this company has considered an even more elaborate system. On receipt of a teletype message from a salesman, a central computer would determine the earliest date by which a prospective order could be filled by plants reasonably near the potential customer—without missing any promised delivery dates on orders previously accepted. This scheme, of course, involves an optimizing program for rescheduling (tentatively) the entire production program for a week or a month at each of several plants, and the selection of the earliest date from among those plants. It is believed that the salesman receiving the inquiry on possible delivery dates would be able to telephone the customer with a firm quotation within ten minutes after transmitting the details of the possible order to the computer.

At one of the participating companies, the manager of systems research had developed a broad program. He described a number of examples of data processing and quantitative techniques that will, or might, be applied in the next five to ten years by the company. These were:

Design. A component part will be available on computers, using a light pen and a cathode ray tube (television) screen. The information would be converted into tapes which could be used on tape-controlled machine tools to make the part. This method could cut the time to design and build the new part from four to nine months to two months, on a routine basis. The computers for these kinds of applications are called "process control" computers. They are more specialized than the general purpose computers used in most management applications.

Production scheduling. The manager of systems research now has a complete design for a corporate scheduling and control system. The system has steps or sections for: corporate planning, plant planning, and plant control. It is believed to have application to many functions in the corporate family.

Top management planning. A part of the plan above is an optimal planning system useful to top management with data arranged so that the top executives can see what numbers to change to allow for potential strikes, sales programs, and other things that were not considered in the basic computer analysis.

General engineering information system. This program will be an information or communication system to speed up engineering operations by giving the right people the right drawings and other information at the right time.

Simulations. These programs will be set up to give provable answers to "what if" questions—where there are now endless arguments based on hunch and opinion. Executives will be able to spend their time on higher levels of management decisions.

Automatic monitoring and control. Shortly a new system will be installed at a subsidiary which will automatically flag production situations requiring action. This system will not control the machines. In one of the other plants, it is expected that the new system now planned will directly control the operations.

Research operations. A system soon is to be installed in the research laboratory so that the test devices will automatically communicate their results to the computer which will print out the data.

Patent information. A computer system for the patent department is being considered which would file and retrieve all kinds of data on worldwide situations concerning patents, trademarks, renewals, and so forth.

It has been made clear that the question for management was not "Is there to be computer centralization?" but "How much centralization is appropriate?" Looking ahead, most of the executives seemed to think in terms of more centralization of computer service rather than less. However, there were important differences in how far this centralization was expected to go.

Some firms anticipated regional computer centers and, perhaps, later consolidation at one data center. Other companies specifically expected to retain some computer capability at their plants, in addition to having a central data processing activity. The reason was that only part of the computer information generated or processed at the plants needed to be transmitted to headquarters.

A third point of view encountered at one company was that in fifteen years the firm would not have any computers. It was expected by the controller that the economies of scale in computers would make it desirable by that time for his company to subscribe to an outside computer service on a time-sharing basis. The telephone company, or some other corporation, would supply the computer service and bill its customers. However, as was mentioned earlier, the larger the computer program or operation, the greater is the chance of error, and the more users with access to the information system, the greater the problem of protecting confidential company data.

While recognizing these advantages and problems, the director of computer services at another firm believed that his company's future requirements for computer capability would be so great that it would function as a "computer service utility." The company computer center would supply various outside customers, as well as internal users, with a full service using time sharing and remote consoles.

The differences in expectations really center upon the volume of usage that is expected and the anticipated economies of scale. The greater the usage and the lower the unit costs for central installations, the more likely we are to see central data centers for large companies, or the extensive use of public utility type computer service organizations.

Decision making, obviously, is one of the areas of greatest interest concerning management information systems. It seems clear that the role of middle management will be at least as important in the future as it is at present. There is good reason to believe that there will be little change in the level of decision making in most firms in the next decade.

It seems likely that the major change in top management decision making will be an increased emphasis on the analysis of alternatives, which will involve the review of a greater number of possibilities than at present, and a more extensive evaluation of the most promising alternatives. Simulations, data summaries, optimizing techniques, and computerized projections will play an important part in the testing of these alternatives. However, the availability of such management analysis tools will place still greater emphasis on questions and judgments concerning "what is reasonable?" or "what is practical?" or "how?" and "when?" in reaching decisions. Thus, in the words of one vice president of corporate planning: "Computers don't obviate the need for human judgment. They make it more important than before."

The information and ideas about the impact of management information systems on the enterprise appear applicable to the foreseeable future. Recognizing the computer and operations research as powerful new tools, their greatest contribution will be to allow both middle and top management to function better. Rather than forcing a particular organization structure, the future developments in management information systems are likely to permit greater freedom of choice.

Managements will be able to adopt organization structures that are centralized or decentralized to the extent desired with less concern than ever before about the availability of necessary information. Such an opportunity should significantly enhance the efficiency of management organizations in the years ahead.

SUGGESTED QUESTIONS FOR MANAGEMENT

From this discussion about management information systems, we naturally move to the question, "What should be done?" The specific answers, of course, will be different depending on the problems of the particular enterprise. However, some general questions can be raised by top management to aid in evaluating the present situation and in developing possible improvements.

The importance of probing questions should not be underestimated. Many times, a problem or opportunity goes unrecognized until the appropriate question is raised. The questions below are intended as illustrations of "first round" inquiries that may prove useful:

1. What is the return on investment for our data processing activity? How does this compare, project by project, with the return on investment forecast when each project was proposed?
2. How do the cost of computer and operations research projects done by our central group compare with the cost of using outside organizations?
3. Where do the ideas come from in this firm for computer and operations research projects? How are they evaluated and by whom?
4. What is being done to explore applications of mathematical decision aids, simulation, data processing, and automatic monitoring or controls, to line activities? How are the line organizations and executives involved in this?
5. How do we determine what data processing and operations research capability should be decentralized to our plants and divisions?
6. How do we assure that all the assumptions are reasonable for the problem at hand when working on operations research or computer projects? How extensive is our use of executives with relevant business experience on task forces for computer system or operations research projects?

7. What are we doing to assure that our senior and middle management executives understand the potential applications and the limitations in decision making of computer equipment and of operations research methods?

8. How are we developing an understanding of the business and its problems in our computer and operations research specialists? What provision is made to give these personnel opportunities to move into line assignments and vice versa?

9. What measures do we have about the level of understanding or the degree of progress we have achieved concerning question groups 7 and 8 above?

EXTERNAL AND EMPLOYEE RELATIONS

10

External and employee relations have been combined in this chapter because of their overlapping areas of concern. It is difficult to discuss such topics as race relations, collective bargaining, or stockholder relations and employee participation plans without covering some elements of both external relations and employee relations. The various subject headings in the chapter have been selected in recognition of these joint interests and their prospect for increased attention from top management in the future.

191

SHIFT IN EMPHASIS

The greater scope and variety of functions, increased staff size, and greater attention from top management during the past decade all demonstrate the impressive increase in emphasis on external and employee relations in the companies studied. The extreme case encountered was a more than sevenfold increase in personnel and budget for one public relations department. In none of the companies visited do the external relations or employee relations activities now receive less emphasis than before.

The reasons for this increase seem to be: (1) increased involvement of government in the affairs of the business community, (2) greater use of national collective bargaining on labor contracts and the attendant publicity in news reporting, (3) a larger and more diversified stockholder group, (4) a broader interpretation of the social responsibilities of business, and (5) a shift in the emphasis of management concerning external and employee relations from a narrow, defensive approach to a broader strategy of anticipating problems and changes.

This strategy shift is illustrated by the creation in one company of a separate long-range planning group in the public relations department, and by the appointment in another leading firm of a corporate relations committee headed by a senior vice president. In employee relations, collective bargaining strategy is now commonly worked out months in advance. Executive reference information is developed and public opinion is courted long before actual negotiations begin. In some cases public tours of plants and facilities are especially encouraged in the months prior to contract termination to forestall erroneous claims about working conditions. On a longer term basis, joint labor-management task forces have been created in at least one industry to work on mutual problems starting more than two years before contract expiration.

ORGANIZATION POSITION AND ACTIVITIES

In most of the participating companies the external relations and the employee relations organization reported to the chairman or president of the company. In some firms one or both of these functions was directly under an executive who reported to the president. The reporting level appeared to be a reflection of the importance attached to the public relations and the employee relations functions in the particular enterprise and the degree of top management involvement. In one company with crucial external problems, the head of the public relations activity discussed business matters with the chairman almost every day on which the latter was at headquarters. In other cases, the public relations activity chief might go for days without any specific need to contact the president or chief executive officer.

Generally, the external or employee relations organization at headquarters provided policy guidance and professional assistance to the various plants and divisions. Where plants or divisions had their own public relations or employee relations personnel, the senior people were usually trained or recommended by the headquarters organization. However, the plant or division public relations and employee relations representative generally worked directly for the line executives at their locations.

The authority for the public relations department or group was usually limited to advice and counsel, although there was a number of activities in which it exercised a veto as to content and timing of public announcements. The executive bulletin from one of the participating firms gives a representative sample of the area of jurisdiction:

1. Public relations should be consulted whenever any activity affects newspapers, magazines, radio, or television.
2. Public relations assistance should be enlisted on speeches to outside audiences that may get publicity from press, radio, or television. Speeches should be cleared with public relations.
3. The following activities should be cleared through public relations:
   a. Acquisitions and dispositions
   b. Product introductions and withdrawals
   c. Plant openings and closings
   d. Operating changes which have an effect upon community employment

A major addition to this typical pattern for handling external relations was displayed by one large firm which recently established a corporate relations committee, alluded to earlier. This committee is chaired by a senior vice president; its other members are two executive vice presidents, the vice president of personnel, the vice president of public relations, the legal counsel, and the corporate secretary.

The committee functions as the policy-developing (but not necessarily policy-setting) body of the company on external affairs. It does not replace the public relations department but generally deals with topics in advance of their presentation as matters for public relations action. This corporate relations committee is one response to the increasing need for planning ahead in external relations and the need for top management participation to make this forward planning effective.

An unusual feature of the committee is that its chairman has refused to permit a staff to be assigned. When the committee decides that something must be done, the implementation of the program is given to one or more of the major functional groups or product divisions of the company. Frequently these programs require coordinated efforts by several teams within the company. The committee reviews the progress. Several advantages are claimed for this arrangement: (1) It saves money and avoids empire building. (2) It gives the line and functional groups a greater interest in external relations activities because the details of the program and its implementation are their creation. (3) It allows the assignment of whatever combination of talents may be required to do the job. (4) Perhaps most important of all, the membership of the committee assures that the measures have the backing of senior line and functional officials.

The backing of top management is also obtained in the employee relations area by use of senior executive committees. However, here the executives are discussing problems already known to be important. The corporate relations committee is distinctive in this study for its role in identifying problems not previously labeled as important.

The employee relations function generally included hiring, training programs, wage and salary administration, collective bargaining, insurance, credit union, pension programs, cafeteria or food service, and health and medical services. In a few cases plant security and industrial engineering were also a part of the employee relations organizations. Presumably industrial engineering was included because of its importance in establishing work standards, methods, and the basis for setting relative pay rates on jobs.

In employee relations, differences in titles of the senior functional executives often reflect the degree of central authority concerning employee relations matters. Among the participating companies these titles ranged from director to executive vice president. Regardless of title the top employee relations executive always had direct access to the chief executive when required. During important labor negotiations several of the companies arranged for a committee of senior officers to be available, when needed, to consider developments and approve new moves by the company negotiators. In one case the top officers of the company actually moved into a special set of living quarters to be available day or night for consultation during negotiations. In other cases the senior officials were kept informed of progress and problems but usually were not personally involved in day-to-day developments. An outline describing one company's decentralized labor contract negotiation methods is included as the first Appendix at the end of this chapter.

The variations in the degree of top management participation in the day-by-day negotiations were apparently a reflection of several factors: (1) the financial importance of the contract terms being considered, (2) whether bargaining was to set a new industry pattern or simply to modify a local plant contract, and (3) the relative importance of the company's senior labor relations executive in his company and in the industry.

The status of the senior external relations executive also influences the scope of his activities. These activities tend to be even more varied than those described for employee relations. External relations activities cover a wide range of problems and functions, including such topics as bigness, safety, overseas nationalism, pollution, buildings, contributions, public understanding, product information, plant visits, publications, annual reports and the annual stockholders' meeting, political education, community projects, contacts with public officials, educational aid, role in industry associations, and so forth. Obviously these items involve many different departments and groups in any large corporation. It is not surprising, therefore, to find that in all the companies in this study, great emphasis is placed on coordination to provide effective planning and action on these varied external or public relations matters.

The second Appendix at the end of this chapter gives the agenda for a monthly meeting on the external affairs of one company, along with comments by the committee chairman on several of the items discussed. This further illustrates the range and importance of the external matters that must be considered, coordinated, and acted upon in the present business setting.

In addition to company headquarters and plant offices for external relations, several of the companies studied maintained a Washington, D.C. office and certain regional offices. These were normally headed by a representative of the president's office or of the public relations staff, often with the title of vice president. These offices serve as clearing houses for information desired from the area and as the "home base" for the resident spokesmen of the firm. One large company has not had a Washington representative for many years; however, senior officers of the company feel that this has been a mistake. On the other hand, none of the firms maintaining a Washington office has any intention of withdrawing it. This is consistent with the growing importance of the federal government in business activities and the large companies' increasing "need to know" about government data and policies.

Outside public relations firms were sometimes employed by the participating companies. Usually these were for special projects of limited time duration. Their use seems to be similar to that of outside legal counsel to supplement the work of the law department of a corporation.

COMMUNITY AFFAIRS

All the companies studied encourage their employees and officers to take an active part in community affairs. This involves everything from Red Cross and Community Chest fund drives to Boy Scouts and elective public office. Ten years ago, many of these firms were neutral or discouraged employees from participating in civic affairs.

In the last few years several of the firms have sponsored political action courses for employees, and their graduates have frequently become active in local affairs. Most of the companies will provide time off for campaigning for local offices, but expect that if the employee is elected the position will not interfere with his work in the company.

These community assignments have sometimes posed serious problems for the individual and/or the company. One example cited was the alleged conflict of interest by a school board member (a company executive) in the selection of equipment for new schools. In another case, the mayor and several other local officials were all executives of one company. This ultimately led to charges that the company was trying to run the town.

Another problem was the unanticipated increase in the workload of a public office. An executive of the largest company in a community was appointed to the local airport commission. Subsequently plans were launched to develop the airport into a major regional air terminal. The resulting workload for the members of the commission seriously interfered with the ability of the executive to perform his normal functions for the company. While withdrawal from the commission was a possibility, senior executives in the company were reluctant to endorse this, since it would imply company opposition to a project in which the whole community was deeply interested.

A third type of problem resulted for a large company in the South which had a policy of nondiscrimination toward color in hiring or advancement. This firm was the largest employer in a particular community, and various groups pressured the local management to use (or not use) the substantial economic power of the company to coerce smaller local firms to serve all persons and to provide equal employment opportunities. No matter what decision the management of the large company made, an important segment of the community would bitterly attack it.

In another case involving race relations, a big company was the victim of a local campaign to import unskilled colored workers from another area. The big company had already taken the lead in establishing special arrangements to assist minority group members in its training programs and to provide jobs, but this was not considered to be enough by the leaders of the local pressure group. As a result of an unfortunate decision by a junior official who was dealing with the pressure group, the top officers had to take charge personally of the matter. In spite of their efforts, the company received considerable unfavorable national publicity and suffered severely in the community. This is another example where being the largest employer in the city, or the largest firm in the industry, seemed to be a definite disadvantage in external and employee relations.

Careful review to anticipate possible difficulties and the assignment of experienced executives to handle novel or potentially dangerous situations seem to be the best way to avoid or minimize these problems. Once enmeshed, there frequently is no easy answer, and the company may have to "write off" unfavorable publicity or unexpected expenditure of executive time as a kind of contribution to community welfare.

STATE AND NATIONAL AFFAIRS

The companies participating in this study appear to have developed a more favorable attitude toward state and national affairs in recent years. The most frequent requests are for temporary or regular assignment of executives to committees or to administrative posts in government. Occasionally there are problems concerning elective office.

One large firm has a definite policy of active cooperation when asked to make executives available and goes to surprising lengths to protect the interests of the employee. He is not released unless he wishes to accept the appointment, and if the post requires complete separation from the company he is given a separation payment equal to the difference between his current salary and the government salary for the period of his government assignment. There is, of course, no way in which the separated employee can be protected when promotions must be made and he is no longer in the firm. On the other hand, his government service may give him background that will make him a more capable or more knowledgeable executive in later years.

In political campaigns, problems often result when the candidate for election is a company employee or some of his active supporters are associated with the company. The most effective defenses against the claim of company influence are often a well publicized policy of encouraging political activity by employees supporting *all* major parties and action to minimize attention to the company affiliation.

The reasons for these more mature or public-spirited company attitudes about outside activity seem to be a blend of corporate good citizenship and a belief that if government officials understand business problems better, government action concerning business is likely to be more intelligent.

CORPORATE INFORMATION

Another major area in which there has been substantial change in recent years is the development and distribution of corporate information. Financial reports are more revealing, company magazines are more numerous and more elaborate, product information and speeches are more widely distributed. In almost every area of public interest, the corporations studied are providing more information now than in earlier years. This greater flow of information apparently results from: (1) the increased recognition by management of the advertising and public relations value of company information, (2) the growing number of new products and their more rapid obsolescence, (3) the greater demands of government regulatory agencies, and (4) the tremendous increase in the number of persons who have a legitimate interest in many details concerning a firm. This includes members of the growing family of new stockholders, representatives of the security analysts or other financial groups, and potential customers for the firm's expanding product line. Employees' stock purchase programs and bonus plans have, of course, created a special interest on the part of employees to know more about their company. Since most, if not all, of these factors probably will continue to operate, it seems likely that we will see still more emphasis on corporate information and external relations in the years ahead.

MANAGEMENT-LABOR RELATIONS

In discussing changes in the last decade, we cannot overlook the substantial improvement in management-labor relations. Perhaps this improvement results in part from the fact that both management and labor have begun to spend more time planning and looking ahead. Perhaps the experience of recent years has convinced many members of the negotiating teams that they can trust the men on the other side of the table, or perhaps the dollars and cents value of labor stability has made a deep impression on both groups. Whatever the reasons, there appears to be a feeling of mutual respect and trust between the executives of most of the companies and their union representatives.

As union officials have learned more about the companies with which they are negotiating, they have also come to understand more about the company problems. This has no doubt led to more intelligent negotiations. In some cases, both national and local, union leaders have been able to discuss company problems so well that they have had difficulty in retaining the confidence of their union members.

Management's improved understanding illustrated by the fact that some of the firms visited have successfully resisted union organizing efforts since World War II. Specific comments on this score include: "We have found that there is a definite correlation between the feeling of insecurity and labor conflict." "No lay-offs is believed to be the major reason the firm was never unionized." Interestingly enough, these ideas have successfully been combined with a demand for efficiency. In the first company quoted, the basic philosophy has changed from a feeling of obligation to keep all employees on the job to a belief that management has a responsibility to the people remaining in the organization to run it efficiently and thus afford better wages. The second company has also met the efficiency problem directly. It uses product market strategy plus a combination of retraining, transfer, early retirement, and separation to maintain high efficiency with no lay-offs and excellent labor relations.

Reviewing the numerous successful examples of labor-management relations among the fifteen companies surveyed, the key to their success seems to be that they have been careful to provide wages and benefits that are competitive with those of leading rivals, good working conditions, and fair treatment. In fact, at one of the un-unionized companies the large size of the employee relations staff was explained by pointing out that they had to provide all the services for their employees that both a company and a union would normally offer. At another company, a careful check is kept on the wage rates of major rivals, and pay increases are instituted by the company when it begins to lose position. In still a third firm, the emphasis is on resolving labor difficulties promptly, informally, and at the lowest practical level—recognizing the great cost of letting small problems grow large.

With improved understanding on both sides and a feeling of mutual trust, employee relations may provide more constructive action in the years ahead than we have been accustomed to see in the past.

APPENDIX: OUTLINE OF DECENTRALIZED LABOR CONTRACT NEGOTIATION METHODS USED BY A PARTICIPATING COMPANY

The vice president of personnel in this company commented as follows:

1. We want to give as much authority as possible to the operating departments, but we need to maintain a certain amount of centralized control.
2. The employee relations office develops the procedures to be followed during contract negotiations.
3. The plant managers actually carry on most of the negotiations with the unions.
4. We follow a general rule that we are always open on wages. We have had some discussion lately, however, about the desirability of negotiating with a view to having wages closed for a three-year period.
5. Each plant manager has a general idea of what is expected of him. For example, he may be informed that the approved guideline is an 8-cent increase per hour.
6. The vice president serves as a monitor of all labor relations policies that have been approved by the executive committee.
7. The general manager of a plant may present a new situation, for example, one that looks like a strike, to the executive committee for discussion. The general manager benefits from the opinions presented by members of the executive committee and then makes the decision. He may be given such advice as "Don't cave in; don't make a major issue of a minor point," etc. The important thing is that the general manager is responsible for making the decision.

8. All matters pertaining to fringe benefits come to the attention of the executive committee.
9. None of our plants built since World War II is unionized. There have been four elections at one plant, but the union has still been unable to get sufficient votes to be approved for bargaining purposes. On an overall corporation basis, there are 40 percent nonunion, 55 percent members of independent unions, and 5 percent members of national unions.
10. Our philosophy on labor relations is that if we have any kind of a problem involving our employees, we should deal with it today. Over a period of ten years we have not had a single stoppage strike.

APPENDIX: AGENDA FOR A MONTHLY MEETING OF A CORPORATE RELATIONS COMMITTEE WITH SOME NOTES BY THE CHAIRMAN

1. *Rising food prices*
   Issues: What should the company's position be?
               What should the company do?
               What is the responsibility of the trade association?
   Action: It was decided to publicize the causes of price increases.
2. *Possibility of wage-price controls*
   Comment: This came up through the personnel department.
   Action: Recommended change by U.S. Department of Commerce was considered and approved.
3. *Political candidate's visit to company headquarters*
   Comment: This came up from secretary of the corporation.
   Issue: Should we invite political candidates for governor?
   Action: Problem was discussed with chairman; he approved, and it was decided to go ahead.
4. *Council for sound state constitution*
   Comment: Company helped found this organization.
   Action: Company is going to cooperate. Company sent leaflets to all employees.
5. *Packaging legislation*
   Comment: Previously some restrictive measures of the bill were removed.
   Issues: What should company be doing under new law?
               Is there a need for follow-up on what company officials said they would do on a voluntary basis?
6. *Business internship program*
   Comment: This was a university proposal. Ten-week pilot effort to be conducted next summer. Participants to be 50 young men between junior and senior years in college who are majoring in political science, history, and so forth.
   Action: Company decided it would take two interns.

7. *American host program*

    Comment: One of the company executives had been studying misconceptions that teachers in Europe have about the United States. Plan is that teacher being sponsored pay only his expenses to and from the United States. Program has been going on for three years.

                Another corporation got teachers from locations in factory towns in Europe where the company had plants and put them in locations in the U.S. where the company has factories.

    Action: The company concluded that the international division should sponsor these teachers and pick up half the cost. Committee chairman will check this out with international division.

8. *Consumerism program*

    Comment: Report given on things going on, such as a meeting with magazine editors on consumerism.

9. *Miscellaneous*

    Comment: Effective citizens organization discussed.

                Ohio politics discussed.

                Political action course (classes) at company discussed.

SELECTION AND DEVELOPMENT OF EXECUTIVE PERSONNEL

11

The chief executive officers of every company visited expressed primary concern over their company's short-term and long-term plans and programs for the selection and development of executive personnel. Although the degree of top-executive involvement varied considerably in the fifteen companies studied, it was crystal clear at every company that this activity merited a top-priority position in terms of the president's time and attention. One president expressed this by saying: "The selection and development of managerial and executive talent will be our number one problem during the next ten years." Another chief executive officer said: "People are the basis of our success. The only way to make everyone in the corporation take a strong interest in the development of people is for me to lead the way in becoming personally involved in the selection and development of the young men who are destined to become the future leaders of the corporation."

There was general recognition of the increasing need to accelerate the flow of top-quality executives to meet the new managerial challenges of an expanding economy and to cope with significantly more complex problems caused by technological and social changes. Frequent mention was made of the constant shortage of imaginative, flexible, and broad-gauged managerial personnel with a capability in general management. Perhaps this increasing awareness of the need for general management capabilities has resulted from the multiplicity of changes in the nature and demands of the executive's job. Typically, managerial and technical employees are better educated and their expectations are vastly different from those of their counterparts of a generation ago. They are more mobile and they expect to be managed by consent rather than by coercion. Changes of this nature require management to have more sophisticated behavioral and communication skills and a more enlightened understanding of the social and economic value systems of individual employees.

Changes in the internal environment of business have had an important impact upon the job of management. The introduction of the project-or-program concept of management in many industries has placed increased emphasis on coordination, and this, in turn, has altered the nature and use of staff activities. Domestic and international competition has increased within and between industries. Growth through acquisition and mergers, plus diversification, dispersion, and decentralization, has generated new and more complex managerial problems which have intensified the need for more flexible and sophisticated executives. The introduction of new tools and techniques in the area of data processing and information technology has increased the demand for executives with a broad range of managerial capabilities.

With the increasing range and complexity of managerial problems, there is little wonder that there has been considerable turmoil during recent years in the area of executive selection and development. Although the requirements for successful management during the past few years may have been quite different among the fifteen companies studied, certain practices and trends were evident in the companies that appear to be doing the most effective job of selecting, appraising, and developing their executive personnel. The most pertinent developments that have been gleaned from interviews with executives of the participating companies are described in this chapter under the following headings:

1. Requirements for success in top management
2. Planning and organizing for effective selection, evaluation, and development
3. Selection and early identification of potential executive personnel
4. Appraisal and evaluation
5. Development of full potential

REQUIREMENTS FOR SUCCESS IN TOP MANAGEMENT

During the past twenty years many studies have been made in an attempt to discover the personal characteristics that distinguish successful from unsuccessful executives. Although no single distinctive profile of the successful executive has emerged, suggestions have indicated that successful executives tend to possess certain qualities normally not found in less effective ones. The positive qualities most frequently mentioned in these studies include: drive, initiative, objectivity, flexibility, imagination, decisiveness, emotional stability, skill in human relations, skill in analysis, communication skills, mental alertness, good judgment, sense of dedication, willingness to take risks, and breadth of knowledge and interest.

Comments by executives. In the present study, which included interviews with over 260 executives, there was general agreement that most of the qualities listed above are extremely important for success in top management positions. All the top executives were cognizant, however, of the dangers in attempting to draw a rigid profile of an effective executive with a view toward matching candidates against this profile. One chairman of the board expressed his concern on this matter as follows: "One of the few things in this field that we have learned to accept without question is that widely different people function effectively as executives. There is no simple stereotype."

Some other typical comments from top-level executives in the participating companies emphasize that the requirements for success in management are action-oriented, broad in scope, and difficult to identify in advance of performance.

Chairman of the board and chief executive officer. How will he work with people? What kind of a personality does he have? Can he make a decision? Is he so analytical that he doesn't know on which side he is? Is he ambitious and willing to take on new challenges? What is the evidence of this? Is he overambitious to the extent that he will sacrifice others to improve his own promotion prospects?

Chairman of the board. The most important things we look for in selecting men for major executive assignments are:

Performance. Has he done well in all of his assignments?

Line experience. No one has or no one ever will run this business unless he has had real experience in the operating end of the business.

Stamina. Does he have the energy for sustained hard work? Will he stand up under pressure?

Character. Is he forthright and honest? Does he have high moral standards?

Loyalty. Will he put the company's interest ahead of making a record for himself?

President. For the senior positions in the corporation, outstanding performance by the candidates being considered is assumed. The selection, therefore, is on such factors as experience needed for the job, the personality of the candidate, and the way he has handled and developed his people in previous assignments.

Executive vice president of manufacturing. If there is anything you need it is the development in a man of the "sense of manufacturing urgency." You must develop the ability to be impatient at times. The man who will be successful as a manager must develop a recognition of the importance of time.

Chairman of the board and chief executive officer. The future general managers will be those who have "drive" and who are "dedicated plus" and who have a fair degree of intellectual ability. It isn't too important what their background is or what their experience is.

Vice president of finance. In looking for a person who can fill the position of vice president of finance, I look for a person who (1) can get the job done, (2) can roll with the punches and work with people, and (3) has a broad background and knowledge of business, the industry, and our company.

President. Among other things, a candidate for a top position should have a certain feeling of "controlled restlessness" coupled with a permanent feeling of dissatisfaction with performance.

Chairman of the board and chief executive officer. Great leaders in business must have the capacity to visualize, conceive, imagine, and resolve. We have a lot of good people, but we need a few great people. They excite the others.

The generalist versus the specialist. During the past few years many claims have been made by professors and by technical specialists to the effect that the channels of mobility into top management positions will be changed with a larger percentage of the future top executives coming up through information and computer technology. Similar claims have been made for scientists in view of the increasing importance of research and technological development.

This issue was discussed in depth with the top executives of the participating companies and with the executives in charge of data processing and computers, operations research, and research and development functions. There was almost unanimous agreement by the top executives in general management and by the top functional executives that the channels are not likely to change materially. If the specialist desires to advance into a high position in general management, he will normally be required to obtain broad operating experience. The following comments by a chairman of the board are typical of the views expressed by top executives in all the participating companies:

Top management is involved in the selection of department managers throughout the world. The trend is to cross-fertilize and to move people from one function to another. The demand for growth has forced this process. We insist upon a policy of looking for the best man wherever he is—inside the company or outside. We have also made it very clear to the specialist that if he plans to go anyplace with the company, he has to become more of a generalist.

A more detailed discussion of the generalist-specialist dichotomy is included in Chapter 12, "Road to the Top."

PLANNING AND ORGANIZING FOR EFFECTIVE SELECTION, EVALUATION, AND DEVELOPMENT

When the original study, *Top Management Organization and Control,* was made, formal executive selection and development programs, including replacement charts, backup schedules, personal inventory records, and scheduled individual personal development plans were almost nonexistent. Considerable progress has been made on this front, particularly during the past ten years. In Chapter 3, "Long-Range Planning," it was pointed out that one of the areas that has shown great improvement is that of corporate manpower planning at the managerial and executive levels. The identification and planned development of key personnel has become a vital part of the total long-range planning activity in all the fifteen corporations included in the present study. Replacement charts, backup lists, and individual development plans for each executive position are the rule rather than the exception today.

Among the companies visited, however, there was considerable variation in the degree of centralized planning and control of executive selection and development activities. Some of the participating companies possessed highly structured, formal programs with strong centralized functional guidance and coordination. Others selected, evaluated, and developed their executive and managerial personnel largely on a decentralized basis with active participation by line management and with a minimum of coordination and control by the corporate functional staff.

Use of committees. Four of the fifteen companies use top-level committees in the administration of their executive selection and development programs; two of these companies have established special committees, whereas the other two utilize their regular executive committees to perform this function. The remaining eleven companies rely upon line management with the assistance of corporate or divisional staff personnel. All fifteen companies have a functional corporate staff executive to provide service and overall coordination.

In one of the companies that uses a special top-level committee, the chairman of the board, the president, and three executive vice presidents are members of the committee. The committee meets every week for approximately two hours during which time the various operating divisions present their executive promotion, replacement, and development plans. Each year the committee reviews the qualifications of approximately 1,500 individuals and approves appointments to the top 225 positions at the corporate and divisional levels. A more detailed description of this company's program is included at the end of this chapter in the example of Corporation A.

The special committee in the second company includes the chairman of the board, the president, and the vice president of industrial relations as permanent members. Other senior vice presidents participate as members of the committee when their areas are considered. Once a year, all factory managers, chief engineers, works managers, and key functional managers are reviewed by this committee for promotion, transfer, and development. This company, which is organized on a functional basis, has 45,000 employees and a sales volume of over one billion dollars.

Of the two companies that use their regular executive committee to select and evaluate executives, the committee in one company reviews and approves appointments for the top 150 executives and managers of the corporation. The selection and evaluation process includes the executives from the president down through the assistant divisional managers and the assistant directors of the various functions of sales, manufacturing, control, and research in the operating divisions. This worldwide company has over 100,000 employees and a sales volume of over $3 billion.

In the second company the executive committee, with the president as chairman, is directly involved in reviewing the qualifications and appointments of the top 300 executives and managers. The president talks with all appointees at the divisional manager level and above prior to the time of appointment. He describes his personal involvement in the following words: "If I have the right man as division manager, my job is much easier. I dignify the job of division manager by insisting on talking with each individual before he is promoted." This company has over 130,000 employees with 65 decentralized operating divisions. Complete personal inventory records are maintained by the corporate staff department on the top 10,000 management and professional personnel. Replacement schedules and individual development plans have been developed for approximately 900 individuals. A more de-tailed description of the methods and techniques used by this company in administering its program is included in the example of Corporation B at the end of this chapter.

Administration without the use of a committee. In the companies that do not use a special committee to evaluate executives for promotion, the chairman of the board and the president are directly involved with the appropriate line and staff executives in appointing key executives.

In one of the companies, the chairman and chief executive officer and the president spend a full week each year, in July, to meet with the group vice presidents and divisional managers and discuss overall manpower plans and evaluate the past performance, future potential, and individual development plans for approximately 700 individuals. They spend another week in January with the group vice presidents and divisional managers to review their recommendations with respect to bonus allocations. It is significant to note that the bonus allocation reviews, which emphasize past performance, are held at a separate time from the other evaluations, which include a review of past performance but stress future potential and forward planning.

The president of another participating company has complete organization charts on his wall, including the pictures of the top 250 executives in the company. He knows these men personally and keeps close watch on their progress and development. He commented upon his involvement as follows:

> When I look at people, I go pretty deep in the organization. People represent the heart of our business. We have two visits a year with each division, once with the board of directors and once with the president's corporate staff. When I meet with the divisions with my staff, we have a closed meeting and we go over each division's replacement chart for all key people. We may spend from two hours to a half-day on this, and a lot of questions are asked.
>
> I also approve all salary changes for employees who are earning over $20,000 a year. This gives me an opportunity to keep in close touch with approximately 1,000 of the top people in the corporation. I have been doing this for the past ten years.
>
> In the case of key men, who I think have great potential, I put them on a two- or three-year rotation basis to give them experience in different functions and with different kinds of problems. Whenever possible we try to team up men with different backgrounds. For example, I think it is ideal if you have two men in a box, one with an engineering or scientific background and another with a general business background.

In a third company, the president focuses primary attention on approximately 200 high-potential individuals through a very informal "Five Key Men" executive selection and development program. Several years ago, this company had a highly centralized formal program with a multiplicity of personal inventory records, colored replacement charts, tests, and periodic evaluation forms for every supervisor, manager, and executive. At the request of the president, this system was replaced with a very simple "Key Five" program wherein each division, plant, and foreign subsidiary is required to submit the names of five individuals within their organizations who have the greatest potential for positions as divisional managers. The corporate director of personnel maintains personal inventory records of all "Key Five" individuals, but the line organization is responsible for the administration of the program. The pressure comes from the president who is constantly asking questions about the progress of the "Key Five" men. This company, which has approximately 35,000 employees located in over 140 plants throughout the world, has been very successful in implementing a decentralized philosophy of management.

It is clear from the illustrations given above that no one plan or organization can or should be applied to all companies. Each company should work out its executive selection and development program according to its particular needs. The chief executive normally is directly involved in determining these needs and in implementing the program.

Recent changes and future trends. In spite of the wide divergence in methodology and structure in planning executive development programs, there was a consensus among the executives visited that certain significant changes had taken place during the past few years in administering these programs within their corporations. The improved changes and future trends most frequently mentioned included:

1. Increased personal involvement and commitment by top management.
2. More effective integration at the executive level of manpower planning and corporate long-range plans and operations.
3. Greater use of an improved professional corporate staff service, which includes a more sophisticated information system for use in manpower planning.
4. Improved selection and early identification of young men with top management potential.
5. A more realistic approach to executive appraisal encompassing separate evaluations on past performance and on long-term future potential.
6. Increased emphasis upon development programs geared to the personal needs of each individual and including considerable personal involvement by top management.

SELECTION AND EARLY IDENTIFICATION
OF POTENTIAL EXECUTIVE PERSONNEL

In all the participating companies there was appreciation by top management of the increasing complexity of future managerial problems and challenges. This recognition was coupled with a realization that one of the most important responsibilities of senior executives is to develop a capability in their subordinates of being able to identify, recruit, and develop those rare individuals with the potential leadship qualities required to assume top management responsibilities in the 1990s.

Recruitment of college graduates. One of the most significant changes in recruitment practices during recent years has been the increased involvement of line executives in the actual recruiting and interviewing process. The companies with the most successful college recruitment programs have experimented with several new techniques. Some follow the practice of having recently hired college graduates return to their former colleges in advance of their corporations' recruiting visits. The alumnus visits informally with students and faculty members in an attempt to identify the outstanding candidates in the present graduating class and to encourage them to sign up for interviews. Prerecruitment visits of this nature by alumni who know the students and faculty have proved to be very effective. Several companies have established summer intern programs for a select number of graduate students who have completed the first year of a two-year M.B.A. program. These students are assigned to work on special projects under the direction of one or more top executives. Companies that have used this technique and the participating students are very enthusiastic about the intern programs. When the students return to the campus, they tend to become ambassadors of good will for the company among their fellow students.

Several of the companies visited reported that they are cooperating with leading graduate schools of business in providing current case material for use in classes. Two of the companies are participating in the development of major case studies on the overall strategies, plans, and programs of their corporations. Students spend considerable time studying the special problems of the industry and the particular company; afterward they write group reports that are submitted to the president. The president and a select group of executives review the reports and visit the school to meet with the students. This cooperative educational venture provides excellent training for future managers and, indirectly, serves as a very effective recruiting aid for the corporation.

Opinions are divided concerning the value, from a recruiting standpoint, of having a formal corporate training program for college graduates who aspire to become managers. One of the participating companies has had such a program for over 30 years and is very well satisfied with the results. Other companies have experimented with formal training programs but have discontinued them on the grounds that the best training should be geared to the needs and capabilities of each new employee. There was a general feeling among most of the top executives interviewed that the really top young action-oriented college graduates are not interested in spending one or two years in a formal, corporate management training program. The trend during the past ten years has been toward the discontinuance of such programs or toward making them shorter and much more flexible.

Obtaining experienced executives from outside. All the fifteen companies visited adhere predominantly to a policy of promotion from within. In a few instances, where special capabilities are not available within, they hire experienced executives from outside the company. The presidents and/or chief executive officers in several companies, however, expressed the opinion that their responsibility was to identify and select the best possible men wherever they may be, inside the corporation or outside. The chairman and chief executive officer of one company made the following comments on the indirect benefits of going outside for experienced executives: "Occasional hiring of top talent from outside the company adds vigor and a fresh point of view to the organization. It also serves to prevent complacency and to improve competitive performance."

In Chapter 7, "Mergers and Acquisitions," mention was made of top management's concern over the quality and depth of management in the companies being considered for acquisition. In many instances one of the major advantages of a particular acquisition is the top managerial capability in the company to be acquired.

Early identification of executive potential. There was unanimous agreement by all executives interviewed that early identification of executive potential is an essential requirement for the continuous successful operation of their companies. They also concurred, however, that the task of identifying the young "comers" while they are in their twenties or early thirties is extremely difficult and risky. Frequently when young executives are appointed to positions of considerable responsibility at an early age, the older and more experienced executives resent this "crown prince" concept. In addition the young men may suffer from being moved too fast too soon. Although the executives are fully aware of the potential dangers of early identification and promotion, most of them feel that the long-term advantages far outweigh the potential risks.

Typically, the young men with exceptional executive capability and promise are identified in two major areas—performance and potential. The most frequently mentioned bases for evaluating performance include: (1) achievement in meeting predetermined objectives; (2) success in handling particularly difficult assignments or in performing effectively during critical incidents involving unusual time or emotional pressures; (3) results obtained in selecting and developing subordinates; (4) success in planning, organizing, directing, controlling, and motivating; (5) effectiveness in working with others at all levels—both within and outside the organization; (6) evidence of dedication and loyalty to the corporation. In evaluating potential, young executives normally are appraised on additional factors such as: creativeness, judgment, background, stability, flexibility, decisiveness, health, and intellectual capacity.

Techniques used by top management to identify young men with exceptional capability varied among the participating companies. The companies that appeared to be doing the best job of identifying and evaluating the young "comers" are those with a high degree of top management involvement in this activity. This involvement is evidenced in many ways, including: (1) top management's participation in planning and evaluating both short-term and long-range plans; (2) assignment of key young men to committee memberships or special task forces and evaluation of their performance; (3) use of "assistant to" positions to obtain firsthand evaluations of performance in a wide range of activities; (4) requiring subordinates to submit lists of "key men," "comers," or "high potentials"; (5) review and selection of young men to attend advanced management courses; (6) observation of presentations made by young executives; (7) participation in manpower planning, management reviews, and bonus allocation meetings.

In one of the most successful companies included in this study, the chairman of the board and former president described how young men with unusual capability were spotted through the use of "skimmer charts." Such a chart consists of a list of everyone who is making $20,000 a year or more. Separate charts are made up for each operating department. The names are arranged on the chart by age groups and salary and a line is drawn across the chart connecting various percentage points for each age group, thus "skimming off the cream." The president gives greater attention to the younger executives. For example, in the 32-year age group, 30 percent of those earning $20,000 a year or more are shown above the line. In the 55-year age group, only the top 5 percent of those earning $20,000 or more are shown above the line. The skimmer charts provide a guide for the president, members of the executive committee, and the general managers of departments to use in spotting competent individuals. They also point out situations where particular departments may have clusters of outstanding individuals in certain age groups, and/or discrepancies among the various departments. This relatively simple approach has been used successfully by the past three presidents of this corporation. The present chairman of the board and past president made the following comment on the importance of identifying competent young executives: "The heart of our business is people, and knowing the capabilities of comers. We try very hard to have an element of youth always present in top management. The skimmer chart gives me a chance to see who sticks his head up."

In several companies studied, "assistant to" positions have been created at the president and chairman of the board levels with a view toward using these positions to identify and evaluate young executives who appear to have top management potential. Normally the young executive is given a wide range of assignments during the twelve or more months that he is in this position. He then is transferred into a position with operating responsibility. The top executives who have used this technique are enthusiastic about the results, and they plan to continue the practice.

During the interviews a few executives questioned the value of developing lists of high-potential young men or in selecting one or two men each year to send to year-long programs. They felt that the identification of a few individuals at such an early stage in their careers was dangerous to the company and to the individuals. In contrast, however, the executives at companies that have developed "comer lists" and have participated in such programs spoke enthusiastically in favor of both practices.

In the companies visited there was little evidence that tests were being used extensively to identify young executives with top management potential. In fact, many executives were very skeptical about the value of tests for this purpose. The president of one company said, "We have taken the I.Q. test scores off the evaluation forms. It is the consensus of management that this information tends to do more harm than good. The important thing is 'can he get the job done effectively?' "

A vice president of personnel commented as follows upon his company's experience with tests as a predictive tool for management success: "We have been giving intelligence and personality tests to applicants for approximately fifteen years. We do not have a very impressive correlation of test results and success on the job. We are thinking seriously of abandoning the use of tests."

In another company, however, the top executives spoke rather favorably about the possibilities of using tests and questionnaires as effective devices to identify managerial and executive potential early in a person's career. This company has been engaged for many years in a research program designed to develop additional tools for identifying managerial talent. Top management has made a significant commitment of time to the program. Over the past ten years, hundreds of managers at all levels have served as guinea pigs in this effort. A series of tests and questionnaires has been developed for measuring such things as application of good judgment to problems, early maturity and independence, breadth of interest, initiative, ambition, adaptability, objectivity, stability, and sensitivity to other people and their needs. The chairman of the board of this company made the following comment about this research:

> Some promising results have been obtained, suggesting that we have a helpful means of determining among younger men their likely degree of success in management. There is, of course, skepticism about this direction of things. I think that this skepticism is rooted for most of us in the respect we develop over the years for the great variety and uniqueness of each individual. This quality makes us question whether such devices can actually measure man's potential managerial worth. In any event, we are using our research results as supplementary to our conventional approaches. It may be that the greatest role they will play for some years

will be in helping us to avoid overlooking promising management potential we would otherwise miss.

APPRAISAL AND EVALUATION

The increased emphasis that has been placed upon "management by objectives," target setting, short-term goals and long-range planning activities during recent years has indirectly caused substantial improvements in the appraisal and evaluation process. In every company visited, top executives expressed the opinion that their management appraisal and evaluation programs were more practical and effective than they had been a few years ago. The vice presidents of personnel and/or the directors of management selection and development all agreed that the major reason for this improvement has been top management's increased concern and involvement. This direct involvement by line management has had the effect of placing greater emphasis upon performance and results rather than upon personality traits. As a consequence, employee appraisals are more work-centered, timely, and meaningful to the individual and of greater practical value to the company.

Formal programs. There is a great variation in the degree to which the appraisal and evaluation programs within the various companies are formalized. Several companies have complete replacement charts, personal inventory records, and regularly scheduled appraisals for every member of management. Others utilize formal succession or replacement charts only at the higher levels of management, but appraise all managerial and salaried personnel once or twice a year, usually in conjunction with salary reviews or bonus allocations. In a few of the fifteen companies, however, the evaluation process consists primarily in the development of "key men" or "high potential" lists for promotion purposes.

Nature and scope of top management's involvement. In each of the companies studied, the chairman of the board and/or the president participate in or review the evaluations of performance and potential. They typically are concerned with the incumbents and candidates for the top three or four levels of management. The number of individuals involved ranges from a high of 1,500 in one of the largest companies to a low of approximately 50 in one of the smaller companies, with a median of 350.

In addition to becoming directly involved in the formal evaluation process, the chairman and/or president and, frequently, members of the board of directors have the opportunity to appraise the capabilities of executives by observing presentations made to the ,executive committee or to the board of directors. One of the participating companies has its entire board of directors and its president visit each major division or subsidiary once a year, at which time the major part of the day is spent reviewing the potential of individual executives in light of the division's manpower plans. Another company holds some of its directors' meetings at different plant locations throughout the world to provide an opportunity for the directors to see the operations and to become acquainted with key operating executives. A third company holds a meeting of its top 100 officers at headquarters once a year. Members of the board of directors are present, and thus have an opportunity to observe presentations and evaluate officers.

Several of the chief executive officers interviewed said that they spend a considerable portion of their time visiting the operating divisions to obtain firsthand evaluations of the performance and potential of executive personnel. One president indicated that he spends approximately one-fourth of his time in this way; another president, one-third of his time.

Counseling as part of the appraisal process.   Only two of the fifteen companies indicated that counseling and/or interviews between the superior and subordinates were part of their formal evaluation programs. Several companies have experimented with this technique, but have eliminated it as a required procedure. In the companies with decentralized operating divisions, the general manager of the division normally decides whether individual counseling should be a required part of the appraisal process. In most instances, discussions of evaluations with the manager being appraised are not required; this is particularly true at the higher levels of management. The vice president of personnel in one of the companies described line management's lack of enthusiasm for counseling as follows:

> Formal periodic evaluations are becoming less popular. The executives tend to be action-oriented individuals and therefore do not like to be counselors. They are uncomfortable when they have to sit down periodically and talk about the weaknesses of individuals as related to personality traits. They resent the fact that they have to call a man in and

say, "It's time that we have a talk!" These action-oriented men prefer to evaluate men in the normal course of work on the basis of their specific performances.

This vice president also cited the example of their asking 50 middle-level managers if they had been counseled by their superiors. The vast majority said "no." They also said, however, that they would have liked to have been counseled by their superiors. When the same 50 executives were asked whether they counseled their subordinates, the vast majority again said "no." The attitudes reported in this survey tend to indicate that there may be a wide gap between counseling theory and practice.

Most significant changes in appraisal and evaluation. Changes that have had the greatest impact during recent years include: (1) Increased involvement by top management, (2) improved integration of evaluation with work-centered accomplishments, (3) decreased emphasis upon use of tests and of personality evaluations, (4) increased use of pooled judgments in evaluating key managerial personnel, (5) separation of past performance and future potential evaluations, (6) improved personal information systems and more sophisticated use of central personnel services.

DEVELOPMENT OF FULL POTENTIAL

When the chief executives in the participating companies were asked what they felt to be their single greatest challenge in the years ahead, there was almost a unanimous response: "The development of people." A considerable portion of their time is devoted to the task of developing the potentialities of all members of management. The chief executive, through his personal involvement in executive development activities, is the pacesetter for the entire organization. If he creates a strong image as a developer of men, other executives follow his lead.

The nature and scope of executive development programs vary substantially within the companies visited. At one extreme are the companies that rely almost entirely upon on-the-job development, supplemented by voluntary self-development on the part of the individual through outside courses. At the other end of the spectrum are several companies that designate specific two- to four-year development programs for every manager or executive included in their replacement or succession charts. The companies that appear to be getting the most effective results from their executive development programs are those in which top management is directly involved and in which specific development plans are outlined for each individual executive or manager.

Although it is generally accepted that "people learn to manage by managing," there are various supplementary techniques that assist in the development process.

Internal development. Many methods are utilized by the participating companies for the internal development of executives. The most frequently mentioned are: on-the-job coaching; job rotation; committee, task force, and project assignments; use of "assistant to" positions; putting two men in one organizational box; conferences and seminars; and formal company-sponsored training programs.

1. *On-the-job coaching.* The most effective education or development must be done by the individual himself. His superior can inspire, coach, create an image, establish a favorable climate, suggest, advise, and lead. Effective development, however, depends upon the degree to which the subordinate responds to his superior's coaching and leadership. Under ideal conditions, on-the-job training is perhaps the single most effective method of internal development. The importance of self-development is illustrated by the following comments made by a chairman of the board to a new president: "You are a young man with a lot of energy. I want you to learn this job fast. There are twenty-four hours a day and seven days a week. Go to work."

2. *Job rotation.* Every company visited recognized the long-term value of job rotation in training future general managers. The companies with the most successful executive development programs start job rotation at a fairly early period in an individual's career. Companies that have autonomous, decentralized divisions normally have more active and effective job rotation programs as compared to companies with functional types of organization.

Several presidents indicated that they are directly involved in implementing transfers and job-rotation assignments, particularly among key executive personnel. One president described his involvement as follows: "We have a rather informal program for the development of management. I spend a substantial portion of my time in selecting and moving people. The divisions frequently are reluctant to give up good men, so I have to get into it. We expect to expand our rotational program."

Another president mentioned that the management of his company had been rather complacent when he assumed the presidency. He decided to jar things loose by rotating several executives at the divisional general manager level. Although this was a bold move for a new president, it worked out very well for this company at that particular time. Discussions with the general managers who were rotated indicated that the "merry-go-round" movement was beneficial in that it created a new climate that encouraged competition on the basis of who could contribute most to the corporation rather than who could claim most for his division.

In one of the larger corporations visited, the vice president in charge of a major division meets with his key executives and with the corporate vice president of personnel to plan and implement rotational moves for key men in 30 plants. The pictures of the men and the organization charts are displayed on a magnetic board. Detailed personnel records are available in the room. These facilities make it easy to try out different moves on the board. The technique has been very effective in providing diversified career development assignments and in planning sequential or "domino-type" replacements.

3. *Committee, task force, and project assignments.* Most of the participating companies used special assignments to develop key young executives. Assignments of this type provide an excellent opportunity to broaden the individual and to determine how well he functions under increased responsibilities. Project management, in particular, is a very effective device to develop general management capability.

4. *Use of "assistant to" positions.* Several top executives in the companies visited have experimented with the use of "assistant to" positions for developmental purposes. Their reactions have been enthusiastic, and they intend to continue the practice. All agree, however, that if this technique is to be successful the top executive must do a very careful job in selecting the individual, in defining his responsibilities, and in training him so that he will be able to work effectively later in a position at a lower managerial level in the organization.

5. *Team management.* In a previous chapter mention was made of the effective use of executive committees as a device to obtain breadth of vision and judgment. Obviously, membership on such committees contributes materially to the personal development of each individual. A number of companies in the present study have experimented

with another technique to develop general management capability and balance at the top level. One company shows the president and the vice president in the same organization box. Another company shows the chairman of the board, the president, and two executive vice presidents in the same box. In both instances the motive behind this rather unconventional structure is to provide an opportunity for development in general management. Frequently, when there are two or more individuals in the same organization box, they will have different experience and/or educational backgrounds; one may have a technical background and the second a finance or marketing background, for example.

Several other companies, which have decentralized operating divisions, show the general manager and the assistant general manager of the division in the same organization box. The assistant position is used for development purposes. Generally, the two individuals in these positions will have come up through different functions within the division.

6. *Conferences and seminars.* During recent years there has been an increase in the number of top-level conferences and seminars held by management. Several companies hold annual meetings for corporate and top divisional management away from their headquarters offices. Typically, the objectives and plans for the year are discussed, and various special presentations are made. The climate is ideal for informal discussions. One of the participating companies publishes the results of its annual conference in book form for distribution to all management personnel.

7. *Company training and educational programs.* A galloping technology, accelerated social and economic changes, and a shortage of qualified managerial talent have exerted new pressures on top management for improved and expanded company training and educational programs. Discussions with executives in the companies visited revealed their genuine concern over the need for continuous education and training after an employee joins the company. There was general recognition among the executives that the more automated a manufacturing system becomes, the higher are the skills required to operate and maintain the system.

All the fifteen participating companies have internal company-sponsored training programs; however, the nature and scope of the training activities vary tremendously.

Six significant changes have taken place recently in the internal training activities of the participating companies:

1. More attention is being devoted to programs and courses for the middle and higher levels of management.
2. Greater emphasis is being given to planned educational and training programs for each individual according to his particular needs.
3. Greater stress is being placed upon learning how to learn, think, communicate, and adapt in a changing economic society.
4. Educational and training directors and line managers are devoting more attention to evaluating the contributions and results of specific training courses and activities.
5. Substantial improvements have been made in training methods through the use of new tools and techniques such as closed-circuit television, computer games, improved visual aids, and programmed learning.
6. Top management and the training directors have become aware of the need for experimentation and research to obtain better understanding of the learning process and to obtain more effective results from in-company training programs.

External developments. Significant progress has been made in advanced management education since the first courses were offered during World War II under the Engineering Science Management War Training Program. Today, thousands of managers and executives are attending special advanced management programs sponsored by leading universities and colleges. All the companies studied are presently sending executives to one or more university programs. It was clear from discussions with executives that this type of development will be continued and perhaps increased. The major objective of most advanced management programs is to provide an opportunity for participants to broaden their knowledge and to improve their skills so that they may become more effective general managers.

In addition to having executives attend advanced management seminars and programs, a number of companies have recently adopted a policy of encouraging executives to participate in civic and governmental activities. If necessary, leaves of absence are granted for those involved. There is a strong feeling among the top executives in the companies visited that experience of this type in the long run will be of great benefit to the individual, to the company, and to society.

KEY QUESTIONS BEING ASKED BY TOP MANAGEMENT

1. Are top-level executives personally involved in and concerned with all aspects of the program? Do they recognize this activity as one of their primary responsibilities?
2. How effective is our integration of manpower planning with our long-range operating plans?
3. Do we have a highly qualified corporate executive who has specific responsibility for overall coordination of this function? Does this individual have the unqualified respect and confidence of other executives and managers at all levels? Has he had operating experience in addition to his background in personnel?
4. Is our corporate personnel staff performing functions that could be done more effectively by the line organization?
5. Are we doing everything possible to keep our program simple? What controls and reviews do we have to prevent excessive red tape and paperwork from killing the program?
6. Are we selecting, as potential executives for the 1990s, young men who have accumulated knowledge and developed skills that may rapidly become obsolete? Are we giving "lip service" to the value of the generalist while we continue to hire only specialists? Or are we selecting young men who have been educated in how to learn, how to think, and how to adapt to change?
7. Is our management willing to accept the risks and criticisms involved with the early identification of the few truly outstanding individuals who possess unusual potential for future leadership in general management positions?
8. Are we taking full advantage of the use of "assistant to" positions and special assignments for developmental purposes?
9. What are we doing to ensure that young managers obtain the necessary breadth of knowledge and understanding at an early stage in their career development through job rotation and transfer?
10. Is our management and executive development program geared to the needs of each individual and to the needs of the corporation? Is there an appropriate balance between training for present and future needs?

11. How effective is our program in identifying individuals who are "bottlenecks" and in getting them out of the system? Do we exercise sufficient courage and wisdom in taking advantage of provisions available for early retirement?
12. What is our image with universities? Are we viewed as a progressive company that is willing to participate in and experiment with new techniques such as: exchange faculty fellowships, internships, case development, visiting lecturers, affiliate programs, and research assistant programs?
13. What, if any, progress has been made on the research front to improve the effectiveness of our selection and development activities?
14. What significant changes have been made in our executive selection and development program during the past five years? What changes do we anticipate in the next five years?

EXAMPLES OF SUCCESSFUL EXECUTIVE SELECTION AND DEVELOPMENT PROGRAMS

Most of the companies visited have effective executive selection and development programs. The scope of this study does not permit a detailed comparative analysis of the various programs. The program of one corporation, which is very complete and well coordinated for its autonomous subsidiaries and divisions and its parent corporation, is described below as Corporation A. This program includes the use of both corporate and divisional committees, a management incentive plan, early identification of key personnel, separate appraisal plans for management and top executives, individual personal development plans, and replacement charts at all levels.

Specific parts of the programs of two other corporations are also described below. The Corporation B program illustrates how one corporation is making effective use of new information techniques to provide the decentralized divisions with up-to-date information on all members of supervision and management. In Corporation C, special attention is devoted to manpower planning and development activities.

Corporation A. The executive selection and development program of this corporation was chosen for more detailed description for several reasons: (1) The corporation has had a major organizational change recently from a highly centralized functional organization to a decentralized organization with autonomous operating subsidiaries and divisions plus a centralized parent organization with overall control. As a result of this change, considerable emphasis has been placed upon the early identification and development of men with potential for positions in general management. (2) The corporation, a leader in its industry, has been extremely successful in recruiting and developing key executive personnel. (3) The program includes an effective balance of professional staff guidance, centralized top management control, and decentralized autonomy and administration. (4) There has been a high degree of top management participation in both the development and the administration of the program. (5) Most of the new selection and appraisal techniques have been incorporated in the program.

Nature and scope of the program. The overall direction and control of the program is the responsibility of the top management of the parent corporation. This direction and control is carried out through a committee on executive development with the chairman of the board, the president and three executive vice presidents as members. An executive development coordinator for the parent corporation works closely with the operating subsidiaries and with the parent committee, which meets once a week for at least two hours and is primarily concerned with the identification, evaluation, and development of people.

Personal history records, individual development plans, and replacement charts are used throughout the corporation. The replacement charts show two candidates who are ready and two or more who are potential candidates for each management and executive position. Each subsidiary organization makes up "A" and "B" lists. The "A" list includes those who have potential qualifications for general management or for membership on the board of directors of a subsidiary. The "B" list is made up of younger executives with long-term potential in general management. The committee on executive development reviews 1,500 individuals on replacement tables each year and approves the appointments to the top 225 positions as well as the individual development plans for all key executives. The committee also establishes salary guidelines for the subsidiary organizations.

The corporation has an incentive bonus plan that includes the top 600 executives. Part of the bonus is based upon performance; the other part, made up of stock options, is based upon the comparative potential of individuals. Bonuses range from 10 to 40 percent of base pay. The coordinator of executive development works with the operating executives in putting the recommended bonus plan together for submission to the committee for approval.

Each subsidiary operating organization and each major geographic division has separate committees on executive development. They perform for their organizations in the same manner as the central committee does for the parent corporation. There is a strong participation by line management at all levels. The following example illustrates how the plan operates:

In one of the subsidiary organizations with 10,000 managerial, professional, and technical people, each operating unit, such as a factory, identifies its key people by five-year age brackets. The top management for each factory places their key men in rank order for each age group—the number one man, the number two man, and so forth, in terms of long-range potential. A four-year development program is required for each man on the list, which normally would include about ten men in each age bracket. These high-potential lists are submitted to the subsidiary headquarters from all operating and functional organizational units. Top management of the subsidiary organization reduces the list from approximately 225 to 60. The list of 60 high-potential candidates plus proposed individual four-year development plans are submitted through the corporate executive development coordinator to the committee on executive development. Individuals included in the top 60 list may be transferred to another subsidiary or to an assignment in the parent corporation to provide additional background and understanding for future positions in general management.

Appraisal and evaluation. Two separate appraisal forms are utilized in evaluating management and executive personnel. The first form, used to appraise management, consists of six parts plus provision for comments by higher levels of management who review the forms. The appraisal information included under parts 5 and 6 are not reviewed with the individual who is being appraised.

Part 1. Appraisal on four basic elements of performance including:
a. *What he accomplishes* in terms of quality of work, quantity of work, cost objectives, profit objectives, and developing people.
b. *How he works* in getting his job done. This includes an appraisal of his performance in planning, organizing, delegating, working with others, communicating, and analyzing.
c. *What he is.* This includes an appraisal of his effectiveness in leadership, judgment, initiative, drive, and dependability.

d. *What he knows*. This includes an appraisal of the man's performance as related to his knowledge and understanding of the work that he supervises, related work, company philosophy and objectives, and new developments in his field or profession.

Part 2. Appraisal of overall performance on a scale of 1 for outstanding to 5 for unsatisfactory.

Part 3. Analysis of major strengths and weaknesses.

Part 4. Identification and description of improvement and development needs.

Part 5. Appraisal of capacity for advancement in present organization. This appraisal indicates whether an individual is ready for promotion and if so to what position or positions and at what time in the future.

Part 6. Appraisal of capacity for advancement in another organizational unit. In this part of the appraisal, specific mention is made of the organizational unit and position for which the indvidual is qualified.

The second appraisal form is a "review of executive characteristics." It was designed by the corporation to assist management in analyzing and reporting their opinions about the qualifications of employees who have the potential for positions as top-level managers, members of boards of directors, or chief executive officers. This appraisal is not intended to evaluate present job performance. It provides an opportunity to bring together judgment from several observers concerning the degree to which an individual possesses and utilizes some of the characteristics frequently present in top-level executives.

This appraisal form includes nineteen executive characteristics selected by the corporation as those most frequently possessed by their successful top-level executives. The characteristics that were identified after several years of research by the corporation are:

1. Articulateness
2. Commitment
3. Creativeness
4. Decisiveness
5. Developing others
6. Drive
7. Flexibility
8. Initiative
9. Intellectual abilities
10. Judgment about business matters
11. Judgment about people
12. Leadership
13. Managerial abilities
14. Motivation
15. Physique and health
16. Problem-solving ability
17. Self-development
18. Self-discipline
19. Stability

When an appraiser uses the form he compares the employee with a "reference population norm group" of the highest management people with whom he is familiar. The norm group may be a board of directors, executive officers of subsidiary organizations, department heads, corporate functional managers, or some other group. The job level or reference group is indicated at the end of the form. The individual being rated is given a numerical score from 1 to 100 on each of the nineteen characteristics. For example, if the appraiser feels that the individual exceeds 80 percent of the reference group on charactristic number one he records a rating of 80 beside that characteristic.

In addition to appraising the individual on the degree to which he possesses each characteristic, the appraiser also includes a rating of 1 to 5 on how the individual applies each particular capability.

Individual development plans. The individual development plans are a vital part of the corporation's program. Each plan includes up-to-date information of the person's functional and management strengths and potential, recommended job and training assignments to aid in reaching the highest potential, information on personal characteristics where change is desired, and specific recommendations on development plans for the individual over the next four-year period.

Corporation B. This corporation, which has approximately 65 autonomous operating divisions, has an organizational philosophy of decentralized profit responsibility with a limited amount of centralized control from corporate headquarters. The corporate staff departments have accepted and are dedicated to the theory that they can make the greatest contribution to the success of the corporation by providing top-quality professional services to meet the specific needs of the operating divisions of the corporation.

The executive selection and development program of the corporation is one of the most complete and highly organized of the fifteen companies studied. Complete personal history, promotability, replacement, and individual development records are maintained for approximately 10,000 management and professional personnel. Primary attention, however, is given to the top 900 individuals, and the president is personally involved with the selection and promotion of the top 300 individuals.

The corporation has a management council which meets once a year away from the corporate facilities. The meeting is attended by the top executives at the corporate and operating levels and lasts two days. During the first day, the present year's problems are discussed. During the second day, future plans and programs are reviewed. The results of the meeting are published each year in book form for distribution to key management personnel.

In a corporation that operates under a philosophy of decentralized decision making, it is essential that the operating executives have complete and up-to-date information prior to making their decisions. This corporation appears to be doing a very effective job in utilizing new techniques and improved data-gathering systems to provide this information.

Through the use of the centralized computer center, corporate personnel staff supplies operating executives with complete and up-to-date information on all management and professional staff so that they can make effective decisions on promotions and replacements. Key personnel promotability registers, coded replacement charts, and key management personnel review forms provide a wide range of pertinent information for use in manpower and organizational planning. A sample of the review form illustrates the type of information that is available on short notice for the use of operating and top management executives. (See the accompanying Exhibit.)

Corporation C. For the past twenty years this corporation has been an industry leader in the field of executive selection, evaluation, and development. The basic philosophy of management is geared to the concept of decentralized autonomous operating divisions and/or subsidiaries with centralized coordination and control. During the past few years, corporate personnel staff has worked effectively with the various divisions to develop the most effective overall executive selection and development program for the corporation. At present, every major division has an active program which includes personal inventory records, backup lists, replacement charts, and individual development programs.

Top management at the corporate level is very much involved in manpower planning. The chairman of the board and the president have made it very clear to the subsidiary executives that their primary responsibility is to select and develop high-potential managerial personnel. The corporate personnel staff recently made a detailed study of past and present management development and training activities and came up with the following recommendations:

Recommendations to the operating companies:
1. Conduct both short-term and long-term manpower planning.

KEY MANAGEMENT PERSONNEL REVIEW

FUNCTION CODES

A — Administration	F — Field sales	L — Law, patent	Q — Reliability
B — Business systems	G — General management	M — Manufacturing	R — Research
C — Controller	I — Personnel & public affairs	N — Marketing	S — Service
E — Engineering		P — Purchases & traffic (incl. credit)	T — Treasury
K — Multi-function			

PROMOTABILITY CODES

Not Evaluated:
T — Time remaining H — Health A — Asgn. under 6 mos. O — Other U — Fully utilized

1 — Outstanding 2 — Very high 3 — Satisfactory

EXECUTIVE REVIEW CODES

Gen. Mngmt	Functional	Multi-func.
GA — Available	FA — Available	KA — Available
GL — Later	FL — Later	KL — Later
GD — Develop	FD — Develop	KD — Develop
C — Continue	PR — Problem	

Table no.   **EXPLANATORY NOTES**

Explanatory note	Section / Field	SMITH	JONES
	PERSONAL DATA — NAME	SMITH	JONES
	(code)	CB	AB
	BIRTH DATE M / Y	9 / 05	6 / 24
Total employment date — Jones joined the Company in 1948	TED Y	26	48
	PRESENT POSITION — TITLE	ASST TO G M	DIV MFG MGR
Smith's Position Grade is Corporate Grade A minus 1	GR	D	
Smith was assigned to his present position March 1962	DATE M / Y	3 / 62	10 / 64
2 — Jones has 9 or more years experience in Manufacturing	EXPERIENCE — FUNCTION 1		9M
2 — Jones has 3 years experience in Engineering	FUNCTION 2		3E
2 — Jones has less than one year in Marketing	FUNCTION 3		0N
Jones has had one or more assignments in Headquarters	ASSIGN — HQ		X
Jones has had assignments in two different Groups	ASSIGN — GR		2
Jones has had assignments in three different Divisions	ASSIGN — DIV		3
Jones has attended BMC	TRAINING — BMC		X
Jones is recommended for WPC	WPC		R
	MMP		
Smith has attended an AMP	AMP	X	
6 — Jones speaks German	LANGUAGE		K
Smith's abilities are fully utilized	PROMOTABILITY — NOT EVALUATED	U	
2 — Jones has outstanding promotability to a multi-function position	1ST POS		1K
2 — Jones has very high promotability to a higher level Manufacturing position	2ND POS		2M
2 — Jones has long range promotability to a General Manager position	LONG RANGE		G
Jones appears on two different Replacement tables	NO. REPL. TABLES		2
The Executive Review Code is examined and approved during the Review Meeting	EXEC REVIEW		

COMMENTS

2. Ensure that a sufficient number of young employees with potential are brought in to meet future needs.

3. Set a target to have at least 20 percent of the supervisory personnel under age 40 in five years.

4. Carefully identify backup candidates with long-range potential. The identification of men with high future potential should be carefully reviewed by higher management levels to be sure that the individuals named are those on which greater expenditures should be made.

5. Work out and follow a plan of development for each individual who has potential. There should be more job rotation at all levels. Participation in outside executive development programs should be continued.

6. Assign responsibility for development and provide rewards for results. Development of executive replacements is a line responsibility. The best indication that a line manager has met his responsibilities is that he has developed a strong replacement for himself and also a reservoir of competent people with potential for future growth.

7. Establish a management development committee under the chairmanship of the president of each company to meet at least three or four times a year.

Recommendations to the corporate officers:

1. Follow up to ensure results. A corporate review of progress should be made annually and the following items should be examined:
   a. What additions and deletions of future potentials have taken place since the last review?
   b. What, if any, functional areas require particular attention?
   c. Are there specific development plans for each individual who has been identified as having a high future potential? Are they being implemented?
   d. How many rotational assignments have been completed?
   e. How many employees have been selected for attendance at outside advanced management programs?
   f. How many young salaried people under age 40 in nonengineering areas have been employed since the last review?

2. Corporate functional vice presidents should review the development activities in depth in their counterparts' organization at the subsidiary level.

3. Corporate industrial relations personnel should be available at all times for advice and counsel to the subsidiary company presidents and to the corporate functional vice presidents.

ROAD TO THE TOP

12

The corporations included in this study had sales in 1967 of $60.0 billion, total assets of $51.1 billion, employed 1,920,000 persons, and produced 7.64 percent of the gross national product. The corporations and executives studied represent fifteen different industries, and each company is in a position of top leadership within its industry. All the companies manufacture and distribute on an international basis.

In a highly competitive society such as ours, industry leadership must be earned through aggressive action, clear foresight, and the

233

productive efforts of all employees at every level within the organization. The continuing success of the individual companies studied can be traced in no small part to the dynamic and inspirational leadership of the top-level executives who have major responsibilities for the planning and implementation of corporate strategies and programs. This chapter focuses attention upon the personal backgrounds and experience of the executives who are the top management of the fifteen corporations studied.

There are many ways to define top management. One way is to draw a line on a company's organization chart and to designate the individuals above the line as top management. Another method is to say that top management comprises the board of directors, the president, and everyone reporting directly to the president. In this study the authors have defined top management as the board of directors and those full-time executives who are involved continuously or frequently in most, if not all, of the twelve following responsibilities:

1. The determination of company objectives.
2. Long-range planning to attain objectives.
3. Establishment of basic policies to implement the long-range plans.
4. Development of an organization structure and its continuous modification to conform to future plans.
5. Coordination of activities of the enterprise.
6. Selection of qualified personnel for key positions.
7. Provision for a continuous flow of qualified personnel.
8. Adoption of effective means of control.
9. Setting of short-term goals.
10. Appraisal of overall results and current performance.
11. Application of corrective measures as performance falls short of predetermined goals.
12. Prudent management of the corporate income, that is, that portion of the income available for discretionary action—what is left from gross income after obligatory expenditures such as payroll, materials and services, taxes, and interest.

In the present study the authors have interviewed more than 260 executives and have analyzed over 400 complete personal information histories of top-level executives in the participating companies. These interviews and personal history analyses provide an excellent current source of information for a study of the top executive's educational and experience backgrounds and of their patterns of progress on the road to success in top management.

After analyzing the personal histories, the authors selected for special study 310 individuals who clearly meet the qualifications specified above for membership in top management. The executives chosen are a very select group in that they represent the top 310 individuals out of a total of 1,920,000 employees in the fifteen companies studied. A breakdown of the group by titles and numbers is shown below:

Titles	Number	Percent	Cumulative percent
Chairman, members of boards, presidents	42*	14	14
Executives and senior vice presidents	37	12	26
Presidents of subsidiaries	47	15	41
Corporate group vice presidents	17	5	46
Vice presidents and/or general managers of divisions	81	26	72
Corporate functional vice presidents	86	28	100
TOTAL	310	100	

*Includes 14 chairmen of boards, 13 full-time members of boards, and 15 corporate presidents. Outside or part-time board members are not included.

Eighty-three (27 percent) of the group are members of boards of directors; 224 (72 percent) are line executives with multifunctional and, in most cases, profit responsibilities. The remaining 86 (28 percent) are top corporate executives who are responsible for the planning, direction, and control of major functions on a corporate-wide basis. The functional executives included in this group are the corporate vice presidents of finance, marketing and sales, manufacturing, engineering, research and development, and industrial relations. All these men, in addition to having major responsibility for their particular functions, are very much involved with the total managerial problems of their corporations.

In this chapter the authors will describe the "road to the top" through an analysis and portrayal of the personal, educational, and experience backgrounds of the selected top executives. Career patterns, the generalist-specialist dichotomy, and special problems of career development will be discussed, and comments will be made on possible future changes in the channels of mobility into top management positions.

PERSONAL AND EDUCATIONAL BACKGROUNDS

A description of the personal and educational backgrounds of the top executives includes analyses of the age distribution, number of years with their companies, number and kinds of educational degrees and honors, and major fields of study.

Age. The median age of the 310 executives studied was 57, with a range from 35 to 75. The median ranged from a low of 51 at one company to a high of 60 at another. The ranges also varied by company, with the narrowest range from 51 to 66 and the widest range from 35 to 63. The age distribution of executives for all companies is shown in Figure 1. Further details are given in the Appendix at the end of this chapter.

Years with company. In the fifteen companies studied there was little evidence of any proselyting of managerial talent from other companies, particularly at the top management level. It has been a rare exception when a top executive has been brought in from outside the company. When this occurred, it was done to acquire specialized talent not available within the particular company or to meet unusual demands caused by expansion or organizational changes.

The promotion-from-within policy followed by most of the participating companies tends to produce a rather stable group of managerial personnel with relatively long seniority with the company. The managerial skills, company and industry knowledge, and mature judgment required by top management take many years to develop.

The median number of years that top executives have been with their companies was 30. Twenty-five percent of these executives have been with their companies 35 or more years and about 3 percent have been employed by their companies for less than ten years. The information analyzed gave no evidence that there was a managerial revolution in progress or that there were any "shortcuts" on the road to top management.

Education. The 310 top executives earned a total of 388 degrees; 87 percent earned one or more degrees, and most of the non-degree holders completed some work at the university level. Thirty-two percent of the executives earned two or more degrees, and 8 percent have Ph.D. degrees. A percentage distribution by types of degrees is shown

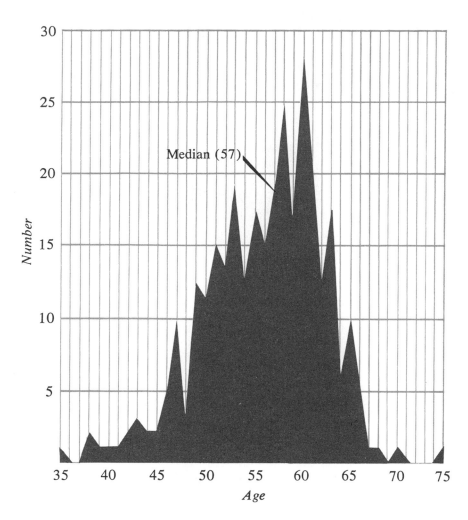

FIGURE 1. *Top management age distribution*

in Figure 2. See the Appendix for detailed breakdown by types and numbers of degrees by job classifications.

The educational backgrounds of the top executives varied somewhat. In the companies where a high degree of technical knowledge is required, the top executives tended to have a larger number of advanced degrees. In one of these companies, for example, six of the nine members of the executive committee of the board of directors and 50 percent of the general managers of the operating departments have Ph.D. degrees.

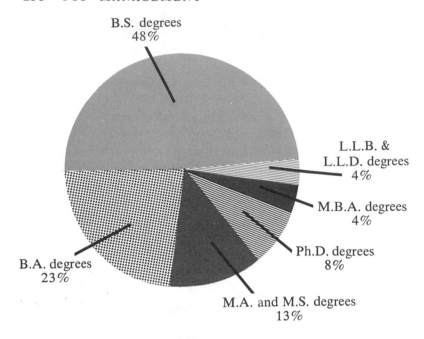

FIGURE 2. *Top management academic degrees*

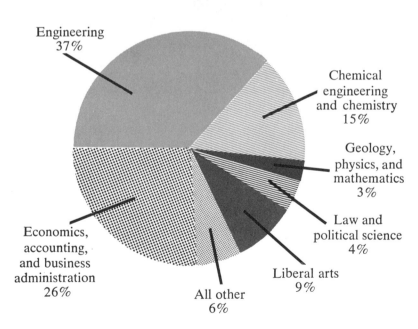

FIGURE 3. *Top management major fields of study*

An analysis of the major fields of study of the 310 executives indicated a heavy concentration in the technical areas of engineering and chemistry. This, of course, would be expected in that the fifteen corporations studied are all large industrial companies requiring rather extensive technical knowledge. A breakdown of the educational fields of study is shown in Figure 3, and a detailed breakdown is given in the Appendix at the end of this chapter.

The 310 executives studied were elected to over 100 memberships in honorary scholarship societies and fraternities. There were twelve Phi Beta Kappa, twenty Tau Beta Pi, twenty Sigma Xi, and thirteen Phi Lambda Upsilon members among the executives. Twenty-seven of the executives received one or more honorary doctoral degrees.

Personal characteristics. The personal educational achievements of the top executives were supplemented by a broad range of activities and honors in civic, industry, community, and charitable endeavors. A large number of the executives were members of the boards of directors of other companies, and many served as trustees for educational institutions.

During the hundreds of hours spent by the authors interviewing the top executives and analyzing their personal histories, certain general impressions were formed. First, this select group of top executives is made up of dynamic, optimistic, hard-driving, action-oriented individuals who are dedicated to creating new opportunities for growth and progress in a free and competitive society. Second, by example they have established within their companies a climate marked by objectivity, high standards of performance, personal integrity, fairness, and an intelligent, sympathetic understanding of social values, of individual rights, of political issues, and of economic problems. And third, the executives who have been most successful in providing effective leadership for their companies possess a built-in humbleness, simplicity, and unselfishness in their managerial behavior.

They are a restless group of intelligent, outgoing men dedicated to the cultivation of excellence within their organizations. In accomplishing their missions, they have placed the interests and demands of their companies well above those of family and self.

EXPERIENCE BACKGROUNDS

The personal experience backgrounds of the 310 executives were analyzed in several ways. Attention was given to the line and staff nature of the experience, to the number and types of functional assignments, to special task force or committee assignments, to multidivisional experience, and to a comparison of the experience patterns within the various companies.

Line and staff experience.   Seventy-two percent of the 310 executives studied are in line positions. The remaining 28 percent, although formally in charge of particular functional activities at the corporate level, are also involved in certain line-type activities as members of special task forces or committees. A large number of the line executives have had some staff assignments during their careers; however, the major portion of their work experience has been in positions that carry line and profit responsibility. Frequently their staff assignments came early in their careers. A somewhat smaller percent of the executives who are now in the staff-type positions have had line management experience during their careers. In those corporations that operate with a functional organization structure, the movement of individuals from staff to line positions is an exception. In the corporations organized on the basis of decentralized profit responsibility, the movement back and forth between line and staff positions is much more prevalent.

Analysis by functions.   The personal histories of the executives studied were analyzed in relation to: the first function in which each executive worked, the function in which each executive spent the greatest number of years, the last function in which each executive was engaged prior to his assignment to a position with general management responsibilities, and the number of major functions to which each executive was assigned during his career.

The functions or fields included for analysis are: engineering, production, physical sciences (for example, chemistry, physics, geology), research and development, accounting, finance, sales and marketing, employee and public relations, and legal relations.

The largest percentage of the top executives started with their companies in either the technical functions of engineering, chemistry and/or research, or in production. The combined first jobs in these three areas made up 56 percent of the total first jobs. The second most prevalent area of concentration for first jobs was in accounting and finance, which represented 21 percent.

Sales and marketing followed in importance with 14 percent. All other functions accounted for the remaining 9 percent. See Figure 4

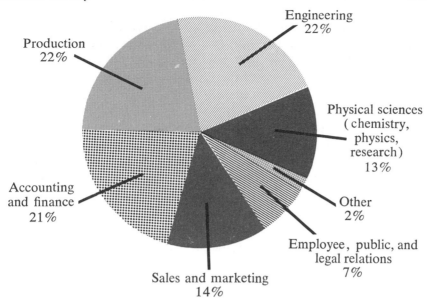

FIGURE 4. *Top management first jobs*

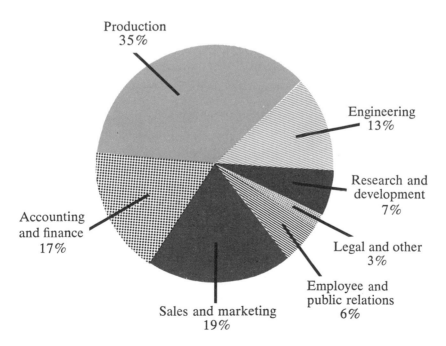

FIGURE 5. *Top management primary fields or functions*

for a comparative picture of the executives' first jobs by functions. Details are given in the Appendix at the end of this chapter.

The personal history of each executive was analyzed to determine in which function he has spent the greatest number of years during his career with the company. The results of this analysis of primary functions are shown in Figure 5 and in the Appendix. Production accounted for the largest percentäge (35 percent); sales and marketing was second (19 percent); accounting and finance was third (17 percent); engineering was fourth (13 percent); research and development was fifth (7 percent); all others represented 9 percent.

In terms of the functions from which executives were promoted into their positions in general management, the relative importance of the functions did not change (see Figure 6). Production and sales and marketing were the major areas from which the executives were promoted into general management. In making this analysis, the 86 corporate functional vice presidents were not included. Further details are given in the Appendix.

It is significant to note that in all three of the above comparisons of first jobs, primary functions, and functions prior to being promoted

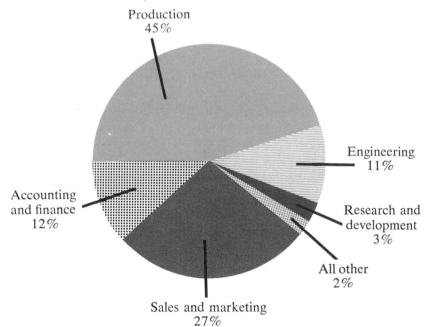

FIGURE 6. *Functions from which top management was promoted into general management*

into general management, the technical and production areas together represent over 50 percent. It is quite apparent that the most heavily traveled "road to the top" is in the technical and production fields of activity. The next most likely way to the top is through sales and marketing, followed by accounting and finance.

A fourth analysis of functions was made to determine the extent to which the top executives have obtained major multifunctional experience prior to their present positions. Figure 7 shows the percent of top management that has had major multifunctional experience. The top executives themselves emphasized the importance of multifunctional experience. Without question, such experience is extremely valuable, but apparently it is difficult to implement on a broad-scale

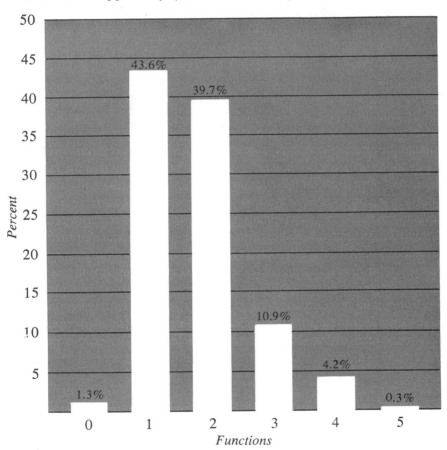

FIGURE 7. *Functions prior to promotion into present top management positions*

basis. Of the 310 executives, only 15 percent have had experience in three or more functions, and approximately 44 percent have had experience in only one function. The group having the largest percent of their members with single functional experience was the one that included the corporate functional vice presidents. There was not as significant a difference as one would expect to find in the number of functions in which the line executives and the staff executives had experience. In most instances the pattern of movement back and forth between the functions was greater in the case of line executives. For example, there was considerable movement from production to engineering and back to production. It was also common to see back-and-forth movements between engineering and sales and between production and sales. The greatest concentration of single functional experience was found in the fields of accounting, finance, and law.

Many of the companies visited utilize a variety of techniques to provide young executives with a breadth of understanding outside their functional jobs. Committee, task-force, project assignments, and participation in advanced management development programs have been used effectively for this purpose.

Multidivisional experience. Several of the companies have planned programs to give executives experience in more than one operating division, and in many instances executives have had assignments in as many as four different divisions prior to their assignment to a general management position. One company follows a practice of using the position of assistant divisional manager as a training position. In this company, when the executive is promoted to division manager, he frequently is transferred to another division. The following example of the work experience of one executive is illustrative of a career pattern that includes both multifunctional and multidivisional experience.

Years	Job title	Organization unit
4	Methods engineer	Division A
1	Superintendent of methods engineering	Division B
1	Assistant product engineer	Division B
4	Assistant factory superintendent	Division B
1	Assistant branch manager (sales)	Division B
2	Branch manager (sales)	Division B
3	Manufacturing manager	Division C
6	General manager	Division C
3	Vice president for manufacturing	Corporate level
4	Group vice president	Corporate level

VARIATIONS IN CAREER PATTERNS

There was considerable variation in the career patterns of executives in the companies studied. In the companies with a high technology requirement, greater emphasis was given to assignments in research, engineering, and manufacturing. Several companies in this category follow a practice of using periodic assignments in central research or in development engineering to keep operating executives up-to-date with the "state of the art." A few companies that have a high engineering technology alternate assignments between engineering development and sales to bring about better coordination of efforts and to provide greater breadth of understanding among the young executives being developed.

The nature of the particular company's organization structure also has a bearing upon the career patterns of executives. In the functional type of organization there is a tendency for an executive to remain in a single function until he reaches the vice-presidential level.

Several companies indicated that they have made major changes in their organization structure during the past few years. Some companies which previously had highly centralized functional organizations made major changes to decentralized structures with divisional autonomy. These changes have resulted in increased emphasis being put upon multifunctional and interdivisional job assignments for the purpose of developing a supply of executives with general management capabilities.

Another variation in the career patterns among the participating companies was the degree of emphasis given to particular functions such as sales, finance, research, engineering, or manufacturing. Companies with a high proportion of consumer-type products normally tend to give greater emphasis to the sales and marketing functions.

A few companies have followed a practice of giving their top industrial relations and public relations executives multifunctional and operations experience prior to their assuming top corporate responsibility for their functions. The industrial relations executives who had the opportunity for this experience valued it highly.

THE GENERALIST–SPECIALIST DICHOTOMY

Most of the executives interviewed expressed strong support for broad training and experience as a prerequisite for success in general management. There was an equally strong feeling, however, that a certain amount of depth of education and experience was also necessary. Most of the companies have followed a practice of hiring, as future general managers, individuals with a technical or engineering background. These individuals are given sufficient time to prove their capability in a certain specialty and are then given the opportunity to broaden as generalists through a variety of work assignments of a multifunctional and/or interdivisional nature.

Some executives expressed the opinion that too much general training too soon was often more hindrance than help. Others were very much concerned about the dangers of overspecialization and of the lack of breadth of certain executives, particularly in the fields of accounting, finance, and research.

There appears to be no simple answer to the question "How much specialization?" There is a wide gap between theory and practice. As a practical matter, it is very difficult to make interfunctional and interdivisional transfers between certain functions that have a high knowledge requirement.

A LOOK AHEAD

Top management's job requires a mixture of knowledges, skills, attitudes, and values. The required mixture varies by time, by company, and by changing economic, political, and social conditions. The new knowledge required to keep pace with technological change has been considerable during recent years, and the rate of change in the future is likely to increase rather than decrease. In the economic and social sphere, new quantitative and behavioral skills will be needed to achieve desired growth and leadership. The collapse of time and distance barriers will demand new techniques in communication and new knowledges and skills in dealing with international problems.

During the past few years it has been popular to write about the changing concepts of management and to make predictions about the most effective mixture of knowledge, skills, and attitudes needed by top management in the 1980s and 1990s. Some writers have predicted that the next generation of top management will be materially different from those of the past in that they will be required to possess more specialized knowledge and skill in the fields of economics, quantitative analysis, and information technology. A few authors have also predicted that the channels of mobility into top management are likely to change with a larger percentage of future members of top management coming up through new fields such as information technology and research management.

In the fifteen companies studied there was no evidence of any major changes in the paths of progress to the top. There was unanimous agreement by the executives interviewed that in the future, as in the past, the individuals who are likely to be the most successful as top executives will be those with line experience—preferably in production and sales—those who have "learned to manage by managing." They will continue to be action-oriented individuals who possess an educated viewpoint, a willingness to listen and learn, plus a practitioner's desire to create and accomplish.

Although the basic nature of the job of top management is not likely to change materially in the years ahead, certain alterations may take place in the development of executives on the "road to the top." Some of these changes may include:

1. Increased emphasis on management development courses and programs to supplement job experience. The educational activities will provide additional breadth of understanding of the problems of the total enterprise in a changing society. Attention will also be devoted to bringing management up to date in specialized fields such as information and computer technology, financial analysis and control, research and development, and the behavioral sciences.
2. Improved techniques in and increased attention to the early identification of individuals with top management potential.
3. Increased emphasis on the planning of individual development programs for executives.
4. Increased use of ad hoc committee and task-force assignments for development purposes.
5. Increased and earlier job rotation to obtain multifunctional and multidivisional experience.
6. Greater recognition of the need for general management capability at an earlier period in an executive's career. The demand for this capability has resulted from:
   a. An increase in the use of project and program management.
   b. The development of new venture or new product development departments.
   c. Increased use of the profit-center concept of management.
   d. New developments in the use of computers and information systems.
   e. More extensive use of task-force assignments.
   f. More sophisticated long-range planning by line executives.

7. Increased use of the assistant divisional manager position to provide the first experience in general management.

8. Increased attention to improving communications and coordination between the research and development department and the engineering, production, and sales personnel.

9. Emphasis upon a broader education and experience for top functional executives, particularly in the fields of accounting and finance. This will result from their increased participation in long-range planning activities, from greater emphasis upon the profit-center concept of management, and from improved educational programs.

There may be other changes in career planning and development in the future. The authors feel, however, that the road to the top will not change significantly in the foreseeable future. The mixture of required knowledges, skills, and attitudes, or the relative importance of the different functional experiences, may be altered to meet new demands of the company, of the industry, or of our society.

In large industrial companies such as those included in this study it is very likely that the majority of future top management positions will continue to be filled by men who have had technical educational backgrounds in engineering or in the physical sciences, plus supplementary education or training in the major functions of business—finance, production, sales and marketing, and control. Their career patterns are likely to include more, rather than less, multifunctional and interdivisional experience, and their understanding of the social and economic problems of our society is likely to be greater than that of their predecessors. Tomorrow's top managers will be specialists, but they will be specialists in the art and science of general management.

APPENDIX: TABULATED DATA ON TOP MANAGEMENT

Age distribution

Age	No. of executives	Cumulative no. less than age indicated	Percent less than age indicated	Cumulative no. more than age indicated	Percent more than age indicated
75	1	309		0	
74	–	309		1	
73	–	309		1	
72	–	309		1	
71	–	309		1	
70	1	308	99.4	1	.3
69	–	308		2	
68	1	307		2	
67	1	306		3	
66	5	301		4	
65	10	291	93.9	9	2.9
64	6	285		19	
63	17	268		25	
62	12	256		42	
61	21	235		54	
60	28	207	66.8	75	24.2
59	16	191		103	
58	25	166		119	
57 (*Median*)	19	147		144	
56	15	132		163	
55	17	115	37.1	178	57.4
54	12	103		195	
53	19	84		207	
52	13	71		226	
51	15	56		239	
50	11	45	14.5	254	81.9
49	12	33		265	
48	3	30		277	
47	10	20		280	
46	5	15		290	
45	2	13	4.2	295	95.2
44	2	11		297	
43	3	8		299	
42	2	6		302	
41	1	5		304	
40	1	4	1.3	305	98.4
39	1	3		306	
38	2	1		307	
37	–	1		309	
36	–	1		309	
35	1	0		309	
TOTAL	310				

Years with company

Years	No. of executives	Cumulative no. less than yrs. indicated	Percent less than yrs. indicated	Cumulative no. more than yrs. indicated	Percent more than yrs. indicated
50	1	309		0	
49	–	309		1	
48	2	307		1	
47	1	306		3	
46	–	306		4	
45	1	305	98.4	4	1.3
44	7	298		5	
43	1	297		12	
42	5	292		13	
41	6	286		18	
40	7	279	90.9	24	7.7
39	12	267		31	
38	19	248		43	
37	10	238		62	
36	6	232		72	
35	9	223	71.9	78	25.2
34	20	203		87	
33	20	183		107	
32	12	171		127	
31	15	156		139	
30 (*Median*)	18	138	44.5	154	49.7
29	10	128		172	
28	12	116		182	
27	13	103		194	
26	9	94		207	
25	10	84	27.1	216	69.7
24	4	80		226	
23	3	77		230	
22	6	71		233	
21	14	57		239	
20	8	49	15.8	253	81.6
19	6	43		261	
18	4	39		267	
17	3	36		271	
16	4	32		274	
15	3	29	9.4	278	89.7
14	7	22		281	
13	3	19		288	
12	3	16		291	
11	3	13		294	
10	3	10	3.2	297	95.8
9	1	9		300	
8	2	7		301	
7	–	7		303	
6	4	3		303	
5	1	2		307	
4	2	–		308	
TOTAL	310				

Academic degrees

EXECUTIVES RECEIVING DEGREES

Number of individuals	Number of degrees	Percent of individuals	Cumulative percent of individuals
20	3	7	7
78	2	25	32
172	1	55	87
40	none	13	100
310		100	

NUMBER AND TYPES OF DEGREES

Type of degree	Number of degrees	Percent of degrees
Ph.D.	31	8
M.A. and M.S.	49	13
L.L.B. and L.L.D.	15	4
M.B.A.	17	4
B.S.	188	48
B.A.	88	23
	388	100

DISTRIBUTION OF DEGREES
BY JOB CLASSIFICATION

Degree	Chairman of board	Full-time board member	Corp. president	Exec. and sr. vice pres.	Corp. functional vice pres.	Corp. group vice pres.	Pres. of subsidiary	Vice pres., gen. mgr. of div.	Total
B.A.	6	5	7	12	35	5	9	7	86
B.S.	8	6	8	20	48	11	30	57	188
Ph.B.	–	–	–	–	1	–	1	–	2
M.A.	1	–	1	3	5	–	1	–	11
M.S.	–	4	2	4	9	3	6	10	38
M.B.A.	2	1	2	2	4	3	1	2	17
L.L.B.	1	–	–	1	8	–	2	1	13
L.L.D.	1	–	–	1	–	–	–	–	2
D.C.S.	–	1	–	–	–	–	–	–	1
Ph.D.	1	6	1	2	9	1	2	8	30
None	1	2	1	5	8	1	8	14	40
TOTAL DEGREES	20	23	21	45	119	23	52	85	388

No. of degrees held									
3	1	4	2	3	7	1	1	1	20
2	5	4	3	7	27	5	11	16	78
1	7	3	9	22	44	10	27	50	172
None	1	2	1	5	8	1	8	14	40
TOTAL PERSONS	14	13	15	37	86	17	47	81	310

Major fields of study

Technical		Number		Percent
Engineering		114		37
Chemical eng. and chemistry		45		15
Geology, physics, and math.		10		3
SUBTOTAL			169	55
Economics, accounting, business administration				
Economics		18		
Accounting and finance		15		
Business administration		49		
SUBTOTAL			82	26
Law and political science				
Law		11		
Political science		2		
SUBTOTAL			13	4
Liberal arts		28	28	9
All other		18	18	6
TOTAL ALL FIELDS			310	100

DISTRIBUTION BY JOB CLASSIFICATION Field of study	Chairman of board	Full-time board member	Corp. president	Exec. and sr. vice pres.	Corp. functional vice pres.	Corp. group vice pres.	Pres. of subsidiary	Vice pres., gen. mgr. of div.	Total
Engineering	4	2	5	12	22	10	18	41	114
Chem. eng.	1	2	–	2	2	1	5	4	17
Chemistry	2	4	1	2	4	–	5	10	28
Geology	–	–	–	–	1	–	3	–	4
Physics	–	–	–	–	2	–	–	1	3
Mathematics	–	–	1	–	1	–	–	1	3
Finance	–	–	–	–	1	–	–	1	2
Economics	3	1	–	3	7	1	1	2	18
Accounting	–	–	2	1	6	1	2	1	13
Business adm.	2	1	6	8	13	2	6	11	49
Law	2	1	–	1	5	–	2	–	11
Polit. science	–	–	–	–	2	–	–	–	2
Liberal arts	–	1	–	4	17	2	2	2	28
Other	–	1	–	4	3	–	3	7	18
	14	13	15	37	86	17	47	81	310

First jobs

	Number		Percent	
Technical and production				
Engineering	66		21.3	
Research and development	40		12.9	
Production	67		21.6	
SUBTOTAL		173		55.8
Nontechnical and nonproduction				
Accounting and finance				
Accounting	51			
Finance	13			
Total accounting and finance		64	20.7	
Sales and marketing		44	14.2	
Employee and public relations		14	4.5	
Legal		7	2.2	
Other		8	2.6	
SUBTOTAL				44.2
TOTAL ALL FIELDS		310		100.0

Primary fields or functions*

	Number		Percent	
Technical and production				
Engineering	41		13.2	
Research and development	23		7.4	
Production	107		34.5	
SUBTOTAL		171		55.1
Nontechnical and nonproduction				
Accounting and finance				
Accounting	34			
Finance	19			
Total accounting and finance		53	17.1	
Sales and marketing		60	19.4	
Employee and public relations		17	5.5	
Legal		6	1.9	
Other		3	1.0	
SUBTOTAL		139		44.9
TOTAL ALL FIELDS		310		100.0

*Primary fields or functions are those in which the executive has spent the most time during his career with the company.

Functions from which top management was promoted into general management*

Technical and production	Number	Percent
Engineering	24	10.7
Research and development	7	3.1
Production	100	44.7
SUBTOTAL	131	58.5

Nontechnical and nonproduction		
Accounting and finance		
Accounting	9	
Finance	18	
Total accounting and finance	27	12.0
Sales and marketing	60	26.8
Other	6	2.7
SUBTOTAL	93	41.5
TOTAL ALL FIELDS	224	100.0

*Top executives included are those who have multifunctional or general management responsibilities. Eighty-six top corporate functional executives are not included.

Functions prior to promotion into present positions

Job classification	None*	One	Two	Three	Four	Five	Total
Chairman of board	2	5	7	–	–	–	14
Full-time board member	–	4	6	2	–	–	12
Corporation president	–	5	4	5	1	–	15
Exec. and sr. vice pres.	1	17	14	4	1	–	37
Corp. functional vice pres.	–	44	34	3	5	–	86
President of subsidiary	1	22	17	5	1	1	47
Vice pres., gen. mgr of div.	–	31	33	12	5	–	81
TOTAL	4	135	123	34	13	1	310
PERCENT	1.3	43.6	39.7	10.9	4.2	0.3	100

*Executives with no prior functional experience with their company went directly into general managerial positions when they joined their company.

INDEX

Acquisitions (*see* Mergers and acquisitions)
Administrative vice president (*see* Executive vice president)
Advertising in international operations, 147
Age of executives, 236, 249
Agents, foreign, 159–160
Annual conference on corporate objectives, 44

Antitrust action, 128–129
and international operations, 141
Appraisal of executives, 217–219
"Assistant-to" positions, 215, 221
Audits, 33
Authorization, product, 111

Balance of payments, 141–142
Bank relations, example of policy on, 30–31

Benefits, overseas, 157
Board of directors, 3–4, 44, 73–76
  compensation of members, 76
  composition and functions, 7, 74–75
  of foreign subsidiaries, 147
  trends, 7, 76
Budget:
  as control device, 2, 23–24
  preparation, review, and approval,
    24

Career patterns of executives, 245, 254
Centralization, 60, 85
  activities under, 69–70
  versus decentralization, 68–71
  impact of information systems,
    175–176
  trends in, 70–71
Charters, 127
Chief executive officer, 2, 3, 5, 22, 33,
    42, 69
  and external and employee relations,
    192–193
  and international operations, 146
  and research and development, 79
  role:
    in mergers and acquisitions, 130
    in organization structure, 58–59
  and selection of executives, 203–204,
    209–210, 217
  span of control, 60, 61, 63
College recruitment of executives,
    212–213
Committees, 5, 71–73
  executive, 72, 209, 221
  external and employee relations,
    typical agenda, 201–202
  external relations, 193–194
  functions of, 73
  on mergers and acquisitions, 130,
    131
  types of, 72–73
  use in selection of executives,
    208–209
Communication and computers, 182

Community affairs, 196–197
Computers, 166, 180–183
  auxiliary equipment, 181–182
  capacity and cost, 180
  and communication facilities, 182
  flexibility and speed, 180–181
  impact of, 175–180
  and organization structure, 64
  problem solving by, 170
  in product line planning, 105–107
  role in long-range planning, 55–56
  software, 182–183
  top management ignorance of,
    167–169
  trends, 183–189
Conferences, 222
Consummation of merger or
    acquisition, 131, 132
Contact directors, international
    operations, 146
Contributions, policy on, 28–29
Control:
  automatic, 170
  and direction of product line, 9–10
  inventory, 110–111
  span of, 60–61
Control devices, 2, 23
  audits, 33
  budget, 2, 23–24
  corporate policies, 2, 27–32
  financial reports, 34
  personal, 33–34
  on pricing, 33
  profit and loss, 2, 24–25
  promotions, 33
  return on investment, 2, 25–27
  salary and promotion reviews, 33
Controlled decentralization, 68–69
Coordinating subsidiary, 162–163
Corporate information, 198–199
Corporate objectives, 2, 23
  annual conference on, 44
  review of, 43
Corporate policies, 2, 27–32
  criteria for, 27
  examples of, 28–32

Corporate research centers, 86–87
Cost of international operations,
    138–139
Counseling in executive appraisal,
    218–219

Data processing, example of policy on,
    31–32
Data processing centers, 172–174
Decentralization, 5, 60, 85
    versus centralization, 68–71
    controlled, 68–69
    impact of information systems,
        175–176
    trends in, 70–71
Decision making and information
    systems, 188
Delegation of authority, 2
Design, product, 185, 186
Distribution and international
    operations, 139, 143
Diversification, 129

Education of executives, 236–239,
    251–253
Employee relations (*see* External and
    employee relations)
Evaluation and appraisal of executives,
    217–219
Executive committee, 72, 209, 221
Executive council, 72
Executive vice president, 5–6
    functions, 6
    multiple, as organizational device,
        61–62
Executives:
    age of, 236, 249
    appraisal and evaluation of, 217–219
    background of, 236–239
    career patterns, 245, 254
    college recruitment of, 212–213
    development of full potential,
        219–224
        external, 223–224
        internal, 220–223

Executives (*cont'd*):
    early identification of, 213–214
    education of, 236–239, 251–253
    experience, 239–245
        functional, 240–244, 254, 255
        line and staff, 240
        multidivisional, 244
    functions of, 19
    generalists versus specialists, 207,
        245–246
    nature of, 19–21
    personal characteristics of, 239
    selection and development of,
        16–19, 203–232
        changes and trends, 211
        by highest executives, 209–211
        importance, 203–205
        management questions on,
            224–225
        methods and sources, 212–217
        planning for, 207–211
        requirements, 205–207
        successful programs, 225–232
        use of committees in, 208–209
    successful, qualities of, 17
    testing of, 215–216
    years with company, 236, 250
    (*See also* Top management)
Experience, executive (*see* Executives,
    experience)
External and employee relations,
    14–16, 191–202
    centralization and, 69–70
    and chief executive officer, 192–193
    committees on, 193–194, 201–202
    community affairs, 196–197
    corporate information, 198–199
    increasing emphasis on, 192
    influence of government on, 14–15
    involvement of top management in,
        194–195
    and long-range planning, 54
    management-labor relations,
        199–201
    organization, 192–196
    state and national affairs, 197–198

Fact finding in merger or acquisition process, 130–131
Finance and control in international operations, 150–153, 164
Financial reports, 198
Five-year planning cycles, 34–41
Foreign agents, 159–160
Foreign currency problems, 152
Foreign representatives, 159–160
Foreign subsidiaries, 12, 147, 161–163

Generalism versus specialization, 245–246
Geographic organization, 2, 5
Government:
  employee involvement, 196–198
  influence:
    on external and employee relations, 14–15
    on international operations, 11, 139–142
Group vice president (*see* Executive vice president)

Identifying prospects for merger or acquisition, 130
Income management, 2, 34–36
Information systems, 13–14, 166–190
  applications, 170–171
  and decision making, 188
  developing, problems in, 167–170
  impact of, 175–180
  management questions on, 189–190
  and middle management, 176–178
  and organization structure, 64
  in product line planning, 105–107
  providing service, 172–175
  role of top management, 178–180
  technology, 180–183
  trends and future, 183–189
Initiation of merger or acquisition, 130
International divisions, 160–161
International operations, 11–13, 137–165

International operations (*cont'd*):
  advertising in, 147
  and antitrust action, 141
  changing conditions in, 144–145
  and chief executive officer, 146
  contact directors, 146
  costs of, 138–139
  direction of, 146–147
  and distribution, 139, 143
  effect of politics on, 139–140
  finance and control, 150–153, 164
  government policy, 139–142
  importance of, 137–138
  labor in, 138–139
  language problems in, 156
  long-range planning in, 153–154, 164
  management questions on, 164–165
  market characteristics, 142–144
  marketing, 142–144, 147–148, 164
  manufacturing, 148–149
  organization, 158–165
  organization structure and, 12–13, 71
  personnel for (*see* Personnel for international operations)
  pricing in, 152–153
  and product line, 12–13
  research and development, 149–150, 164
  and taxes, 140
  top management functions, 145–158
Inventory control, 110–111

Job rotation, 220–221

"Key men," 18

Labor in international operations, 138–139
Labor contracts, example of policy on, 29–30
Labor relations, 199–201
Language problems in international operations, 156

Line executives:
    and information systems, 168–169
    role in long-range planning, 3–4,
        44–45, 53
Long-range planning, 3–4, 37–56
    comprehensiveness of, 41–42
    and computers, 55–56
    examples of, 48–53
    exceptions to five-year cycles, 39–40
    and facility requirements, 40–41
    five-year projections, 39–41
    importance of, 37–38
    in international operations,
        153–154, 164
    role:
        of central staff, 45–47, 53–54
        of line executives, 3–4, 44–45, 53
        of top management, 3, 42–44, 55
    trends in, 53–56

Management:
    involvement in executive evaluation,
        217–218
    line (*see* Line executives)
    middle, impact of information
        systems, 176–178
    by objectives, 54–55
    relations with labor, 199–201
    team, 221–222
    top (*see* Top management)
Management council, 72, 73
Management information systems (*see*
    Information systems)
Managers:
    product, 6, 64–65, 108–110, 117
    program, 6, 65–67, 108–110
    project, 6, 65, 108–110, 117
Manufacturing, foreign, 148, 164
"Market province" concept, 123–127
    establishing provinces, 124
    evaluating, 127
    objectives of, 125
    working relationships in, 125–126
Market surveys in international
    operations, 148

Marketing:
    foreign, 12–13, 158–159
        (*See also* International operations,
            organization)
    in international operations,
        142–144, 147–148, 164
    world, by product line, 163–164
Marketing outlook, derivation of, 41
Mathematical techniques, 183
Mergers and acquisitions, 10–11,
        128–136
    checklist on, 133–136
    committees on, 130, 131
    fact finding in, 130–131
    negotiation in, 131
    policy on, examples, 28, 129–130
    product line expansion by, 128–129
    role of chief executive officer in, 130
    steps in, 11, 129
    top management involvement,
        129–132
    trends in, 133

Natural-resource companies, planning
    by, 41
Negotiation, 199–201
    in merger and acquisition process,
        131
New facilities, planning for, 40–41
New products, 8
    research and development, 90–91

Objectives, management by, 54–55
On-the-job coaching, 221
Operations research, 166,
        170–171, 184
Organization structure, 4–7, 57–76
    arrangement of, 58–60
    board of directors in, 73–76
    centralization versus
        decentralization, 68
    committees, 5, 71–73
    and computers, 64
    decentralized, 5
    departmental groupings in, 63–64
    executive vice president in, 5–6

Organization structure (*cont'd*):
  and information systems, 64
  and international operations, 12–13,
    71
  planning departments, 6–7, 67–68
  and product line control, 112–113
  product managers in, 64–67
  reasons for modifying, 58–60
  as research and development subject,
    85
  role of chief executive officer in,
    58–59
  span of control, 60–61
  vice presidents in, 61–63

Patent information, 187
Personal characteristics of executives,
  239
Personnel for international operations,
  147–148, 154–158, 165
  foreign nationals, 157–158
  key, 147–148, 154–158
  problems of living abroad, 156–157
  recruiting and selections, 155
Pilot projects, 148
Planning:
  of external and employee relations,
    192
  future developments, 185, 186
  long-range (*see* Long-range
    planning)
  product line (*see* Product line,
    planning)
  in public relations, 15
  in selection of executives, 207–211
Planning committee, 73
Planning cycles, 4, 39–41
  five-year, 39–41
  and product line, 40, 41
  ten-year, 54
Planning department:
  organization of, 6–7, 67–68
  role in long-range planning, 45–47,
    53–54

Politics, effect on international
  operations, 139–140
Pricing:
  as control device, 33
  in international operations, 152–153
  and product line planning, 104–105
Problem solving by computer, 170
Product authorization, 111
Product design, 185, 186
Product line:
  cost control, 118
  direction and control of, 9–10,
    101–102, 107–114
    trends, 114–118
  expanding by merger and
    acquisition, 128–129
  and international operations, 12–13
  "market province" concept,
    123–127
  obsolescence in, 118
  planning, 103–107, 112
    balance and emphasis, 103–104
    pricing and timing, 104–105
    use of management information
      systems, 105–107
  and planning cycles, 40, 41
  programs on, examples, 119–123
  world marketing by, 163–164
Product manager, 6, 64–65, 108–110,
  117
Product organization, 2, 5
Product safety, 111–112
Product transition departments, 90–91
Profit and loss as control device, 2,
  24–25
Profit and loss statement, 25–26
Program manager, 6, 65–67
  functions of, 66–67
  in product line control, 108–110
Project manager, 6, 65
  in product line control, 108–110,
  117
Promotions as control device, 33
Public relations (*see* External and
  employee relations)
Public relations firms, 196

Race relations, 197
Record keeping, 170, 171
Representatives, foreign, 159–160
Research and development, 7–8,
    77–100
  allocations for, 87–88
  central, 8
  and chief executive officer, 79
  establishing objectives and
      philosophy, 78–85
  importance of, 81–83
  in international operations,
      149–150, 164
  and new products, 90–91
  organizing, directing, and
      controlling, 85–91
  policies and practices, 94–100
  trends in, 8–9, 77–78, 91–94
  types of, 83–85
Research centers, corporate, 86–87
Return on investment, 2, 25–27

Safety, product, 111–112
Salaries, 33, 69
Scheduling, 186
Seminars, 222, 223
Simulation, 170–171, 187
"Skimmer charts," 215
Software, 182–183
Span of control, 60–61
Spare parts, control of, 110–111
Special assignments in executive
      development, 221
Subsidiaries:
  coordinating, 162–163
  foreign, 12, 147, 161, 162
Systems selling, 126–127

Tariffs, 139
Taxes and international operations,
    140

Team management, 221–222
Ten-year planning cycle, 54
Testing, executive, 215–216
Timing, product line planning, 105
Top management:
  background for, 236–239
  defined, 234–235
  experience for, 239–245
  future trends, 246–248
  generalist versus specialist, 207
  ignorance of computers, 167–169
  involvement:
    in external and employee
        relations, 194–195
    in international operations,
        145–158
    in mergers and acquisitions,
        129–132
  in product line planning, 105
  requirements for success, 205–207
  role:
    in information systems, 178–180
    in long-range planning, 3, 42–44,
        55
    in management of corporate
        income, 3
    in overall control, 2
Training programs, 222–223

Unions, 16, 69, 199–200

Vice president for administration, 62

World marketing by product line,
    163–164

Years with company, executives, 236,
    250